A Stake in the Outcome

A Stake in the Outcome

Building a Culture of Ownership for the Long-Term Success of Your Business

Jack Stack

and **Bo Burlingham**

Currency

New York London Toronto Sydney Auckland

A CURRENCY BOOK
Published by Doubleday
a division of Random House, Inc.
1540 Broadway, New York, New York 10036

Currency and Doubleday are trademarks of Doubleday,
a division of Random House, Inc.

Book design by Erin L. Matherne and Tina Thompson

Cataloging-in-Publication Data is on file with the Library of Congress

ISBN 0-385-50507-8

PRINTED IN THE UNITED STATES OF AMERICA

First Edition: April 2002

Currency Books are available at special discounts for bulk purchases for sales promotions or premiums. Special editions, including personalized covers, excerpts of existing books, and corporate imprints, can be created in large quantities for special needs. For more information, write to Special Markets, Currency Books, 280 Park Avenue, 11th floor, New York, NY 10017, or email specialmarkets@randomhouse.com.

10 9 8 7 6 5 4 3 2 1

This book is dedicated to the big players, past and present, who have understood the competitive advantage of a culture of ownership, including Sam Walton, Herb Kelleher, Bob Beyster, Tom Watson, and Ewing Kaufman. They knew in their hearts and minds that only ownership could close the gap between the haves and the have-nots, and they've shown the way for the rest of us.

This book is also dedicated to all the members of the Stack and Burlingham families, without whose support and encouragement it would never have been written.

Contents

Acknowledgments

It would take more space than we have here to acknowledge everybody who has helped shape this book and the thinking behind it, but there are at least four groups of people who deserve special recognition and thanks.

One group we think of as the *contributors*. They include, first and foremost, Janet Coleman, the managing editor of *Leader to Leader*, the quarterly publication of The Drucker Foundation, who shepherded us through the process of creating the original manuscript. She was there through thick and thin, asking the right questions, offering common-sense feedback, providing calm, level-headed guidance throughout. We would not have made it without her.

Inc. magazine's editor-in-chief, George Gendron, also played a vital role, coming in at critical points in the process to offer invaluable editorial advice and encouragement. (That means he made sure we didn't kill each other.) Gary MacDonald of Kingston Technology Corp. was our indefatigable lab tester, who not only read and marked up an early version of the manuscript but also tried implementing the ideas in some of the companies he works with. His observations were extremely helpful in making the revisions.

Sam Kaplan, president of Central Chase Associates LLC in New York City, was a great resource, especially when it came to sorting through the reasons that companies are bought and sold. Norm Brodsky, the venerable entrepreneur and *Street Smarts* columnist, provided the kind of sage counsel we've come to expect from him over the years. We're indebted as well to Tim Bellanti and Jeff Johnson, who gave us feedback and criticism along the way, and to Dennis Balcom, who helped us keep it all in perspective.

Corey Rosen, the founder and guiding spirit of the National Center for Employee Ownership, has been a pioneer on the issues we write about here, as well as a wonderful resource and a great friend. He's also bloody accurate on the complexities of equity sharing, and accuracy is vital when it comes to ownership. Bill Fotsch and David Lough kept us on our toes at all times. Art Kleiner offered helpful feedback and insight into the wider world of business. So, for that matter, did our friend and colleague John Case, who has done more than any other individual to document the open-book phenomenon as it has emerged over the past ten years.

Of course, there were also a lot of key contributors from the SRC family of businesses. Ryan Stack and Jim Carrigan provided important research on several of the episodes we've written about and made us focus on the hard questions we had to answer. Becky Lane was, as usual, the voice of reason. She greased the wheels with the able assistance of Sarah Dennis and Linda McHaney. Dennis Sheppard deserves special recognition for keeping us together, on track, and moving forward, while helping flesh out many of the stories and checking up on our accuracy. In that regard, we also received tremendous help from Beverly Willis, Alexis Brown, Jeff Payne, Denise Bredfeldt, Steve Crowder, Eric Paulsen, Marty Callison, Mike Carrigan, Gary Brown, Rich Armstrong, Tom Samsel, Dave Lahay, and Joe Loeber.

Finally, we are indebted to Roger Scholl and his colleagues at Currency Books, Stephanie Land and Sarah Rainone. Together they helped us improve the manuscript in countless ways. We also want to thank publishing manager Rebecca Holland, book manager Chris Fortunato, and designers and typesetters Tina Thompson and Erin L. Matherne for their excellent (and speedy) contributions.

Then there are the *players*. The great experiment we write about in this book has been, as noted, a collaborative enterprise. We've drawn extensively on the advice and experiences of the practitioners who are leading the way to a new business paradigm.

Some of them contributed the stories we've used in the "Field Notes" scattered throughout the book. They include Bill and John Palmer of Commercial Casework, in Fremont, California; Leslie and Sam Fishbein of Kacey Fine Furniture, based in Denver, Colorado; Joe Knight, Joe Cornwell, Joe VanDenBergh, and Reid Leland of Setpoint, in Ogden, Utah; Bruce Nims, Jan Baird, and Missy Viewig of Nims Associates, based in Decatur, Illinois; Steve Weatherford of Daryl Flood Warehouse and Movers, based in Carrolton, Texas; and Bruce Thurston of Charlton & Hill Ltd., in Lethbridge, Alberta.

We received valuable feedback from those people and from other great business practitioners, including Martin Babinec of Trinet Group, based in San Leandro, California; Todd Parnell and Cyd Blackburn of The Bank, in Springfield, Missouri; Jay Burchfield of The Trust Company of the Ozarks, also in Springfield; Joe Jenkins of Jenkins Diesel, in Springfield; Bruce Kelling of Tiburon Inc., based in Fremont, California; Steve Petersen of Petersen Inc., in Ogden, Utah; Eric Harvey of The Walk the Talk Company, in Dallas, Texas; John Cappelletti, Paul Studebaker, Greg Zamin, and John Blatnik of Putman Media, in Itasca, Illinois; and Gary Davis and Gary Olds of Jim's Formal Wear, based in Trenton, Illinois.

The third group consists of the *teachers* who have helped us learn some of the most important lessons in building a culture of ownership. You will find many of their names in the pages of this book. They are people with whom we shared the struggle, and we will always think of them with respect and affection. In particular, we'd like to single out Dan McCoy, Dan Rorke, Stan Golder, George Stone, George DiPrima, Mike Ingram, Mike Carrigan, Lee Shroyer, Doug Rothert, Dave Lahay, and the RSC guys—Ralph, Doug, Bill, and Joe.

Most of all, we want to thank the people at the center of our lives. Without them, none of this would matter. Betsy Stack and Lisa Burlingham, who have the patience of saints, somehow managed to bear with us through the long process of bringing this book to fruition. Ryan, Katie, Meghan, Timmy, and Kylie Stack and Jake and Kate Burlingham gave us constant support, not to mention a sense of purpose. Our deepest hope is that this book will play some small role in making their world a better place.

A Stake in the Outcome

1

A Culture of Ownership

There's a great experiment going on in business today that involves literally thousands of companies and millions of people, but it's one of the best-kept secrets around. I know about the experiment because my company, SRC Holdings Corporation (formerly Springfield ReManufacturing Corporation), is part of it. For twenty years now, my colleagues and I have been trying to develop a particular type of culture at SRC. In the process, we've come into contact with thousands upon thousands of people who are trying to do the same thing at their companies.

A lot of those people have visited us here in southwestern Missouri. By conservative estimates, we've had more than 4,600 people from 1,600 companies come to see what we're doing and learn about the Great Game of Business, the management system we've developed to teach everybody in our company about business and to turn our employees into owners. That's prompted *BusinessWeek* to label SRC a "management Mecca." Another 5,000 people from 1,700 companies have attended the various conferences we hold for current and would-be practitioners of open-book management, which is the generic term for what we do. There we've been joined by our kindred spirits in the corporate world, including some of the most revered companies around—Southwest Airlines, Harley-Davidson, VeriFone, Outback Steakhouse, AES Corp., Whole Foods Market, Kingston Technology, and ServiceMaster, to name a few. (You can find examples of the lessons we've learned from some of these companies in the "Field Notes" we've included throughout this book.)

Meanwhile, the book we wrote about our management system in 1992 has sold more than 200,000 copies and has been translated into Russian, Spanish, Hungarian, Chinese, and Korean. People have applied the principles of the Game to an awesome array of businesses—from oil companies to hair salons, from Internet start-ups to roller-coaster manufacturers, from fast-food chains to law firms, landscapers, software developers, woodworking companies, furniture retailers, mining operations, even not-for-profit social service organizations.

Not just in the United States, either. SRC has become famous in places we once barely knew existed. There are companies in Zambia and Malaysia that practice the Great Game of Business. The Australian *60 Minutes* did a segment on our company, and it became one of the program's most requested videotapes. Delegations have come to see us from as far away as India, South Africa, Singapore, the United Kingdom, Sweden, Japan, wherever—all interested in finding out as much as they can about the way we do business.

At a certain point, you have to ask yourself Why? What could all these people be looking for, and why would they trek all the way to the Ozarks to find it? I like to think of SRC as a leading-edge business, but let's face it: We're not a high-flying star of technology, and we don't live in a hot zone of the new economy, or even a major metropolitan area. While we do have our own Internet-based subsidiary, most of the companies we operate are involved in the making and selling of engines and engine components, an old-economy industry if there ever was one.

Nor can you explain the interest by our business success alone. Yes, we've done well. A share of SRC stock that was worth 10 cents in 1983, the year we started, had an appraised value of $81.60 as of January 31, 2001, an increase of 816,000 percent in eighteen years. During that time, we've grown from $16 million to $160 million in sales; from 119 to more than 900 employees; and from one company to twenty-two. After losing $60,000 in our first year, we've had seventeen straight years of unbroken profits. It's a good record, and I'm proud of it, but many companies can marshal equally impressive growth statistics, and they don't all acquire the kind of notoriety that we have.

There are some other numbers, however, that I suspect get closer to explaining why people come to Springfield to see us. When we started in 1983, we had just thirteen shareholders—me and the twelve other managers who'd scrounged around and come up with the $100,000 we needed to make a down payment on the factory where we worked. Today we have 727 shareholders, all employees, just five of whom have stock from the original buyout. The other 722 shareholders own 64 percent of the business, valued at $23 million.

That transfer of ownership is the result of an odyssey we began two decades ago. During that time, we've worked long and hard to foster an environment that brings out the best in people, giving them the confidence, the courage, and the self-esteem to do what they're capable of. How? Mainly by trying to be as loyal to them as they've been to the business and thereby creating a place where they can feel more secure.

There's a level of mutual trust and respect at SRC that doesn't exist in a lot of companies. It comes from everything we've done to build our culture. It comes from being honest with people, from telling them about the realities of business, from having principles and sticking by them, from trying to be fair. I suppose it's also important that we've avoided mass layoffs, but it's more important that we've done it together, by keeping our promises to one another, by living up to our mutual commitments. We've treated people like the capable, intelligent adults we know they are. We haven't protected them like children. We've created a society built around rules we all know and understand—some of which we've developed, but many of which we've gotten from the marketplace. They're the basic rules of business, the things we have to do to survive and prosper in a competitive economy.

Out of all this has emerged a special kind of corporate culture—what I think of as a culture of ownership. It's that culture, I believe, that is drawing all those people to Springfield. They want to see it, feel it, smell it, and taste it, and they want to find out how to create something similar in their own companies.

The Definition of a Culture

So what exactly *is* a culture of ownership, and where does it come from? The term, I admit, is tricky to define. It's a little like what a Supreme Court justice once said about pornography: It's hard to say exactly what it is, but you know it when you see it. By that standard, if no other, we can all think of companies we're familiar with that have an ownership culture. Southwest Airlines comes to mind. Harley-Davidson and Home Depot do as well. So, for that matter, do Herman Miller, the $2.2-billion furniture maker, and Whole Foods Market, the $1.8-billion natural foods grocery chain, and Science Applications International Corporation (SAIC), the $5.9-billion employee-owned defense contractor.

Each of those companies has a distinctive corporate culture you quickly become aware of when you walk into one of their facilities or spend time around their employees. There's a sense of pride, identity, direction, and purpose. People know they're part of something bigger than what they do on a day-to-day basis. They belong to something, and it belongs to them. They have ownership, and it's a two-way street.

But while most people can recognize an ownership culture when they see it, they have many misconceptions about what it takes to develop one. There's a common belief, for example, that it's all about owning stock. Equity-sharing certainly plays a crucial role, but you don't get an ownership culture simply by giving stock to employees. We've seen a lot of that in recent years, and more often than not the result has been disappointment and misunderstanding.

Part of the problem has been the tendency of companies to use stock merely as a form of compensation—a carrot to get people to work harder. In a company with a strong culture of ownership, stock is more than compensation. First and foremost, it's a vehicle for change. The goal is not just to reward people for the work they do, or to maximize profits for their own sake, or to enhance shareholder value, improve cash flow, or whatever. Rather, equity is used to involve people in the process of making a difference in the world.

Why? Because business is not an end in itself. It's a means to an end. It's a tool that allows us to accomplish the things that matter most to us, and those things must transcend business to have real meaning and value. The precise nature of those loftier goals will vary from company to company, and even from person to person, but you must have them. They are what makes ownership worth caring about.

And to be an owner, a true owner, you have to care. Owners do not follow a job description. They don't just put in their time. They have something bigger they're working toward, and they feel a sense of responsibility about accomplishing it. They go beyond mere problem solving and look for creative, innovative ways to reach their goals. They are independent-minded, freethinking people, leaders not followers, and they know how to take the bad with the good. Indeed, they're often at their best when the going gets tough. They have what it takes to reach down and find the inner sources of strength that allow them to keep moving forward, no matter what gets in their way.

At SRC, we wanted to have a culture that would draw out those qualities in the people who work here. But to build such a culture—and to sustain it—you must also have a company that comes through on the promises it makes to its employees. It's relatively easy to create an illusion of ownership by handing out stock or stock options. It's far more difficult to give people the tools they need to realize the rewards that ownership can provide.

We've been trying to figure out how to do that for the entire time we've been in business. It has been a long, slow, difficult journey, filled with pitfalls and obstacles, and we haven't yet reached the end of it. Perhaps you never do. But we've been able to overcome a lot of the obstacles, mainly because we've put so much effort into teaching people about business, creating mechanisms that have allowed them to learn about the complexities of ownership as they've been engaged in the process of building an enduring company.

Those mechanisms are the building blocks of the Great Game of Business.

Continuous Learning

I want to be clear about what I mean by the word *mechanism.* I'm talking here about a regular process, program, or routine that has become an integral part of our management system—our 10-20-30-40 bonus program, for example, or our high-involvement planning process, or our weekly huddles. We wrote about several such mechanisms (including those three) in our first book, *The Great Game of Business.* Since then, we've developed several more, some of which we'll discuss later on in this book.

All of these mechanisms serve more than one function. To begin with, they're management tools. The bonus program provides incentives to achieve certain goals; the planning process produces an annual plan; the huddles are essential means of communication; and so on.

In addition, the mechanisms allow us to delegate a tremendous amount of authority and responsibility by giving people the information they need to make decisions that are in the best interests of the company, both short and long term.

Then, too, the mechanisms embody our values and transmit our culture to new employees. With the weekly huddles, the scoreboards and charts on the walls, the constant chatter about hitting targets, it doesn't take long for someone to figure out what we stand for.

Those are all valuable functions, and I could probably come up with others. It's important to understand, however, that by far the most critical function of the Great Game mechanisms is education. They are the tools we use to promote continuous learning in every corner of the organization. They are the means by which we make informal business training a regular part of our day-to-day routines.

Let me say a few words here about informal training, which I've always found to be better, cheaper, and more effective than formal training.

I like to use a fishing analogy. You can do all the research in the world on bass fishing. You can find teachers who'll tell you everything they know. You can read every fishing magazine, study every fishing book, and watch Jimmy Houston haul them in every Saturday morning on ESPN. But it won't mean anything until you go out on a lake and start throwing a lure. When you feel that first bite—or have that first backlash—you'll begin to learn about fishing.

I'm not saying that formal instruction is worthless, just that it's overrated. According to an authoritative study conducted by the Center for Workforce Development, formal training programs account for only about 30 percent of what people know about their jobs. The rest they pick up informally from the people they work with—at the coffee machine, in the lunchroom, during breaks on the floor.

Those findings aren't as surprising as they may seem at first glance. Think about how it works in most organizations. When new people come in, they usually get some kind of job orientation. Somebody explains their benefits and tells them what's expected on the job. But who gives them their *real* orientation? How do they find out what's *really* expected? They learn, all right, but not in any formal training session. I'm reminded of a story I heard once from a guy who worked in a giant automobile factory. I'd asked him how new employees find out what they have to do to be successful. "It's real simple," he said. "Somebody tells them, 'Keep your nose clean for ninety days, and you'll have a job for life.'" Talk about transmitting a culture.

The point is that job-related learning goes on whether or not we're aware of it. People learn through a whole series of events that most companies don't even recognize, and so they never figure out how to leverage the process. They don't see how much training you can do outside of any formal training program.

I believe that people learn when they participate in games or work in teams. People learn when they have meetings or interact with customers. When you talk with your supervisor, you learn. When you mentor another employee, you learn. When you report to your peers, you learn. When you come up with a replacement so that you can move on to another job, you learn.

That's the informal training process. Through it, people learn interpersonal skills—how to communicate, how to handle themselves in a group, how to deal with different personalities. They learn how to fit into the company's culture, how to live up to expectations. They learn how to innovate, how to create new products and services. They acquire the practical skills they need to do a particular job, as well as the mental skills they can use wherever they go: the ability to solve problems, to think critically, to integrate tasks, to compete and win. Some people are extraordinary at winning. Why? Mainly because they've learned how—through informal training.

This is a critical point that, for some reason, I have a hard time getting across to people who want to understand the success of our management system. They focus on the design of the bonus program, or the selection of a critical number. They think it's all about finding the right incentives. Wrong. *It's all about leveraging the informal training process, using the regular routines of the company to promote continuous learning.* A bonus program may help you hit certain goals and put some extra money in the pockets of your employees, but you'll miss the greatest potential benefit if you don't make the connection to learning.

I don't believe you can build a durable ownership culture without some such system of ongoing business education. Nobody can think and act like an owner without understanding the basic rules of business, and most people don't understand them. We use the Great Game of Business to teach people those rules. We start with the idea that there are two things every company must do to stay in business: make money and generate cash. Through the informal training mechanisms of the Game, employees learn about all the subtle and not-so-subtle challenges of doing those two things in the various industries in which we compete. From there, people move step-by-step up the ladder of business complexity, eventually confronting the ultimate challenge of building an enduring company capable of transferring ownership—and wealth—from one generation of owners to another.

And the system works. It works brilliantly. People really do wind up with a damn good business education—whether or not they realize they're getting one at the time. In the nineteen years since we started the company, we've had dozens of employees rise from the shop floor and the customer-service desk to top management positions, and they're far better qualified than a lot of MBAs I see.

I don't mean to suggest that our line employees are the only ones being educated, either. I think I've learned more than anyone through our system. Then again, most of our managers would probably say the same thing. What's more, none of us would have received that education if we'd relied on formal training to do the job.

When you open your books—*really* open them—you also open your mind, and neither your mind nor your books will be closed again. Why? Because you'll keep discovering things about yourself and your company you wouldn't have known otherwise.

Business is an unfolding drama. You never reach a point at which you "understand" it in the sense of having all the answers. There are always new questions to consider, new discoveries to make, new problems to confront and mysteries to solve. To be good at business, you need to be continuously learning—even if you're Jack Welch. And you need to become extremely good at business if you want to build a company and a culture that will carry on and prosper long after you leave.

The First Rule of Ownership

There's another vital role that the Great Game of Business plays for us. It's the means by which we keep people focused on the fact that we're building a company, not just making products. In the process, we continually remind them of, and link them to, the higher goals behind SRC—the reasons why we're in business.

You absolutely must have some system for doing that if you want to build a culture of ownership. The system doesn't have to be the Great

Game of Business, although you're more than welcome to use it if it suits you. Southwest Airlines, Harley-Davidson, Home Depot, Herman Miller, Whole Foods, and SAIC all have their own systems, which are different from the Great Game and from one another. But you must have some way of getting people to think in terms of the company they're building and the higher goals they're striving toward, rather than just the products and services they're delivering.

Don't get me wrong. I'm well aware that every company has to design, make, and sell things customers want to buy. Otherwise you won't have a business. I'm also aware that great companies tend to be known for their great products and services. But they're the result, not the cause, of greatness. Inspired people can do incredible things. The question is, Where does the inspiration come from? In an ownership culture, it comes from building the kind of company that can let you achieve your higher goals.

That's a fundamental rule of ownership, and I can't emphasize it enough:

OWNERSHIP RULE #1

The company is the product.

If you want to build a culture of ownership, people have to understand that they have a direct role to play in creating the kind of company they want, and that creating such a company is their responsibility and the ultimate goal of the enterprise, the end result of all their efforts.

Now, you might think that such a rule would be easy enough to get across to people, but it isn't. In fact, it usually requires a huge change in the consciousness of employees. Most of them, after all, have grown up either in the old industrial economy or in institutions that operate by its rules and norms. Even many of the self-proclaimed "new economy" companies are managed internally a lot like their old economy forebears. By that I mean that everybody except the senior executives is encouraged to have a narrow focus. Job descriptions, work rules, accountabilities, performance reviews, individual bonuses—they're all designed to make people think in terms of doing the job, performing the function, getting the product out the door. Only the top people are supposed to worry about the company as a whole.

So when you set out to create an ownership culture, you wind up having to fight against all the habits of mind that people have developed in those old-economy environments. You also have to fight against the ways people have been trained to think about their roles.

Most managers, for example, assume that a major part of their job is to manage people. But you can't manage owners, and most people don't like to be managed anyway. One of the basic flaws of traditional management thinking is its emphasis on managing people, which leads companies to spend billions of dollars on implementing management flavors of the month—producing what? A lot of cynicism and resistance to change, and maybe a few good laughs in *Dilbert*. The alternative is to have a system that allows people to manage themselves.

I'm not being naive here. I realize that everyone won't automatically buy into that concept. But many people will—more than you might expect—and the rest can be challenged to make a choice. Do they want to be worker bees or leaders? It doesn't matter what job they hold. They can still be leaders. They can choose to lead by taking responsibility for themselves, seizing the opportunities that the company has to offer, reaching out for their own higher goals—even if they're front-line employees being paid an hourly wage. We have hourly people who've made tens of thousands of dollars by saving up their money and taking advantage of the chance to buy stock in the company. Then again, we also have people who've passed up our stock offerings—and lived to regret it.

In an ownership culture, you need to broaden the concept of leadership and delegate leadership. You need to work on developing leaders at all levels of the organization—improving business knowledge and skills, giving people ownership of the job and responsibility for its execution, pushing them to make decisions, encouraging everyone to reach out and move up. You want a workforce full of people who are fast on their feet and ready to take advantage of the opportunities that come along. That's the only way a company can achieve its strategic goals.

And what do you do if you happen to be a manager in such a company? You challenge people. You encourage them. You tell them the truth. You try to help them understand reality. But you don't manage them, at least not in the traditional sense.

Instead you manage the system. You make sure you're using the mechanisms you've developed, and you look for ways to improve them. You keep measuring and analyzing the results. You constantly ask whether or not you need new mechanisms and, if so, which ones.

Because the system is never finished. There will always be parts of it that need fixing or upgrading, or that haven't been invented yet. There will be, that is, as long as the world keeps changing.

So somehow you need to quantify the performance of your ownership culture, if only to determine how well your system is working. At SRC, we measure our success by the growth and retention of people and the growth of the company. If we have high turnover, or if our people aren't learning, moving up, taking on new challenges, then there's something wrong with our system and our culture. Unless we fix the problem, moreover, we'll be selling ourselves short, not to mention missing out on the long-term business opportunity.

Why? Because, in the future, companies will increasingly be valued on the basis of their people. It's inevitable given the changing demographics of the workforce. Forget about the latest downturn. Economic slumps will come and go, but the population will keep on aging, the employee pool will keep on shrinking, and the competition for talent will intensify. If companies want to maximize shareholder value over the long term, they have to focus on the growth and retention of their people, and there's no better way to do that than by building a successful ownership culture.

Psychic Ownership and "Real" Ownership

At this point, you may be wondering, "What about equity? If you can get all these wonderful benefits by having an effective management system, why bother sharing stock at all?"

That's a good question. In fact, I know a lot of companies that have implemented the Great Game of Business, or something very much like it, without actually giving employees an equity stake in the company. By and large, the results have been excellent. Not only has the company's performance improved, often dramatically, but morale and employee retention have risen as well.

When you spend time in one of those companies, you can't help but be struck by the employees' spirit, loyalty, and knowledge of the business. They talk and act as if they really are owners. What's more, they clearly feel that, on some level, the company is theirs, and they'll tell you so if you ask them.

That's what I think of as psychic ownership. It comes, I believe, from the sense of community that develops when you treat people as responsible adults, capable of understanding how the business works, looking out for its best interests, and contributing to its success. Just by implementing a well-designed open-book management system, companies demonstrate trust and respect, and then the educational process kicks in, transforming both the culture and the behavior of employees—not all of them, but a certain critical mass. Along the way, they become extremely possessive of, and deeply loyal to, the company and its culture.

Psychic ownership is important. It's an essential component of an ownership culture. I hold in high regard any company that has earned such trust and devotion from its employees. But psychic ownership doesn't help a company deal with the biggest issues it faces—like succession. I also believe that businesses miss out on the real potential of ownership if stock is not part of the deal.

Equity is, in fact, a kind of a contract. It defines the terms of a shareholder's relationship to the company that issues the stock. When people get stock in the company they work for, they have something real in their hands, a guarantee that they're going to receive a portion of the wealth they help create. What happens to the stock, and what they ultimately get out of it, are different matters, but they do have the promise in writing, and no one can take it away from them.

Out of that contract come all the wonderful things that equity is capable of providing. It's one mechanism that can absolutely change people's lives. It can make their lot easier. It can help them send their children to college. It can enable them to buy a home. It can support the charities they care about. It can give them something to look forward to in retirement. It can significantly enhance their quality of life in many ways.

And yet there's more to equity than simply the rewards people get from it, because they can receive those rewards only by working together to build something of value. You need a group of people to create a company whose stock can be bought and sold. It's almost impossible for anyone to do it alone.

So equity-sharing is about defining the community. It's about what one person can do for another person. It's not just a set of rewards; it's a reward system. People come together, struggle together, build something together, and enjoy the benefits together. Yes, there are hardships along the way. Life is full of hardships. But when people are working toward a common goal, they can rise above the hardships. They can put aside the petty issues and think at a higher level. They can realize how important they are to one another, and come together as a team, and create something better than what existed before. Because people have hope. They have something to look forward to in their lives.

In the process, you get a place that more nearly resembles how you'd like the world to be: a nicer place, a softer place, a place where people are a little more equal, and so you have a little less envy and guilt. It all comes out of this reward system.

I don't mean to paint too rosy a picture here. Ownership is not all fun and games. You try to have as much fun as possible by creating opportunities to win, but an owner has to learn how to deal with the bad as well as the good. Why? Because being an owner involves responsibility—for making payroll, for protecting jobs, for fulfilling commitments, and so on. You give people ownership in part because you want them to share and accept that responsibility.

The question is Can they handle it? Have you created a culture that enables them to handle it? Any company can do well when times are good. It's in bad times that we find out what businesses are made of.

SRC is actually at its best in bad times, and I believe it's because of ownership. We know how to come from behind because we've done it so often in the past. Whenever the going has gotten tough, we've been able to draw together as a family, figure out what has to be done, and then go out and take care of business.

I doubt that would have happened if a few of us had kept all the stock to ourselves. The other people would have always felt (correctly) that they were working for someone else. By sharing equity, we put everybody in the same boat, and so we could make sure we all were pulling together when the seas grew rough. As a result, we learned we could handle adversity. It tested our mettle and made us stronger.

You miss all that when you settle for psychic ownership or try to get by with phantom equity, which is really just a long-term bonus program. No matter how loyal and motivated psychic owners might be, they aren't complete owners if they don't also have an equity stake, and sooner or later the limits of their ownership become apparent. They hit a wall in their education. They may become better employees, but they never encounter the biggest challenges of ownership, and they don't share in its rewards. In the end, it's equity that provides the ultimate economic payoff of business. Unless employees are responsible, not just for helping the company make money, but also for building its equity value, there will always be a division between the "real" owners and the psychic owners, and over time that division will undermine the culture, stunting the growth of the business and that of its people.

And no one's growth will be stunted more than that of the owners who keep the stock to themselves. I speak from experience here. My entire education as a businessperson has come from struggling with the challenges of making employee ownership work. It boggles my mind to think what I would have missed if we hadn't taken this route.

In the beginning, I knew nothing about business. My partners and I didn't even know how to define success. We thought it was just a matter of surviving. At one point in our first year, we had $8.9 million in debt, against just $100,000 in equity, and barely enough cash to scrape by. So we figured out how to make do with what we had. Through the Great

Game of Business, we taught everybody in the company what it takes to earn a profit and generate cash in an operating business. The result was that we paid down our debt and watched our stock value soar.

But just when we thought we were out of the woods, we discovered a whole side of business we hadn't known about before. It isn't enough to create wealth; you also have to be able to pay for it eventually. In our early years, we'd created a lot of wealth—on paper. What were we going to do when it came time to cash in the paper?

So began the next phase of our journey, which proved to be both the most difficult and the most rewarding. By having to come up with a plan for cashing people out, we were forced to change the entire way that we looked at the business. We had to learn how to view it objectively, to see it as an investor would, from the outside in, and we had to develop a long-term perspective. Clearly, we were going to need a ton of cash in the years ahead to cover our obligations to shareholders. The more successful we became, the more cash we'd need. Somehow we had to figure out how to generate it, not just now, not just this year or next year, but on and on into the future. We had to create a repeatable pattern that would guarantee we'd have the money to pay shareholders when they were ready to leave.

It took more than a decade to come up with the pattern. Along the way, a funny thing happened. We learned the fundamentals of good business. We learned what it really takes to succeed under capitalism. We learned how to create new businesses and how to get people ready to run them; how to generate new sources of cash flow; how to do alliances; how to buy and sell companies; how to turn customers into partners; how to increase the price-earnings multiple on our stock; and on and on. Above all, we developed the courage, the character, and the conviction to be able to handle the future. We figured out how to build certain disciplines into the organization that would get people thinking ahead, thinking strategically, thinking as far into the future as we could go. So as expensive as our equity was, having to pay for it turned out to be the best thing that ever happened to us.

Meanwhile, the world was changing around us. When we began our journey, it was considered a radical idea to share ownership and financial information with employees. Now both practices are commonplace. Almost 20 million people are covered by some sort of broad-based equity-sharing program these days—more than 15 percent of the private-sector workforce—and the numbers are rising fast. As many as half of all private-sector employees could have stock in their companies in the coming years. And even companies that don't share equity search for ways to instill an ownership mentality in employees, encouraging them to "think and act like owners," as the phrase goes.

At SRC, we've come as close as anyone to figuring out how to do that, but it's taken twenty years. I think back to the pessimistic times at the start of our journey, when we'd get daily reports of factories closing, people losing jobs, communities being devastated, and I realize how far we've traveled. We were just a bunch of working stiffs back then. We had only some values we felt we had to live by and a few crazy ideas about how businesses ought to be run. We didn't understand ownership. We'd never heard of employee stock-ownership plans or open-book management. When we tried those things, we didn't know how, or even if, they would work.

But we believed we had to give them our best shot. We had to see if it was possible to build a business around the same democratic values we'd grown up with and come to expect in every other part of our lives. We had to find out whether or not you could share the rewards of ownership, be open with information, treat people with dignity and respect, educate yourself and everyone else, and still have a successful company.

As it turns out, you can—but it ain't easy.

2

Dreaming

I believe Dan McCoy was the person who first suggested that we buy the factory. It was in January 1981. He was controller of Production Operations for International Harvester's Construction Equipment Group, based in Woodfield, Illinois, and one of the people who oversaw the Springfield Renew Center, where I was plant manager.

The factory—which specialized in remanufacturing engines and engine components that were used as replacement parts for construction equipment made by Harvester—employed about 230 people, but we were beginning to realize that our jobs were in jeopardy. A recession had begun, and Harvester was not prepared for it. Hoping to recover the market share it had lost during a long and bitter strike, the company had borrowed a ton of money and ramped up production. The problem was, customers weren't buying, and interest rates were going through the roof.

So disaster loomed. It was clear that none of us was going to escape the crisis. A wage freeze was already in effect throughout International Harvester. Meanwhile, the company—worried about rising inventories—had ordered us to cut back on production.

I was furious about the whole situation, and I was scared of the direction in which we were heading. The next step, I could see, was that we'd be told to start laying people off. "Screw it," I said to McCoy in one of our phone calls. "We're not giving in to this bullshit, and we're not giving up. We're going to find work for people even if we have to go outside the company to get it. I don't give a shit whose feathers we ruffle. I'm going to run this place just exactly like it was my own business."

"So why don't we buy it?" he said.

I'm not sure exactly how I responded. I probably laughed. I certainly thought he was joking. I had just turned thirty-two. I had no independent resources. I supported my family by getting a paycheck every week, and McCoy's situation wasn't much different. Where the hell were we going to get the money to buy a factory? Even if we could, what reason was there to believe that Harvester would sell it to us?

But McCoy was serious. He said there were ways to get the money. What we needed was a strong team and a good business plan. He thought we should talk to our boss, Dan Rorke, the head of Production Operations for the Construction Equipment Group and the guy who'd sent me down to run the Springfield plant in the first place. I agreed.

Rorke loved the idea. We made contact with a Chicago deal-maker named Louis Lichtenfeld, who had a lot of connections in the financial world. He liked what he heard and agreed to help us put together an offer to Harvester. The figure we came up with was $6 million.

That was our first attempt to buy the factory, and it was a resounding flop. Lichtenfeld later told me that, when he met with two of Harvester's top executives to present our plan, they just sat there and looked at him. It was as if they were incapable of responding. By then the downsizing of Harvester had begun in earnest, and the executives were no doubt as shell-shocked as we were by what was going on. Lichtenfeld said it was one of the strangest meetings he'd ever had.

We never did get a clear response from Harvester to that offer. Lichtenfeld eventually gave up and moved on to other deals. Meanwhile, the stresses of downsizing took a heavy toll on Rorke and McCoy. McCoy eventually left Harvester and went to work for an oil rig company in Tulsa.

Rorke lost his job in a company reorganization and moved on as well.

The idea of buying the factory didn't die, however. It was still our best hope, maybe our only hope, and hope was something we desperately needed. Harvester was in turmoil, going through wave after wave of layoffs. Every day brought word of friends losing their jobs, factories being closed, business units being sold. What remained of the company was constantly being restructured. The Springfield factory was moved around like a pool ball that couldn't find the pocket. In the nine months after Rorke's departure, I must have had seven different bosses.

To be sure, even this cloud had a silver lining. Adversity brought out the best in people. There was a spirit of mutual self-sacrifice. After one particularly severe budget cut, for example, we all got together and agreed to close the factory one day a week in order to avoid having to lay people off. For most of us, that meant taking a 20 percent reduction in our salaries—on top of the erosion we'd already experienced because of the wage freeze in effect throughout the company since 1980. Yet nobody complained.

We also tried to drum up new business. At one point, our production quotas slipped so low we were afraid we'd be forced to cut back our hourly workforce. We didn't have a single salesperson on staff, but we still went out and found new customers, signed contracts with them, and generated enough additional work to keep everyone employed—for a while. For a bunch of metal benders to do that on their own was unheard of.

There's a lesson here, and it's the foundation of everything I know and believe about business. People can accomplish almost anything if they have a common purpose, a higher goal, and they all know what it is, and they're going after it together. *Everybody needs to be going somewhere.* People need a destination, or they get lost. If they have one, however, and if it's really their own, there's no telling what they can do. They can survive the darkest hours, beat the longest odds, scale the greatest heights.

That's a fundamental truth I've seen demonstrated over and over again throughout my career. I've seen machinists in Melrose Park, Illinois, transform their department from the least productive to the most productive in the plant out of sheer pride. I've seen copper miners in Zambia perform incredible feats in an attempt to save their company and their country. I've seen all kinds of struggling businesses—retailers, design firms, wholesale distributors, woodworking companies, and on and on—suddenly turn themselves around and take off. I've seen our own people at SRC band together to make sure we didn't have to shut down a plant that had suddenly lost its biggest customer.

A leader can't make those things happen. A leader can only allow them to happen. How? By coming up with a goal that people can believe in and then showing them how to reach it. Doing that is the most important job a leader has.

In the dark days of 1981, we needed a goal to strive for. We needed a way to keep hope alive. I couldn't think of any better objective than buying the factory ourselves. The idea of having our own company was exciting. We could fix everything we saw wrong with business and build our own little city on a hill. It could be a great adventure. On the other hand, I knew the old adage about being careful what you wish for. At one of our meetings, I put the question directly to our managers and salaried people: Did they think we should try to buy the factory?

There was a part of me hoping someone would stand up and say that I was crazy, that it was absolutely nuts to think we could put together such a deal on our own. But nobody did.

Buddy, Can You Spare a Dime?

So we continued our quest. I sent another letter to division headquarters, just to make sure people knew we were still interested in buying the factory. Meanwhile, I searched for investors willing to put up the money to do a deal.

I worked every contact I had and followed up every lead I got. It was like a treasure hunt. A lender in Springfield would look at our proposal and decide it was too risky for him, but he knew another guy with an investment company in Kansas City who might be interested. We'd go together to see the guy in KC, and he'd say the deal was too risky for him as well, but he knew a venture capitalist in Chicago. So it went. Altogether I must have met with fifty potential investors over a period of eighteen months. I traveled to New York, Chicago, St. Louis, San Francisco, Dallas, you name it. Occasionally the investors would fly in to see us.

McCoy sometimes accompanied me to these meetings. I kept in close touch with him after he moved to Oklahoma. He was the only person I knew with the financial savvy to handle the technical aspects of a deal. As for the other managers, they had their hands full dealing with the continuing crisis in the company, but I kept everybody informed. Not that there was much progress to be informed about. The response we received from investors ranged from cold to lukewarm.

Along the way, I got a tremendous education. I'd go in and make my best sales pitch. I'd talk about our terrific record at Harvester, our wonderful plans, our great credentials. I wanted them to see what a fabulous team we had. They weren't impressed. They didn't care about all the courses I'd taken, all the management disciplines I'd mastered, all the wonderful skills I'd acquired during my thirteen years at International Harvester. It made no difference how well we followed the principles of Total Quality Management. It didn't even matter whether or not we were good managers.

I remember arguing with one venture capitalist, coming up with every reason I could think of why he should invest in us. He didn't bother to answer me. "It may be your brains, kid," he said, "but it's my money, and I ain't interested." That just about said it all.

I found their response incredibly frustrating—and also fascinating. They were looking at us from a whole different perspective, one I was completely unfamiliar with, and they were asking questions I'd never been asked before. I'd thought that I knew something about business. I was beginning to get the feeling that I knew very little.

There was one meeting in particular that I'll never forget. It was with Stan Golder, a partner in Golder, Thoma and Co., a leading venture capital firm. We were sitting in his office in Chicago. McCoy and I had just finished presenting our business plan. He sort of flipped through it and tossed it back at us. "It's got no schmozzle," he said. "I need schmozzle."

"What's schmozzle?" I asked.

"It's what you don't have here," he said. "Listen, kid, I want to know about the market. I want to know how big it is and what percentage of it you've got. I want to know how you're going to grow that percentage, what specific steps you're going to take to get a bigger share. And I want to know what that means to me. I want to know how I'm going to get annual interest of 40 percent, compounded, over the next five years and a 500 percent return on equity when I get out at the end of that time. That's schmozzle."

What Golder said was a revelation to me. Maybe it shouldn't have been, but it was. Investors were interested in their money, not in my company! They wanted to know how I was going to help them achieve their financial goals! Eureka!

OWNERSHIP RULE #2

A company isn't worth anything if nobody else wants to own it.

If your aim is to build value in a company, you have to learn how to look at it from the outside in. You can't view it the way most people in business do, from the inside out. You have to see it as investors see it—coldly, objectively, without any sentimental attachments to people, products, buildings, history, culture.

Why? Because people don't put money into a business unless they feel it's a good investment for them. They won't invest in your dream if they don't believe they can earn a good return. If you can't promise them one, they'll look elsewhere.

Not that it's easy to look at your company from the outside in. On the contrary, it takes an enormous amount of discipline and determination, as well as a few whacks on the head. When you're focused on the day-to-day operations of a business, it's almost impossible to step back and look at it objectively. I myself had to learn this lesson all over again about four years into SRC's journey, and I've spent the time since then trying to figure out what to do with it.

Even more difficult was the challenge of getting other people at SRC to see the company the same way. At one point, I put some of them directly in touch with an investment group that wanted to purchase half of the company and let them see firsthand how investors looked at them. In effect, I gave them the same experience I'd had in the early 1980s.

I've since learned that there are actually four different types of investors, and they're arranged in concentric circles, sort of like Dante's circles of Hell. The first circle consists of people who lend because they want to help you build an enduring company; that's a sparsely populated circle. The next one is filled with investors who just want to get in and get out. The third circle has the predators—investors who give you money hoping you'll blow it, at which point they'll steal the company from you for a song. Then there's the fourth circle: the guys who charge you through the nose and break your kneecaps if you don't pay up.

It would have been nice to find an investor from the first circle, but mainly we were looking in the second circle, and—by the grace of God—avoiding the third and fourth. I began to realize that, to get our financing, we had to start thinking more like investors who just wanted to get in and get out. We had to be able to see ourselves as they saw us. We had to learn their language, understand their concerns, figure out how to give them what they wanted—because only then would we be able to get what we wanted.

What's in a Dream

And what exactly did we want? The answer was becoming a bit clearer to me as we continued our fruitless search for capital. Granted, the months were rolling by, and we were meeting with rejection after rejection, but—oddly enough—we got something out of the experience besides frustration and an education in business. We got a chance to dream.

We might have lost that opportunity, ironically, if we'd secured our financing and bought the factory sooner. Reality always intrudes on dreams. Problems have to be solved. Compromises have to be made. Things like human nature and the surprises of the marketplace are constantly getting in the way. When you're struggling with the hard facts of life, you need a dream to guide you—to remind yourself where you're going and why, to help you figure out what you need to do next.

I've come to realize that dreaming is an essential business activity. It may be the most important thing that people do. Why? Because a dream is ultimately the expression of your values. It shows what really matters to you. It defines who you are. And it will stay with you. You'll come back to it again and again as the years pass and ask yourself whether you've been true to your dream. Have you created the kind of company you had in mind when you started? Have you built the kind of career you originally envisioned? We built SRC around a fundamental belief in our people—in their ability to meet any challenge, in the goodness of their hearts, in their desire to help one another succeed. We've stuck with that belief through thick and thin, and it's given us the company we have today.

During the two years from McCoy's idea to "the buy," as we called it, we had plenty of time to think about the kind of company we wanted. A picture began to take shape in my mind. I don't know if I'd call it a vision in the way that businesspeople normally use that term. It was more of a fantasy. It was a dream of creating a really neat company, a place where people would be friends and colleagues, where they'd care about each other and act as if they cared about each other, and where everyone would get a fair shake. You spend a major portion of your life at work. I wanted that portion of mine to be good. I didn't want my work to come at the expense of my family, or at the expense of my principles and beliefs. I wanted to lead a balanced life. I was looking for a life of achievement, fulfillment, opportunities, challenge, competition, and fun, and I wanted to work in a place where I could find those things. I also wanted to be around people who were as happy as I was, who liked coming to work in the morning, who were getting out of it what they were looking for, too. In my dream, this company would be a healthy place, where people enjoyed spending time. It would be the kind of company that other people would look up to as a model and say, "Gosh, that's a neat place to work." And they'd really mean it.

Of course, money had something to do with it as well. After all, we were talking about a business here, not a social club. I was aware, we were all aware, that in business you can make more money if you own the company, and who doesn't want to be financially independent? Moreover, you can create wealth for the people you work with at the same time as you're creating it for yourself. I didn't see why those two goals had to be in conflict. It was going to take everyone to make the business successful, and I believed everyone should share in the rewards.

Nor did I think I was giving anything up by sharing equity. It seemed to me that we'd all wind up richer in the long run if everybody was an owner. Why? Because I thought our people would perform at a higher level if they had an ownership stake. I thought they'd give us an edge that our competitors didn't have.

Besides, if we didn't share ownership, we'd create barriers between owners and nonowners, and I believed it was critical that we eliminate as many barriers as possible. We had to make sure that we were all in the same boat, and everybody's oar was in the water, and we were all rowing. That meant, among other things, that people had to know the financial rewards would be distributed more or less equitably. Otherwise, people wouldn't look at the Big Picture. If they didn't have a share of the pie, they'd have no reason to care about making the pie as big as possible. And making a huge pie was the best way to ensure we'd all get a substantial slice.

But beyond generating wealth, I was thinking about the kind of company we were creating. I wanted a company filled with independent-minded, freethinking people. To me, that meant we all would share the burdens as well as the benefits of ownership. I really didn't want the entire responsibility for feeding everybody. I wanted people to have some responsibility for feeding themselves. I kept reminding them that along with the potential rewards goes the potential of risk. I didn't want them looking at me saying it was all my fault if we failed. Business owners sometimes say, when they want to justify keeping the equity to themselves, "You didn't go through the agony of having to meet payroll every week, and I did." Well, there's some truth to that. I could easily imagine what it was like to face that responsibility alone, and I didn't want to do it. If we failed, I wanted to make certain that we failed on a collective basis.

Mainly, however, I wanted to make people successful. What better goal can you have than for everybody to be a winner? I was looking for pride of ownership, authorship, a sense of accomplishment, satisfaction, meaning in life—not just for me, but for all the people I was working with.

Close but No Cigar

Our dream was looking increasingly like a long shot, however. While we were searching for investors, International Harvester had decided to put us out for bid. I found out from a friend of mine who called me in early 1982 to ask about a tombstone advertisement he'd just seen in *The Wall Street Journal* announcing the availability of International Harvester's Renew Centers to interested buyers. I was shocked. After checking it out for myself, I called one of the people we reported to. "Oh, yeah," he said. "I forgot to tell you. Sorry about that."

In fact, the news that we were on the auction block wasn't necessarily all bad. If the top people at Harvester had finally decided to sell the factory, maybe they would agree to sell it to us. I went to Chicago to plead our case with George Stone, Harvester's divestiture manager, who was in charge of handling the sale. "Look," he said, "there's a whole company we have to think about here. We have to get as much as we can for that factory. We can't do an inside deal without seeing how much someone else might pay for it."

He was right, of course, but the decision put me in an awkward situation. The tombstone drew an overwhelming response from the outside world—much larger, I suspect, than anyone had anticipated—and everyone wanted to come visit us. So Harvester began sending down a steady stream of potential buyers whom we were supposed to show around the Renew Center, presumably doing everything we could to encourage them to make an offer, preferably a big one. Of course, the larger the bids that other people made, the harder it would be for us to buy the place ourselves. Nevertheless, Harvester didn't send anyone else from the company to make the pitch. It seemed odd that I'd be left alone to interview all these people, given my obvious conflict of interest. I handled the situation as well as I could.

Meanwhile, our search for financing continued. But we were running out of leads. Then one day I picked up a copy of *The Wall Street Journal* and came across a long article about a major crisis at the Bank of America. Somehow it had to increase its return on assets. To do that, it was—among other things—attempting to establish a presence in the burgeoning field of asset-based lending, providing capital to companies that were so shaky they couldn't get financing any other way. I figured we fit that description perfectly.

(In an asset-based deal, the borrower does not get a typical bank loan, secured by a company's general credit. Instead the loan is a line of credit secured by the company's assets—inventory, receivables, plant, equipment, and so on. In return, the company pays a significantly higher interest rate and sacrifices some flexibility. These are high-risk loans by definition, after all. To protect itself, the asset-based lender usually takes control of the company's receivables, requiring that customers send checks to a so-called lockbox to which only the lender has access. The lender also imposes a stringent set of conditions, or "loan covenants," consisting mainly of certain financial ratios that the borrower has to adhere to. If, at any point, the borrower's ratios fail to comply with the terms of the covenants, the lender can come in, seize the assets, and liquidate them to get its money back.)

I gave Bank of America a call and was directed to the Midwest office of the asset-based lending division. Lo and behold, the people there were interested—so interested that a banker flew to Springfield immediately to meet with us. He liked what he saw. He was genuinely excited. Finally, after twenty months of searching, we had someone who was willing to go to bat for us.

And not a moment too soon. The crisis at Harvester was nearing a climax. The company had debt payments of $100 million coming due on October 31. If it couldn't come up with the cash, rumor had it that Harvester would be forced into Chapter 11 by its creditors.

So the company was going to have to sell some assets. Our hope was that it would sell its Springfield asset to us.

We were a minnow, however, and Harvester needed a whale. On Halloween came word that the whale had shown up in the form of Dresser Industries,* which had stepped in at the last moment and offered to buy Harvester's entire construction equipment division for $100 million. I wasn't particularly happy about the news, but I was relieved. In one of the company's frequent reorganizations, we'd been moved out of the construction equipment division and into a new engine division. So we were still alive.

Or so I thought.

The death notice arrived a couple of weeks later. I received a call from Dresser requesting that we send along various financial documents as soon as possible. My stomach jumped into my throat. I said, "I can't do that. I don't have permission to give that information to you."

"Well, you'd better hurry up and get permission," the person said, "because we need it right away."

I don't remember whether I called my boss, Russ Freeland, or George Stone, the financial guy who was handling the sale of assets. Whoever I spoke to told me to go ahead and send the information to Dresser. Negotiations were under way.

My heart sank. I didn't need any further explanation. We were in play, and other people were calling the shots. It didn't matter anymore that we had Bank of America behind us. We were just pawns now. Harvester needed Dresser to save it from its creditors, and we were part of the deal. If Dresser wanted us, Dresser was going to get us. There was nothing we could do about it. As high as I'd been before, I felt now as if I'd hit rock bottom. The show was over. The fat lady was getting ready to sing.

---

* Like other companies mentioned in this book, Dresser Industries has undergone several changes of ownership and management in the past twenty years. The Dresser of today is engaged in its own journey to build a culture of ownership.

Saved at the Bell

Not that it mattered, but I later learned that we'd wound up in the deal more or less by accident. Dresser hadn't actually bought anything on October 31 or even promised to buy anything. It had simply delivered a letter of intent to purchase various assets of Harvester's construction equipment division for $100 million—a letter that Harvester could give to its creditors and use to buy time. The next step was for Harvester to draw up a list of the assets it was offering for sale. The two companies would then negotiate a price for each of those assets one by one.

But someone had made a mistake in drawing up the list and included assets of the engine division, such as the Melrose Park plant. Harvester, which had no intention of losing Melrose Park, found itself in the sticky position of having to explain to Dresser that various items on the list were not for sale after all. Naturally, concessions had to be made. We turned out to be one of the concessions.

As a result, I was about to wind up with a new boss, and I can't say I was overjoyed when I found out who he was. His name was George DiPrima, and he was a Harvester veteran whom I'd worked with at Melrose Park. We hadn't gotten along very well back then. I had no reason to think either one of us had changed.

To be fair, I doubt that anyone could have won me over at that point. I was absolutely crushed by the failure of our buyout attempt and the loss of our dream. When DiPrima welcomed me to the Dresser team, it felt as if someone had just kicked me in the stomach.

Dresser Industries was based in Dallas, but DiPrima was operating out of a former Harvester facility in Libertyville, Illinois, which was going to serve as headquarters for the reconstituted construction equipment division. In early December, he flew down to Springfield to meet with our management team.

He told us that the deal was pretty much complete; there were just a few details left to work out. People would be coming in soon to transfer us from the Harvester computer to the Dresser computer. We'd be reporting to him from now on. No, he couldn't tell us anything about wages or benefits, but we'd get that information shortly. Meanwhile, we should start thinking of ourselves as soldiers in the Dresser army.

Over the next few weeks, I shuttled back and forth between Libertyville and Springfield, while the final details of the sale were being hammered out. The more I learned, the more depressed I became. I had hoped that, despite my own disappointment, the sale would at least be good for the people I worked with. After all, they'd be going from a nearly bankrupt company to a healthy one with deep pockets. I assumed that Dresser would lift the two-year-old freeze on wages and benefits, restore what had been lost, and put the factory back on a growth track.

Our new owners had other plans, however. On a trip to Libertyville with our human resources director, Gary Brown, we learned that Dresser intended to continue the freeze indefinitely, and some of our benefits were actually going to be cut. I also ran into one of the honchos from Dallas, who let me know just how uncertain our future was. He indicated that our factory was being acquired for one reason: because it was cheap. The Dresser people bought it, he said, because they realized they could shut it down, liquidate the assets, and still make money on the deal.

That did it for me. I called my wife, Betsy, and told her I was going to quit. She said I couldn't quit. We had three young children and no other source of income. We couldn't afford to miss a single paycheck. I pleaded with her, but she wouldn't budge. She insisted that I keep my job no matter what. Just to be sure, she made me promise to go straight to the airport and come home before I had a chance to do anything rash.

So Brown and I returned to Springfield, skipping a meeting of plant managers I was supposed to attend that afternoon. I later gave DiPrima some lame excuse for my absence. The truth was, I didn't care what he thought. I'd already quit mentally. I felt like a complete loser. I was just biding my time until the sale went through. Then I'd figure out what I was going to do next.

But, for some reason, the sale didn't happen. The negotiations seemed to drag on forever, which I found baffling. We were getting close to Christmas, and I figured everybody wanted to have the deal wrapped up by the end of the year. Why didn't they get it over with? What I didn't realize was just how hard Dresser was bargaining and how angry the Harvester negotiators were becoming.

On the morning of Monday, December 20, I received a phone call from DiPrima, saying that the moment of truth was at hand. "I'm heading into a meeting right now, and we're going to close the deal today. We're making our final offer. If they call you, don't take their calls. You understand?" I told him I understood.

I didn't hear anything for a few hours. Then the receptionist called in and told me that Harvester's lead negotiator, George Stone, was on the line. Technically, he was also still my boss. I took the call.

"We're at an impasse with Dresser," he said, "and we have this letter from you saying you want to buy the Renew Center. I assume you have access to the financing you'll need."

I could hardly speak, but somehow I managed to tell him we did.

"Well, I'll take you at your word," Stone said. "If you can come up with $1 million more than you offered in this letter, we'll do it. We need to get $7 million for the whole thing, and we need to close the deal by the end of the year."

My heart was pounding so hard I could hear it. "Stay there," I said. "I'll call you back." I had to compose myself.

I hung up the phone. I felt as though I was going to pass out from shock. I wanted to scream. I couldn't believe what was happening. We finally had the opportunity we'd been chasing after for two long years!

A Million Here, a Million There

There was just one small detail to resolve: how to come up with an extra $1 million when we had absolutely no money of our own and we'd already borrowed as much as anyone was willing to lend us. We were $1 million short of Harvester's asking price, and we knew we couldn't go to Bank of America for another dime.

But I remembered something I'd heard during my long search for capital. One of the venture capitalists had commented that he would buy anything and pay any price if he could do it with an unsecured promissory note. As long as he didn't have to put up cash—that is, as long as he could repay the note over time out of the earnings of the business—the amount of money involved didn't matter.

What if we agreed to pay Harvester $7 million instead of $6 million but worked out a deal whereby Harvester would get the additional million later? We'd sign an unsecured promissory note, which we'd pay out of earnings. Harvester would, in effect, be lending us the extra money we needed to buy the factory, but Stone could still go to his boss and say truthfully that he was getting the price he'd asked for. I didn't think the bank would object if the note was unsecured. In a bankruptcy, secured creditors are taken care of before unsecured creditors, so the bank would be covered even if we went belly-up.

Stone wanted me to get back to him quickly about the price. So I called him and said, "Listen, we've only got $6 million that we can put into the acquisition itself. We need a little running room." I asked if he'd consider letting us have a year to pay Harvester the additional $1 million. He'd have to give us an unsecured note to avoid problems with the bank, but collecting wouldn't be a problem: Harvester would be one of our biggest customers. Stone agreed, and we had our deal.

3

The Design of a Business

Most people, I know, don't think about the company they're designing when they start out in business. They think about the products they're going to make, or the services they're going to provide. They worry about how to raise the money they need, how to find customers, how to deal with salespeople and suppliers, how to survive. It never occurs to them that, while they're putting together the basic elements of the business, they're also making decisions that are going to determine the type of company they'll have if they're successful.

But a good company, I've learned, is like a good car: It begins with a good design. The company you wind up with reflects the concepts and principles you incorporate at the very beginning.

I knew we needed a new design for SRC, mainly because I could see there was something fundamentally wrong with the old one. I didn't have to look much further than International Harvester for proof. Not that I had any idea what was involved in putting a new design together. I wasn't even sure it was possible. But I knew I'd have to find out—because I'd already promised people more than I could deliver.

My natural inclination is to start at the end and work backward, looking for shortcuts as I go. I'm not sure whether it's a gift or a curse, but it's the way I operate. Give me a toy to build, and I ignore the directions and work from the picture on the box.

Harold Geneen, the legendary builder of ITT, believed that the ability to work backward from a goal was the secret to being a good manager. "You read a book from the beginning to the end," he wrote in *Managing*. "You run a business the opposite way. You start with the end, and then you do everything you must to reach it."

What he didn't mention is that, when you follow this approach, there's a very good chance you'll wind up putting your foot in your mouth from time to time. You'll make promises to people, and then you'll be forced to figure out how to keep them. In the process, you'll learn what you need to know to achieve your long-term goals.

If there are secrets to business success, this is certainly one of them. You move forward in business by running into obstacles and overcoming them. Of course, you'd never know that by reading most business success stories, but any experienced CEO will tell you it's true. Every company confronts an endless series of obstacles, each one new and different. You develop business skills by dealing with them one at a time.

The best businesspeople understand the process. They realize that the bigger the obstacle, the more they're going to learn from it. They welcome the challenge even though they know they won't always be successful on the first try. At least they'll learn what they need to do differently the next time. So, instead of being driven crazy by problems, they can enjoy themselves because they accept that business is all about problems. It's just one long obstacle race. The sooner you learn that lesson, the better off you'll be.

My problem was that I tended to create my own obstacles. It took a while before I began to see them as opportunities to learn. On the other hand, I never let myself get stopped by the obstacles I'd created, and so I learned a lot in spite of myself.

And I was about to get another lesson.

For months I'd been promising people that if we ever succeeded in buying the factory, we'd all be owners of the new company. It wasn't going to be just my show. Each of us would have stock, and each of us would be responsible for determining whether or not it was worth anything. I wanted everybody to recognize from the start that our success or our failure was going to be a group effort, and that awareness had to be incorporated into the design.

By the time Harvester accepted our offer, however, I'd discovered that we might not be able to make everyone an owner, at least not right away. Someone—I don't remember who—had pointed out to me that there are laws against bringing a lot of unsophisticated investors into a deal as risky as the one we were proposing without following some very specific rules of disclosure. To give everyone an opportunity to buy stock, we'd have to become a public company, and that meant going through a long, expensive process under the watchful eye of the Securities and Exchange Commission—a process we couldn't afford and didn't have time for.

There's Always a Core Group

So we came to our first big obstacle. We could avoid the necessity of going public by limiting the number of shareholders, but what about my promise? I'd made a commitment. I'd created expectations. How could we leave people out now without generating a lot of bitterness that could wreck the company before it got started?

And that wasn't the only challenge. Even if we could make people understand the situation, even if we could eventually figure out a way to bring them all in, we still had to decide on the number of shareholders we were going to start out with. Our understanding was that, under Missouri law, we could remain private as long as we didn't have more than twenty-five shareholders, but should we have that many or fewer? Where exactly should we draw the line?

Our attorney, Dennis Sheppard, had experience in these matters. He supported our goal of making everyone an owner, but he made a strong argument for keeping the initial group of shareholders as small as possible. Who was going to be responsible for the debt? What if something happened, and the bankers had to foreclose? They wouldn't like the prospect of having to chase 120 people around, Sheppard noted, or even twenty people. Chances are the bank would insist on having a small, concentrated group of shareholders. If I wanted to bring other people in as owners, he said, I could think about an employee stock ownership plan, or ESOP.

ESOPs were a relatively new invention, one I hadn't heard of. Congress had passed the enabling legislation only a few years before. Under the law, companies receive various tax benefits for setting up special trusts that can acquire and own stock on behalf of employees. The actual shareholder is the trust; the employees are members of the plan and receive the benefits of ownership through the trust. Being an ESOP member is not exactly the same as owning stock directly in the company. For one thing, you're subject to a number of rules and regulations that don't apply to direct shareholders. But the ESOP members do share in the financial rewards of building a successful company, and companies can use an ESOP to create an ownership culture. Today there are about 11,500 such plans, covering 8.5 million employees. Back in 1983, however, there were only a handful.

The ESOP offered us a way around the first obstacle. We could do the buyout with a core group of shareholders and then set up an ESOP to provide an ownership stake to the rest of the people later on. As for the makeup of the core group, it seemed logical to include everyone who was responsible for other people—that is, the management team. Under the Harvester classification system, we had twelve managers and supervisors, and I was planning to bring in Dan McCoy as our chief financial officer. So that gave us a group of thirteen initial shareholders.

No One Likes to Be Left Out

Most outsiders considered it a very large group. Sheppard thought we were pushing the limits of what we could handle and what the bank would accept. Inside the company, however, it was a different story. The initial shareholders became known as "The Lucky 13," and there was a certain amount of resentment directed against them, and against me for selecting them, particularly from employees who'd just missed the cut.

You have to be prepared for those feelings when you select a core group. No one likes to be left out of an inner circle. There will always be people who think they've been passed over unfairly, and they may be right. Some will get over it; some won't. Years later, there will be moments when their bitterness bubbles up in your face, and you'll see how deeply they were hurt way back when.

Our experience taught me two lessons in this regard. First, make your decision in the best interest of the company, then let go of it. You can't please everyone, no matter how much you want to or how hard you try. If you make reasonably good decisions out of pure motives, the vast majority of employees will eventually come to accept and appreciate your decision.

Second, don't give up on the people who feel slighted and angry. We have several people who believe to this day that they were treated unfairly in the buyout—but that hasn't stopped them from making major contributions to the company's success, or from reaping big rewards.

Ownership and Control Are Different

The next part of the design had to do with the issue of control, which people often confuse with ownership. They think that owners automatically have control over decisions. Conversely, I know experienced businesspeople who believe they can't be in control if they don't have at least 51 percent of a company's stock.

Well, that simply isn't true. You can easily separate ownership from control by having two classes of stock. The people with voting stock elect the board of directors. People with nonvoting stock are also owners. They have certain legal rights, and they get to share the rewards. But they don't have a say in electing the board, which is the ultimate authority. Whoever controls the board controls the company.

Although I'd never really understood the mechanics of control before, I'd thought a lot about these issues. Remember, I'd come up through the ranks at International Harvester. I'd started out in the mail room, and I'd worked on the shop floor, and I'd had my doubts about the design of the system from the beginning. In particular, I couldn't justify putting so much power in the hands of the people at the top. I thought it was dangerous. There were no real checks and balances. Back then, most boards were a joke. The top people were pretty much free to do as they wanted. What if they were wrong?

As it turned out, of course, the top people at Harvester had been wrong about several things, with the result that a great company filled with great people had been brought to its knees. If nothing else, the experience had taught me that leaders are fallible. They make mistakes all the time, and I had no reason to believe I'd be an exception to the rule. On the contrary, I was absolutely certain that I couldn't make all the right decisions on my own. What's more, I didn't want the responsibility that comes along with absolute power.

So I was determined to develop an alternative to the top-down, command-and-control business structure that was the norm in those days.

At the same time, however, I knew that we were going to have very little margin for error in the beginning. We'd have to come charging out of the blocks and drive forward. The decision-making process would have to be very clear, very fast, and very direct. In the beginning, there wouldn't be time to work on consensus building, team building.

So I came to the conclusion that, until the company was up and running, we should keep responsibility for the major decisions in the hands of the most experienced people, that is, the senior managers. Not that we didn't want to hear what everybody had to say, but I felt that the final authority, the last word, should remain with a relatively small group, at least in the beginning.

HOW TO CONTROL A BOARD

When you share equity with people throughout an organization, it's important to understand exactly how a board of directors works.

In any company that has one, the board is elected by the shareholders who own voting stock. Indeed, that's the difference between voting and nonvoting stock. All shareholders have a legal right to vote on the big issues that affect their status as owners, including the sale of the company, the purchase or sale of a substantial portion of assets, the issuing of stock options, acceptance of the annual valuation, and so on.

But only the voting stock can be used to elect members of the board, which has the final say on the company's strategy and direction. The board exercises its authority by approving or rejecting the annual plan it gets from management prior to the start of the year, and by making certain key decisions—about hiring and firing the top officers, for example, or approving what the top people earn. Thus, whoever controls the board ultimately controls the company.

In our case, we were all middle managers embarking on our first entrepreneurial venture, and we had yet to see how anybody would respond to the challenge. Although I intended to have a highly participative management process, I thought that—in the beginning, at least—I should have the dominant voice in deciding who would serve on the board.

Under Missouri law, we have cumulative voting for directors, which requires that each voting share gives the shareholder one vote for each position on the board. So let's say you have 10,000 shares of voting stock, and there are seven members of the board of directors. You'd have 70,000 votes altogether. You can use those 70,000 votes however you please, or at least you could under the rules we adopted. In other words, you could cast 70,000 votes for one person, or divide the votes among several candidates. It was your decision.

In fact, we did decide to have seven directors, and we agreed that three of them would be outsiders, which wasn't a hard sell. We knew we had weaknesses in various areas. I argued that we could use the board to address those weaknesses by recruiting outside directors who had the expertise we lacked internally. Everyone else agreed.

Once we'd settled on the outsiders, I knew people would focus their attention, and their votes, on the four insiders. If you have a limited number of votes, there isn't much point in using them on candidates whose election is a foregone conclusion. Besides, some shareholders wanted to be directors and would have no qualms about voting for themselves.

What I wanted was a board with a good balance—not a rubber-stamp board, but not a disruptive one, either. We had some strong personalities on our management team, and they sometimes clashed. I wanted to make sure the conflicts didn't get out of hand and harm the company.

I divided up the voting stock accordingly, reserving 28 percent of the voting stock (140,000 voting shares) for myself, while McCoy got 24 percent (120,000 voting shares) and each of the six senior managers 8 percent (40,000 voting shares). That gave me just enough votes to elect myself and to swing the other seats in favor of the people I thought would create the best balance on the board.

The Logic of Dividing a Pie

So how could we translate all that into a framework of ownership? How much stock would each shareholder get, and who'd have the voting shares?

I struggled hard with those questions, and I didn't get much help from the twelve other members of the core group. Whenever I sounded them out about what they wanted, what they'd be willing to pay for, most of them asked for more. Each person compared his slice of the pie to somebody else's. I kept saying, "It doesn't matter how big your slice is. The question is, How big is the pie going to be? Would you rather own 1 percent of General Motors or 100 percent of our company?" But most people had a hard time putting aside personal issues. It was an extraordinarily frustrating process.

OWNERSHIP RULE #3

The bigger the pie, the bigger the individual slices.

That was my introduction to one of the great challenges of equity-sharing—namely, the difficulty of getting people to think about what's possible rather than focusing on what they have. You give them stock hoping it will motivate them to grow the business. You want them to be thinking, "Gee, how much could this stock be worth in ten years? What can we do to maximize its value?" Instead, they see only what's on their plate right now and ask, "How much did so-and-so get?" It's a disease that leads people to miss some great opportunities. Unfortunately, there's only one cure for it that I know of: the benefit of hindsight.

Finally, I said, "Screw it," took out an organization chart, and tried to think the matter through logically.

Clearly, survival had to come first. It didn't matter how much stock anybody got unless we survived, and we wouldn't survive unless we lived up to the terms of our loan agreement. That meant abiding by the loan covenants and making sure we always had enough cash to cover our expenses. There were two people who bore the major responsibility for making sure those things happened: the CEO and the CFO. I decided that, between us, McCoy and I needed to have at least 51 percent of the voting stock. If push came to shove, we had to be able to take whatever steps we deemed necessary to make sure the company survived.

On the other hand, I had no illusions about our infallibility, nor was I confident that we'd always see eye to eye. So I decided to allocate 48 percent of the voting stock to the six senior managers. I trusted their common sense to come to the rescue if McCoy and I were at odds. And I'd take it as a warning sign if the vote went 52 percent to 48 percent, with McCoy and me on one side and the senior managers on the other. That kind of a split would tell me something was wrong and would force me to take another look at my position. In any case, I figured we'd have enough balance to keep the company on an even keel.

Deciding on ownership stakes was a different matter. Although I thought McCoy and I had to have a majority of the voting stock, I didn't feel that we needed—or ought to get—52 percent of the overall ownership. After playing around with various percentages, I finally came up with 19 percent for me, 17 percent for McCoy, 8.5 percent for each of the six senior managers, and 2.6 percent for each of the five supervisors.

Then I translated those numbers into shares. Since we were putting up $100,000 in equity, I decided we could issue 1 million shares, of which 500,000 would be voting shares. Each share, voting or nonvoting, would be worth 10 cents. We could have had fewer shares, and a higher valuation per share, but I wanted people to feel the stock in their pockets. I wanted it to be growing out of their pockets. I wanted them to know they had a substantial stake in this business, and 10,000 sounds a lot heftier than 1,000. In any case, my piece of the pie came to 190,000 shares, while McCoy's was 170,000 shares. Each of the senior managers got 85,000 shares, and each supervisor got 26,000 shares.

That was just the initial division of ownership. We agreed that we were going to bring the other employees in as soon as possible—through the ESOP and perhaps by other means, if we could find any. In the process, the portion of the company each of us owned would be diluted. Then again, we all hoped that by giving everyone a piece, we'd eventually wind up with a much bigger pie.

Everything Sends a Message

Looking back, I realize there was something else going on in my selection of the core group and my division of the stock. On some level, I was trying to send a message to people in the organization. I can't say I was doing it consciously, but—conscious or not—the message was there. It had to do with my gut sense of how a business ought to be designed. I believed that everyone should be an owner, and that the rewards of ownership should be distributed as equitably as possible. To me, an equitable distribution meant the pie would be divided in a way that reflected the risk people had taken, the responsibility they'd accepted, and the contribution they'd made. The people who benefited wouldn't just be those at the top of the organization chart. Everyone who made a contribution would get a piece of the action. We were at least going to try to be fair.

But it wasn't enough to believe all that. People had to know we were going to act on those beliefs. Otherwise, obstacles would go up. People would think, "We're getting screwed again." They wouldn't see the Big Picture. They'd spend so much time staring at their empty plates that they wouldn't look at the pie, let alone focus on trying to make it bigger.

That's one reason I decided to bring all of the managers in as shareholders—the supervisors as well as the people who reported directly to me. I was trying to say that we weren't a privileged elite. Ownership wasn't going to be limited to the senior people. The group included anybody who, under the Harvester system, was recognized as being responsible for supervising other people. If you fit the definition, you got in. What's more, you'd be eligible for the same stake as everyone else on your level.

The point was that we had rules. There was an order based on merit, logic, and fairness. People might disagree with the criteria we used, but the mere fact that we had criteria sent an important message about the way we intended to run the company.

When you're a leader, how you think and act is as important as what you do. People pay attention to the details, the unconscious messages, the little signals that you send often without realizing it. When I was twenty-three years old, I worked as an expediter at the Harvester plant in Melrose Park, Illinois, and I had an opportunity to watch management from the other side of the street. I could see how people on the shop floor responded when a manager ignored them, or talked to them as if they weren't really there. And I remembered what I'd seen when I later became a manager myself. I became very conscious, for example, about how I said hello to people, about looking them in the eye when we talked. The same thing applies to the decisions you make as leader. It's often not the decision itself, but the thought process behind it that sends the loudest message. People can accept a decision they don't like if they understand that you made it for the greater good of the organization.

I was astute enough to realize that if one group got something others didn't have, the playing field wasn't going to be considered level. In fact, a few people complained loudly about how unfair we'd been. But at least we'd made the statement. We'd established the principle. The challenge was to live up to it.

Success Is Harder Than Failure

Before charging ahead, however, we had to finish the framework. There were three other critical issues we had to address.

First, we needed to agree on a method for determining the value of the stock (and the company) in the future.

Second, we needed a plan for buying back stock that would protect both the cash flow of the company and the interests of the shareholders.

Third, we needed to figure out how to regulate transfers of stock. What would happen to the stock of shareholders who died, or left, or just wanted to sell some shares?

All three of these issues have to do with cashing out—which is, of course, the last thing most people think about when they go into business. If they think about getting out at all, they figure they'll deal with whatever is involved when the time comes. They say, "We'll sell the company" or "We'll go public." But they don't address the tough questions like valuation, which I discovered is one of the biggest mistakes you can make. If you have any other shareholders or partners, you're asking for trouble if you don't decide on a valuation method right at the beginning.

As Sheppard kept reminding us, you have to design a business understanding that your biggest problems won't come with failure. They'll come with success. That's hard. Nobody starts a business worrying about the dangers of success. You think, "I should only be lucky enough to have those problems." But, in fact, success is often more difficult to handle than failure, particularly if you have partners.

We had to consider, for example, what we'd do if our stock value took off, and greed set in. If the company failed, after all, things would more or less take of themselves. No one was going to argue about valuation when we were out of business. What we had to plan for was the possibility that we'd wake up one day with $8 million in equity rather than $8 million in debt. What kind of issues would we be facing then? How would people change? What if some of them left? How would we cash them out without putting the company at risk?

Setting the Value

So we looked at the various possibilities. Should we value the company at two times book value (that is, twice the amount left over after subtracting the company's liabilities from its assets)? How would that work? What was book value liable to be? What if we had a lot more shareholders at the time? What if we went public and our book value suddenly became irrelevant? We tried to think through the logic and play out various scenarios. If the formula didn't have any logic, we threw it out. If the scenario led us to a gray area, we knew we'd have problems.

We realized that whatever we came up with had to be as clear and as clean as possible. We wanted a valuation method that we all found acceptable, and that would allow us to live together harmoniously and separate peacefully, come what may. That is a golden rule of equity-sharing: The clearer you can be up front about your method of valuation, the better off you're going to be.

In the end, our choice was guided by our decision to set up an ESOP, which pretty much required us to have an annual valuation by an independent appraiser, who would look at the company from various standpoints and come up with his best estimate. Afterward, he'd meet with everybody and explain how he'd done his valuation, and we'd vote on whether or not to accept his appraisal. Assuming we voted yes, the stock value would then remain in effect until the next valuation. (Just to be safe, we included a couple of alternative valuation methods we could use if there were no ESOP valuation. It's no doubt important to have such contingency plans in a shareholder's agreement, but we've never had to resort to them.)

It's impossible to exaggerate how important this part of the process is. Trust is a key element of long-term business success, and you can't have trust without honesty and openness. By agreeing in advance to a fair method of valuation, and then by sticking with the process year after year, we were able to create an environment in which trust, honesty, and openness were understood to be fundamental elements of the way we did business. And they came right out of the shareholders' agreement.

The Ten-Year Buyout Provision

We did something else that turned out to be extremely important, although we didn't fully understand its significance at the time. At Sheppard's insistence, we agreed on a formula for cashing out individual shareholders.

To be sure, none of us had given a moment's thought to leaving. The idea never crossed my mind. Nor could I imagine that we'd ever lose any of the original shareholders—except maybe through retirement at some point in the distant future. But Sheppard convinced us we had to address the issue anyway. After all, people would retire eventually. People would even die. All kinds of unexpected things might happen, and we'd be forced to buy back stock that might then be worth a lot of money. What would we do if we didn't have the cash to pay someone's estate $1 million or $2 million in one fell swoop? How could we make sure that we'd be able to meet our obligations without putting the company in jeopardy?

Again, we tried to think the problem through logically. There was no way to know what the company might be worth at any point in the future, but we knew that its value would be some multiple of after-tax earnings. Back then, the Dow Jones Industrial Average was hovering around the 1000 mark, and the average price-earnings ratio of publicly traded stocks was 17. In other words, a public company's stock was, on average, worth 17 times its annual after-tax profit. We guessed that, as a private company, our price-earnings multiple would be somewhere in the vicinity of 10 to 12.

Okay, we said, why don't we agree to buy back stock over a ten-year period? Whenever someone left, or died, we'd determine the value of the stock and draw up a promissory note wherein we'd agree to pay the departing shareholder, or his estate, 15 percent down and the balance, plus interest, in 120 monthly installments.

If our stock was valued at 10 times our after-tax earnings, we should be able to make the payments without running out of cash. In theory, after all, we could buy back 100 percent of the company's stock over a ten-year period and pay for it out of our cash flow. Of course, we'd never be faced with the need to do that. If everyone was cashing out, we'd sell the business. What we were anticipating was the possibility of having to buy back the stock of one or two shareholders—something we could afford to do as long as we gave ourselves enough time.

Everyone agreed, and it was settled.

Buying In and Selling Out

We also thought through how we should regulate stock transfers. What if somebody else wanted to buy the stock? Should people be allowed to sell their stock to other shareholders or to other employees? And what if an outsider wanted to buy in—and was willing to pay substantially more than the company was offering under the valuation agreement? We didn't want a shareholder to be able to hold the company for ransom, say, by threatening to sell his stock to one of our competitors. On the other hand, we didn't want to restrict the market unreasonably or unfairly.

So we decided on some rules to ensure that the company got first dibs on any shares that were put up for sale. If the company didn't want them, the other shareholders and the ESOP, in that order, would have a chance to purchase the shares. Only if the company, the other shareholders, and the ESOP all decided to pass could an outsider buy in.

The Design Pays Off

I don't think I appreciated—I mean, *really* appreciated—the importance of all the work we'd done on the shareholder's agreement until we were faced with the prospect of buying out a major shareholder for the first time. It happened two and a half years later, in the fall of 1985, when we decided to part company with Dan McCoy, our CFO. That was an incredibly difficult moment—agonizing for everyone involved and fraught with danger for the company.

What saved us was our shareholder's agreement, and specifically the buyout provisions. Up to then, I'd more or less taken it on faith that we needed to figure out in advance how we'd go about buying back someone's stock should the need arise. Only when we were confronted with a crisis, however, did I understand that a buyout formula is not just a good idea; it's an essential element of any equity-sharing arrangement.

For those thinking about entering such an arrangement, never, ever go forward without agreeing in advance to a formula you're going to use to cash shareholders out when they leave. I have seen companies wrecked, friendships shattered, people driven to the brink of a nervous breakdown by the failure to follow that simple rule. I shudder to think of the nightmare we would have faced if we hadn't discussed and signed on to the buyout provisions in our shareholders' agreement long before we ever had to use them.

What a well-crafted agreement gives you is the ability to protect the company at a time when passions are running high. You can negotiate from a position of strength. In the end, you may wind up with a formula that's slightly different from the one in the shareholders' agreement, since it's always possible to change the terms of the buyout by mutual consent. There's going to be discussion and haggling no matter what. The important thing is to make sure that you hold all the cards, and you will if your shareholder's agreement has been carefully thought out.

In McCoy's case, for example, we had very different ideas about the price he should get for his stock. Under the shareholders' agreement, we were allowed to buy back the stock at the price set by the last valuation. McCoy felt entitled to a higher price, and we might have been forced to give it to him if he hadn't previously agreed to a very clear and specific formula. Naturally, he wanted us to make an exception in his case and no doubt believes to this day that he got screwed, but we had to do what was best for the company. Thank goodness we could.

On the other hand, we were willing to be flexible about the payout period. Rather than paying 15 percent up front and the balance over ten years, we negotiated a deal whereby we paid McCoy 25 percent up front and the balance over three years. He got quicker access to his money, and we avoided having to pay a lot of interest. It was a reasonable exchange.

And a funny thing happened in the course of paying off our debt to McCoy. We discovered that we could, in fact, afford to buy back stock from time to time. We were generating enough cash internally to cover the cost without having to make sacrifices in other areas. We could still buy machine tools, pay bonuses, and run the company the way we wanted to.

The Test of Time

So how did we do with our business design? I can look back almost twenty years later and say, "Amazingly well." We owe a lot of our success to Dennis Sheppard, who made us think through all the issues very carefully. (See "What to Look for in an Adviser" on page 53.) With his help, we developed a solid framework, by which I mean the basic set of rules you agree to follow as you build the company.

To build a culture of ownership in which employees feel they're part of the company and committed to its success, those rules have to be fair, and everyone has to sign on to them up front. Not that we were right on all the details, but we had rules that allowed us to change the details if we needed to. When we made a mistake, we could go back and fix it. When we ran into an unexpected situation, we could deal with it. When we had a people problem, we could take care of it. We could handle pretty much anything because our framework of ownership was sound.

Not only was the framework right, but so was the process we went through to develop it. We played out every scenario we could think of.

We debated what we'd do if this or that happened. We looked at all the possibilities, good and bad. It's what I call trapdoor thinking. We kept playing the upside and downside, trying to think about what we'd do if something went wrong—or if something went right. We'd take each question, come up with an answer, and then say, "OK, how do we address the what-ifs?"

Over the years, that way of thinking played a critical role in the evolution of our management system. It got us into contingency planning. It became a whole mode of operation inside the company. By constantly anticipating how we were going to handle the downside, we were able to overcome every obstacle we ran into. Why? Because we were prepared.

WHAT TO LOOK FOR IN AN ADVISER

A lot of people—including many lawyers and accountants—will tell you that sharing equity is dangerous. They'll listen to your ideas about the kind of company you want and try to convince you that they won't work, or maybe that they aren't worth the effort. Why? Because lawyers and accountants get paid to keep you out of trouble, and they think it's easier and safer to follow the conventional route, which is true, by the way.

The problem is, the conventional route may not take you where you want to go. Equity-sharing alone won't give you a culture of ownership, but you'll never get beyond psychic ownership if you don't put real stock in the hands of employees, and neither you nor they will get the full rewards that ownership has to offer, for reasons I explained in Chapter 1.

So don't take the advice of naysayers at face value. Yes, there are certain things you have to get right at the beginning, or you could run into big problems later on. While it's important to have professional help, you have to be careful in selecting your advisers. Don't believe people know what they're talking about just because they have impressive credentials.

We didn't know anything when we started out. Fortunately, we had an adviser who did. Dennis Sheppard was exactly the kind of guide we needed, and we were lucky to find him. Not only did he have great credentials, but he also knew what he was talking about. He was a successful young lawyer with one of the top firms in town, and he'd put together a lot of deals. I went to see him the day after Harvester accepted our offer. We hit it off immediately.

For starters, he had a neat solution to my biggest problem at the moment. Harvester wanted us to close the deal by the end of the year, which was two weeks away. We needed at least a month to line up our financing, but I didn't want to let the Harvester people know that. I was afraid they'd think we might not get it, and they'd change their minds about selling us the factory. "Just tell them no offices are open in Springfield between Christmas and New Year's," Sheppard said.

"We can't get any of the documentation we need to complete the sale and satisfy the lender. Tell them there's no choice but to move it to the end of January."

Aside from common sense, Sheppard had three other qualities that I'd urge you to look for in choosing an adviser:

- *You need a good listener who focuses on helping you reach your goals, not on changing them.*

Sheppard is, in fact, one of the best listeners I've ever met. At our first meeting, he had me recount the whole story of our attempts to buy the factory, and he got me to articulate as clearly as I could what I wanted to do. Then he told me about some of the legal boundaries, as well as the practical boundaries, that might get in the way. But I never had the sense he was discouraging me from going forward. On the contrary, it was clear that he really liked the dream. He really wanted us to be successful.

- *You need someone with practical business experience as well as legal and technical expertise.*

You have to deal with a lot of legal and technical issues when you set up your framework of ownership, and it's essential to have a lawyer who knows his or her way around the territory. But technical expertise alone is not enough. You also need to get advice from someone who's been through it before and who knows the pitfalls. We were lucky to have both in one person. Sheppard was not only an experienced lawyer but a guy with real business experience. He'd had partnerships. He'd been burned a couple of times. He'd had to arbitrate disputes. And he'd done a lot of shareholder agreements. He knew how companies got into trouble, and so he could raise the issues that many other lawyers—though perfectly competent from a technical standpoint—would never think of.

- *You need someone who is thorough.*

There's a whole education process you go through in designing a business, and it's important to make sure that you get all the required courses. Sheppard is nothing if not thorough, which is another important trait to look for in an adviser. On the whole, I'd say that it's better to have thorough advice than good advice. You need to have someone who will force you to think through every major contingency you should be anticipating. As long as he or she keeps asking you the right questions, and demanding that you come up with answers, you'll probably be all right.

Sheppard was great at giving us lists of things we had to decide upon. Then he'd take our answers, massage them, and come back with comments and more questions. He'd tell us the pitfalls. He'd pose different problems. He was extremely patient and persistent. He's the type of guy who thinks of everything, and it can drive you crazy. But it was just what we needed.

4

The Hazards of Employee Thinking

There are two extremes in the debate over how companies ought to be run. One extreme says business is business: You can't set up a company on fair principles and run it in a truly equitable manner without getting into trouble. In capitalism, it's a matter of screw or be screwed.

On the other extreme are people who believe that business utopia is just around the corner. If you walk the talk and stick to your principles, everybody will rise to the occasion and love one another, and you'll achieve the peaceable kingdom right here on earth.

I never accepted the first argument, and if I had any illusions about the second, I lost them very early in the game. From the moment we actually started putting the deal together, I found myself dealing with all the foibles of human nature. There were times, in fact, when I thought they might put us under.

OWNERSHIP RULE #4

Stock is not a magic pill.

It doesn't change anybody's behavior, at least not overnight. People don't suddenly put aside their differences and join together for the common good just because they've become owners. When you've spent your entire adult life focusing on a job description, it's difficult to stop thinking like an employee and start thinking about what's best for the company as a whole. Old habits die hard.

I didn't realize how hard it would be to change old habits until the shareholders started turning on one another. The occasion was an all-day meeting of the core group. We had some major issues to resolve before we could launch our new business, and the most difficult involved the other people at the factory. We knew that we couldn't afford to put them all on the payroll without dooming the company from the start. The question was, Which people should we hire—and which ones would be left to fend for themselves?

It was not a subject any of us liked dealing with. I would have been worried if anyone did. Who enjoys making decisions about somebody else's livelihood? But the discussion was difficult for another reason as well. In addition to struggling with tough issues, we were also confronting the need to change the way we thought about our roles and our responsibilities. We had to stop thinking like employees and start thinking like owners.

That was hard. We had been employees for our entire careers. Employee thinking was so deeply ingrained that, for some of us, it was second nature.

By "employee thinking," I mean the habit of focusing on your little piece of the company instead of looking at the whole thing. That's how we'd all been trained. As Harvester managers, each of us had a department, a unit, for which we were responsible. Yes, we'd promoted team spirit, but there was never any question that—together and individually—we had to live up to the accountabilities we'd been given, and that meant taking care of our turf.

As owners, however, we could no longer afford that type of thinking. We had to get rid of the blinders and accept responsibility for the entire enterprise. Of course, we'd continue to have individual accountabilities, but we had to view them in a different light. We couldn't look at them simply as elements of a job description someone else had given to us. We had to see them as our part of a mutual agreement to achieve our common goals.

I considered it obvious that we had to make such a change when we became owners, and I assumed other people did, too. Why wouldn't they? They were going to be shareholders just like me. Once they had stock, I thought, everything else would take care of itself.

So I wasn't prepared for what happened one Saturday in January. We began by working through our worst-case scenario for the coming year, which would tell us how many people we could safely have on the payroll. I felt strongly that we shouldn't bring anyone back whom we weren't committed to keeping, and the other shareholders agreed. We wanted to build a company that would take job security seriously, that would treat loyalty as a two-way street. We wanted to be in the business of creating jobs, not eliminating them. That dream would die in the cradle if we rehired too many of the old Harvester employees and then discovered we didn't have enough business to support them.

Once we had an appropriately conservative sales forecast, we took our budget and began cutting. We hacked away at the numbers all day long. By evening, we still had $550,000 in overhead that had to go. We went around the room, and the managers reluctantly made their cuts—all but one, that is, the head of engineering, who refused to accept any reduction in his staff. That, in itself, wasn't such a big deal. We could handle one shareholder acting like a bureaucratic department head. What took me aback was the escalating conflict his behavior ignited.

The problem was that he had some of the highest-paid employees in the factory. If you dropped one salary in engineering, you might be able to pick up two somewhere else. At first, the other managers tried coaxing him along. "Come on, we've all got to do this." But he wouldn't budge, and you could see the frustration level gradually rise. No one wanted to lose people, after all. This guy wasn't playing by the rules. Pretty soon, the discussion began to get personal. People turned on each other. Tempers flared. Insults were traded. Threats were made. People dug in and defended their turf. Meanwhile, they forgot about cutting the $550,000.

It was the worst meeting of my life—a free-for-all sparked by one guy's refusal to accept the idea that he might have to get by with a smaller staff. No doubt he thought he was protecting his people's jobs. In fact, he was jeopardizing the business, or he would be if he succeeded in defending his little fiefdom. I could see the walls going up all over the place. No one was focusing on what we had to do to survive. And these were the leaders, the role models!

The meeting went until midnight, and the longer it lasted, the more depressed I became. I saw the dream dissolving before my eyes. Afterward I did a lot of soul-searching. **It was clear to me how easily we could destroy ourselves from within, and I realized we might well do so if people didn't give up the habits of a lifetime of employee thinking.** Was the episode a sign of things to come? Were we making a big mistake here? Would people rise to the challenges we were bound to face in the days and weeks ahead?

In the end, I decided I was probably expecting too much, too soon. If we were going to achieve our dream, we'd have to do it with the people we had, and—as potent as equity might be—they weren't going to change all of their habits and ways of thinking in a couple of weeks.

So I did what any CEO would do. I took the decision into my own hands and did what I thought was best for the company. From our sales forecast, I could calculate the amount of gross profit we could expect to earn in the coming year. I then figured out how much of it we should set aside to cover interest, warranty, and net profit. The rest I divided up among the various departments. The department heads were all given dollar amounts that they could spend any way they chose as long as they got the job done and stayed within the budget. I doubt if my approach made it any easier for them to decide which people to bring back and which ones to let go, but at least everyone understood why those decisions had to be made.

It wasn't my idea of a good budget process. I didn't want to tell people what they could spend. I'd hoped we could reach a consensus about what was best for the company, but obviously we weren't ready to operate by consensus. Would we ever be? Time would tell. We'd give the shareholders a chance to get used to the idea of being owners and hope that everybody would start acting accordingly. Whether or not they needed anything other than time, we'd have to see.

FIELD NOTES

Lessons from Companies with an Ownership Culture

Nims Associates, Decatur, Illinois

How do you build spirit when people are widely dispersed, working in different locations, and have little direct contact with one another? A culture of ownership, it turns out, can be the unifying factor, turning a bunch of employees into a team.

Take Nims Associates, based in Decatur, Illinois, a provider of computer-related consulting services that has been practicing open-book management since its founding in 1978 and playing the Game since 1992. In the past ten years, the company's revenues have climbed 1,400 percent, and profits 9,000 percent, while the workforce has grown from 54 to 570 employees.

But fast growth was producing strains, and they were exacerbated by the fact that employees spent almost all of their time out in the field, working with clients. In addition, the company was opening new branches in cities as distant as Minneapolis and Dallas.

Concerned about preserving the ownership culture at Nims, a group of employees decided to take matters into their own hands, putting together what they call their Active Ownership Program. The goals of the program, they said, were to provide informal business education, promote the Nims culture, facilitate interaction and communication, and help people to "feel like they have a stake in the outcome." With that in mind, the group developed a schedule of activities, including regular lunch discussions of business and "Town Hall" meetings with managers and members of the board.

"Ownership is active concern," the members explained in an orientation for new employees. ". . . An owner chooses to constantly grow, and does not wait for someone else to tell him what new skills to learn. . . . An owner builds the entire team."

5

How We Began to Open Our Books and Build Our Ownership Culture

For the shareholders of SRC, as for most people who start their own companies, our first year in business turned out to be a school in which we were taught what it really takes to survive as an independent enterprise. Of course, some people never graduate from that school, and we almost flunked out as well, thanks to a chain of events set in motion before the buyout was even completed. Without realizing it, we'd turned our second-largest customer into our sworn enemy.

Dresser Industries was the new owner of Harvester's old construction equipment division and controlled the distribution pipeline to the former Harvester dealers, now Dresser dealers, who carried our products. We were counting on Dresser for $12 million in sales during our first year—almost half of what we'd forecast for the entire business. What we hadn't counted on was the reaction of the Dresser people when they found out that Harvester had decided to sell the Springfield factory to us rather than them.

I got my first inkling of their feelings the day after the buyout when I telephoned my erstwhile boss, George DiPrima. He wouldn't take my call.

Not a good sign. Instead his vice president of sales got on the line and spelled out the terms under which Dresser would continue to do business with us. The terms were so unfavorable that—had we accepted them—we'd have lost money on every sale and gone out of business within months, if not weeks. When I objected, he told me to take it or leave it.

I thought he must be bluffing. In my view, we were the only people around with experience in producing the remanufactured engines and engine components that the Dresser dealers needed to serve their own customers. Dresser had to maintain credibility with those dealers. Yes, it could develop another supplier, but I figured it would take months to get one up to speed. In the meantime, I figured, Dresser would no doubt follow its own best interests and do the sensible thing—namely, keep buying from us.

I concluded a few weeks later, however, that this wasn't about sense. It was about emotion.

George DiPrima didn't mince his words. "We don't want to have anything to do with you," he said when we finally met face-to-face. "Take your business and go someplace else."

War!

In the beginning, I don't think we fully appreciated the size of the hole we'd just fallen into, but we knew it was very, very big. Of the $7 million we'd paid for the Renew Center's assets, 75 percent had gone to purchase inventory, including both finished goods and materials we intended to make into finished goods—most of which could be sold only through Dresser dealers. Indeed, we figured that, all told, about 80 percent of our inventory was earmarked for Dresser. If it refused to distribute our products, there was just one other way to get them to market. We'd have to sell them directly to the Dresser dealers.

To be sure, that meant competing with Dresser itself, which had lined up another supplier faster than any of us had thought possible. We needed that kind of competition like a hole in the head. On the other hand, we couldn't just write off $4.2 million worth of inventory.

We'd been in business for less than five weeks, and no one was in a mood to surrender. We were ready to take on the world if we had to. If it was war Dresser wanted, war was what it would get.

Fortunately, we didn't know what we were doing. I say "fortunately" because—in retrospect—we probably made the right decision, and we might not have if we'd understood how crazy it was. After all, we were about to go up against a multi-billion dollar giant with virtually unlimited resources and a direct channel to the customers we had to reach, and we didn't even have a sales force. Lee Shroyer, our head of sales, was doing his best, but he was a manufacturing guy like the rest of us. So were the people who worked for him. None of them had any significant sales experience. What's more, they didn't have basic selling tools, such as price sheets, catalogs, information packets, and so on—we hadn't had time to create them.

And even if we were able to put those materials together, even if we could somehow build a credible sales organization, we'd still be operating at an enormous disadvantage. It didn't matter how effective our salespeople were, or how good our products were, or how cheap our prices were. We simply didn't have the clout with dealers that Dresser had, and we never would. But as I said: Fortunately, we didn't realize that, and so we proceeded to get ready for war.

We were also lucky that our bankers gave us some leeway. We had to tell them what was going on. We certainly didn't want them to find out later. When you borrow money, your word comes first, and so you have to protect your credibility. The bank will accept whatever you say you're going to do, but you damn well better have a plan you can deliver on, and if there are any changes in it, you have to let the bank know fast.

So we did that. We told the bank we had problems with Dresser and we'd have to revise our sales projections accordingly. We added, however, that we expected to recoup a substantial portion of the sales by going directly to the dealers.

We didn't waste any time getting started, either. We immediately pulled several employees out of production and put them on the phones. Other people went to work creating sales materials. Meanwhile, Shroyer's team fanned out across the country, visiting every dealer we knew, letting them know that we were in business and ready to help them meet all of their remanufacturing needs.

Yet, for all of our hard work and good intentions, it was strictly an amateur effort, as McCoy kept reminding me. "We may be able to get away with this for a while," he said, "but the bank isn't going to buy it forever. We're going to have to come up with something better, and soon."

"No Surprises"

Our situation was particularly difficult—not to say hopeless—because of one very big and very simple problem. It's the same problem that most start-ups face sooner or later, and it can be summarized in just two words: no cash.

Most people think that profit is paramount in business, and it certainly is important, but cash is king. I'm talking here about the stuff you use to pay your bills every month. I don't think anyone really understands what it takes to succeed in business until you've tried to operate without cash.

To be sure, you might think at first glance that we had access to plenty of cash. In addition to the $6 million we'd gotten to do the buyout, the bank had given us a $2 million credit line. But one of the first things you learn in business is the difference between a promise of cash and its actual delivery. In fact, the bank had advanced us only enough cash at the time of the buyout to keep us going for about three months. To get more, we had to generate receivables.

Under the terms of our deal, the bank would lend us 50 percent of our outstanding receivables from Harvester, and 80 percent of receivables from other customers, up to the limit of $2 million. Whatever we owed on the credit line would be paid down as the receivables were collected and the checks were deposited in the bank's lockbox. At that point, we could take out the cash we hadn't borrowed on those receivables—the remaining 50 percent from Harvester and 20 percent from other customers—and we'd be eligible to borrow more against new receivables.

HOW TO MAKE A BANKER LOVE YOU

When you have a start-up company, you're naturally afraid of doing anything that might alarm your lenders because you're at their mercy. If they lose faith in you, they can cause you all kinds of trouble, maybe even put you out of business, just by calling their loan.

But I didn't fully understand why bankers hate surprises so much until I served on the lending committee of a bank in Springfield in the early 1990s. I realized then that it all has to do with the bankers' perception of your character.

When it comes to borrowing and lending, character is everything. Why? Because character is all that a lending officer knows about. Anyone can come up with a good-looking business plan, and you can tell only so much by going over a set of projections. Even when you check the assets, assess the market, and perform your due diligence, you're mainly searching for clues about the people who want you to lend them money—because you make loans on character and conviction. Can we trust these people? Are they honest? Do they tell the truth? Do they understand the responsibilities they're taking on? Will they live up to their commitments?

I don't think most people realize that when they start out in business. They'd save themselves some trouble if they did. If nothing else, they'd see why it's a good idea to begin developing a relationship with a banker before they need to ask for a loan. It's a lot easier to borrow money from someone who already knows your character. We didn't have that luxury, but we made up for it by bending over backward to maintain our credibility with our bankers at all times, and thereby give them confidence that we were trustworthy people to do business with.

But we couldn't borrow any more money until we'd made the sales and sent out the invoices. Meanwhile, there were certain bills that had to be paid on time no matter what, including our monthly interest payment of $79,000 and a monthly payroll of $215,000.

The bank was as nervous about this situation as we were and expected us to report almost daily on our cash status—what we had on hand, what we'd committed to spend, what we could count on coming in and when. We knew how important it was to give the bank accurate projections. We couldn't afford another surprise like the Dresser deal. We also knew that McCoy and I, who'd drawn up the original forecast, had blown it, mainly by underestimating how angry the Dresser people were and how fast they could move.

My solution was to get more people involved in the process. Partly, I suppose, I wanted to spread out responsibility for the forecast, but I also thought we couldn't be accurate otherwise. McCoy and I didn't have the information we needed. In fact, we didn't even have the means to collect it.

So we began holding daily meetings of the shareholders at which we'd collectively put together a rough income statement on a yellow pad and figure out where we stood in terms of cash. We'd sit in our conference room every morning and gather the latest information from the day before. Our purchasing guy, Dan Plumery, would report on what he'd ordered, what he was getting ready to order, what we owed our top thirty suppliers. Dave Lahay, our materials manager, would say how we stood with inventory, what parts were running low. Doug Rothert, our controller, would tell us what checks had come in and what invoices had gone out. And so it went.

Then, once a week, we'd have a larger staff meeting, including all of the front-line supervisors, to let them know where we stood and to give them a chance to let the rest of us know about anything important we might not be aware of. Afterward, the supervisors would usually hold meetings on the shop floor to fill the hourly people in.

The idea was simply to make sure everyone knew what was going on, how we were doing, and what needed to happen next. Without realizing it, however, we were also laying the groundwork for the open-book management system we later developed—the one that came to be known as the Great Game of Business. We were establishing the principle that everybody had a role to play in making the company successful and that we were all depending on one another to do our part. We were starting to break down the walls of ignorance that keep most companies from tapping into their most valuable resource: the intelligence and creativity of their employees.

OWNERSHIP RULE #5

It takes a team to build equity value.

An ownership culture is built on mutual trust and respect, and it's almost impossible to have either one unless people throughout the company are engaged in frank, open, and honest communication about the state of the business.

Our motto was "no surprises." Over and over, we told people that we couldn't afford even a $10,000 surprise, and by and large we didn't have one. The meetings did more than eliminate surprises and improve our forecasts, however. The relentless focus on cash wore away at habits and attitudes carried over from the Harvester days. People were constantly reminded that cash was everything. They couldn't hide behind budgets and job descriptions and departmental boundaries. We were in survival mode. We did what was necessary to make sure we didn't squander the one resource that could keep us alive.

To drive the point home, we came up with a mission statement, "Don't run out of cash, and don't destroy from within," and I repeated it at every opportunity. I wanted people to be thinking about cash all the time. I also wanted them to understand that the greatest threat to cash—or at least the greatest threat we could control—was internal conflict. We couldn't afford any more meetings in which we tore one another apart over budget issues. If we ran out of cash, we were dead, and we were sure to run out of it if we started fighting among ourselves.

And people rose to the challenge. Everybody did. We pinched pennies so tightly they turned colors. We spent one whole meeting debating whether or not to replace the bushes that were dying out in front of the factory. Was it more important to project a prosperous image for marketing purposes, or to spend the cash on additional machine tools? In the end, we went for the machine tools and gave the guys who wanted bushes enough money to buy seeds.

That was more or less the pattern. We talked about things in minute detail, and we compromised when we could. Was it worth spending

$60,000 on the new copier we needed? What if we could get a financing deal allowing us to pay for it interest-free over five years? Did we want the additional debt? Could we afford the hit to cash flow? And how were we going to transport people to the trade-group convention in Louisville we'd signed up for? We could actually save money by renting a Lincoln Town Car, rather than two economy cars, but would we be sending the wrong message?

I can't say that we always made the right decision, or that everyone liked the decisions we made, but there was a lot of give-and-take, openness, and flexibility, as well as a tremendous feeling of community, which was a direct result of the way we were operating. The more information people had, the less territorial they became. We all knew how dire our situation was on a daily basis and how much we needed one another to survive, and so attitudes began to change. None of us was just an employee anymore. None of us was working to a job description. The company we owned was in trouble, and we needed to do whatever was necessary to save it.

That feeling was contagious. Whenever we had a big order to fill, for example, everybody pitched in. We couldn't afford to pay overtime to the hourly people, and so the managers frequently spent their evenings and weekends out on the shop floor, getting their hands dirty. On regular workdays, we all wore blue jeans and work shoes to the plant, just in case our help was needed—as it often was. We expedited parts. We struggled with labelers. We boxed thousands and thousands of water pumps. Managers would come off the floor saying, "Man, I can't believe what a backbreaking job that is. How can these guys do it for eight hours a day?" Sometimes they'd even think up ways to make the job easier.

Disaster

Although our situation remained precarious, we were able to make some headway and succeeded in reducing our inventory by about $1.4 million during the first quarter. Then disaster struck. Sometime in May, I returned from a trip and sat down with McCoy to find out what had happened while I was away. In the course of the conversation, he mentioned that he'd sent a check for $389,000 to the Internal Revenue Service to cover our tax liability on the inventory sales.

I almost fell out of my chair. "Three hundred and eighty-nine thousand dollars!" I said. "Are you out of your mind? Has the check been cashed?"

"Calm down, Jack," McCoy said. "What are you going to do? Stop payment on a check to the IRS?" We had no choice, he said. There was a quarterly tax payment due, and—because of the profit we'd made on the inventory we'd sold—our accounting firm had told him to send in a check for $389,000.

"And you didn't get a second opinion?" I said. I couldn't believe it. We were all aware that we didn't have that kind of cash to spare. How could McCoy spend it knowing the consequences? The accounting firm couldn't predict what our tax liability was going to be at the end of year. Nobody could. We were a start-up, for Pete's sake. Wasn't there another option?

And why hadn't McCoy talked to me before sending off the check? Why did I have to find out about it after the fact? Okay, I'd been away, but we were supposed to have open communication and no surprises, whether or not I was in town. That was a fundamental principle. What else was going on that I didn't know about?

The next day, we consulted with some tax specialists, who told us we could probably have avoided the payment had we not already sent it in, but now there was nothing we could do—other than change our outside accountants, that is, which we did.

The experience taught me that we had a hell of lot to learn about business. None of us had even thought of the tax angle beforehand, and so we'd gotten trapped by our ignorance.

I also learned that financial decisions are too important to be left completely up to the financial people. McCoy was the smartest finance guy I knew, but he'd made a critical mistake because he acted alone, without consulting the rest of us. That ran counter to everything we believed in. We couldn't let it happen again.

The payment of the tax bill pushed us to the brink of collapse. We were forced to use up the rest of our credit line, thereby increasing our total debt to $8.9 million. Our debt-to-equity ratio reached a mind-boggling 89-to-1, which is the business equivalent of brain-dead. We were flirting with default on our bank loan. Our largest customer was almost bankrupt. Making payroll was touch-and-go.

We were about as low as you can go in business and still be alive. After three months of operation, our net worth was negative—that is, our liabilities exceeded our assets—and the terms of our loan required that we have positive net worth at all times. The bank could close us down at any moment. What's more, we had no fallback position. We'd already leveraged everything in sight. There were no other assets we could borrow against and no possibility of renegotiating our loan. We had a one-way ticket, and once we'd used it, the ride was over. There would be no return home.

The only thing that could keep us alive was cash, and we were having more trouble than ever coming up with it. Harvester, which needed cash as desperately as we did, was paying all of its suppliers as slowly as possible. There were times when we had to send somebody to Harvester headquarters to get the next check so that we'd be able to meet payroll. Meanwhile, we weren't having as much success as we'd hoped in our campaign to sell directly to the Dresser dealers, despite bringing in some high-powered salespeople to help us.

But you can never overestimate the role of luck in business, or maybe it's divine intervention. What ultimately saved us was a factor we hadn't counted on and couldn't have controlled if we'd wanted to: the zeal of our adversaries at Dresser.

I don't know exactly how it happened, but somewhere along the way, Dresser made a critical error. Perhaps DiPrima and his people were fed up with us and let their emotions dictate their strategy—always a bad idea in business. In any case, Dresser made the decision to start buying lots of certain key materials required to remanufacture engines, the so-called cores.

In any type of remanufacturing, the core is the old, worn-out product that serves as your basic raw material. It's what gets recycled when somebody buys a remanufactured product. If the product is a remanufactured engine, the core is the used engine that's being replaced. The purchaser turns it in, and the dealer ships it back to us. We then remanufacture it and sell it—and get another core in return.

It's a great system from an environmental standpoint, but it can drive you crazy as a businessperson, because the inventory is always coming back. You can never get rid of it. As a result, you always have tons of cash tied up in these rusty, old, broken-down engines piled up in a lot behind your factory.

And engine cores are, in fact, worth a good deal of money—for the same reason that empty beer cans can be worth a good deal of money. When you buy a remanufactured engine, a credit for the core is included in the price. That credit works pretty much like the deposit you pay when you buy a can of beer. Just as you can get your deposit back when you return the can, engine buyers can get their deposit back when they return the core. What's more, the supplier has to pay them. No matter that customers almost always buy another engine on which they have to pay another deposit. As the supplier, you have an obligation to refund the deposit on every engine that comes back in. And when you refund the deposit, you are, in effect, paying for the core. So engine cores represent a major investment, though they may look to the uninitiated like worthless junk.

Of course, as an engine remanufacturer, you make money on cores—as on other kinds of raw inventory—by converting them into finished products that can be sold. Moreover, you can't remanufacture engines if you don't have a source of cores. Since Dresser wasn't going to do business with us anymore, it needed other suppliers. One way it could help them was to provide them with cores. So someone at Dresser had the bright idea of offering top dollar to acquire as many cores as possible.

There was just one problem with this strategy: We had more engine cores than we knew what to do with. Cores for Dresser engines constituted about 30 percent of the inventory we'd bought from International Harvester, which had sold them to us at 50 percent of cost. The market value was $800 to $1,500 apiece. Now Dresser was suddenly offering $2,500, and no one had a bigger supply than we did. We might have been naive, but we knew an opportunity when it hit us in the face. We decided to go into the core-selling business.

We proceeded to dump as much of our inventory on Dresser as possible. We couldn't do so directly, of course, because Dresser wouldn't buy from us, so we sold the cores through intermediaries—specifically, friends of ours who were Dresser dealers. We had good relations with several of them from the Harvester era. We offered them a deal they couldn't refuse: 5 percent on every sale without doing anything.

It was such a good deal for both parties that we couldn't stop. When we ran out of our own cores to sell, we began buying them from junkyards. Our people, unlike Dresser's, knew exactly where to look. They'd been doing it for years. They had the best contacts in the market, and we just fed the cores into the pipeline, splitting whatever profit we made with the dealers.

It wasn't a long-term strategy, but it worked well while it lasted, and we made a lot of money. The cash we brought in literally kept us afloat during one of the most perilous times in our history. Eventually, somebody at Dresser had enough common sense to say, "God Almighty, what are we going to do with all these cores?" So the program was terminated. By then, however, we'd already gotten what we needed out of it. Indeed, without Dresser's core-buying extravaganza, we probably wouldn't be here today.

FIELD NOTES

Lessons from Companies with an Ownership Culture

Setpoint, Ogden, Utah

The ability to forecast has always been an important gauge of how well a company is managed. Bankers, for example, view the accuracy of the forecast as the acid test of a company's management, as well as a critical tool for making credit decisions. You can be much more accurate if the people doing the work know what the forecast is and have the information they need to achieve it.

That was the lesson at Setpoint, in Ogden, Utah, a fast-growing, project-based manufacturer of factory-automation equipment and roller coasters. In November 1998, the company was on a growth binge, pushing the limits of its credit line, and its banker was breathing down the CFO's neck. Setpoint, which had been playing its own version of the Great Game of Business since its founding in 1992, had run losses for three consecutive months, but CFO (now CEO) Joe Knight had promised the banker that it would break even in November and return to profitability in December.

When the number for the first week of November came in, however, they showed continuing losses. Knight distributed the weekly income statement to employees and talked to the lead engineer about the danger of maxing out the credit line. The bank could shut down the company, he said.

People knew exactly what to do. When Knight got the numbers for the second week, the situation had been completely turned around. Virtually no work had been done on money-losing projects. Instead, people had focused almost all their attention on the projects with the higher gross-profit margins, so the company had made money for the week.

"How many companies can find out they're losing money in the first week of November and turn it around like that?" asked Knight. "Not many." When he met with the banker, he had the numbers to prove the company was in control.

6

Manageable Failures

Everybody who goes into business wants to be successful. The mistake most of us make is to think that the path to success is a straight line. Every big success, we believe, is the result of a series of small successes. The assumption is that you will eventually get what you want if you just take it a step at a time, going from one small victory to the next, until you reach your ultimate goal.

What we miss are all the failures that play a critical role in every success story. Many of those failures are personal. I'm talking about people not living up to expectations, not rising to the challenge, blowing opportunities, giving up, falling by the wayside. I'm talking about serious miscalculations, grave lapses in judgment, disastrous blunders, severe disappointments, even betrayals. We've had them all from day one.

And yet, as a business, we've grown stronger with every failure. Each attempt has produced benefits for the company, even if the individuals haven't taken advantage of the opportunity we've offered. They may not have come out winners, but the company always gained.

Success is a series of manageable failures. I didn't see that at first. For a long time, I let the failures get to me. I found them very discouraging. They made me question what we were doing. It slowly began to dawn on me, however, that there was an important lesson in the failures.

OWNERSHIP RULE #6

Failures are fine as long as they strengthen the company.

Everything depends on making the company successful. Yes, you want all the players to have a chance at the rewards. But the rewards come only after success, not before. As long as people understand that rule, you can handle the failures. You can learn from your mistakes. The company gets in trouble only when people lose sight of the common goal.

In the course of building an ownership culture, you're going to have a lot of failures, most of which will be people failures. We had our full share. But each failure took us a step closer to our dream, which proved to be very good for everyone who persevered.

The Deal of a Lifetime

One of our most important failures came in the early stages of our equity journey. The loss of the Dresser account got us thinking about putting together a high-powered sales team. We knew we couldn't survive unless we generated a lot of new sales, and we also knew we couldn't get them with the sales force we had, which consisted largely of people we'd pulled off the shop floor. We needed top salespeople with winning track records, superstars who could not only compete head-to-head with Dresser but go out and find new accounts.

But how could we attract that kind of talent? And how could we pay for it? We certainly couldn't afford the salaries that superstar salespeople commanded. We had no money. What could we offer that would get a topflight salesperson to give up a secure, well-paying job and come with a struggling engine remanufacturer in Springfield, Missouri?

As soon as I asked the question, the answer popped into my head: equity.

These days, of course, a lot of businesses attract talent with offers of an equity stake. Indeed, stock options helped fuel the whole Internet boom of the late 1990s, and there's widespread agreement that they can be an important tool in motivating a workforce. Back in 1983, however, only a handful of companies offered equity to employees, let alone new hires, and it was pretty much unheard of for a manufacturing start-up to use equity as recruitment bait. So we didn't have the advantage of being able to learn from someone else's mistakes. But that didn't deter us. Although we'd been in business a grand total of about six months, we charged ahead and made our own mistakes—and learned all kinds of vital lessons in the process.

It didn't take long for a plan to come together. We would set up a subsidiary that would do nothing but sales—not just for SRC, but for other customers as well. We called it the ReManufacturing Sales Company, or RSC for short. SRC would own 60 percent of the new business, and we'd sign up four top-notch salespeople, each of whom would get 10 percent of the stock. That would take care of the long-term reward. In the short term, they'd earn commissions of 5 percent on any sale they made—with 3 percent going to the individual salesperson and 2 percent staying in RSC. While they were getting started, they could take a "draw" that would eventually be paid back out of commissions. We'd also guarantee each of them a base salary. As for financing of the business, they wouldn't have to put up a thing. What we wanted was their energy, commitment, and experience. SRC would underwrite the whole deal.

It seemed like a can't-miss proposition. The people we signed up could hit the ground running. We could drive a lot of sales to them and give them a ton of leads—all the Dresser dealers, for openers. What's more, if RSC succeeded, and if it helped make SRC successful, the new company would itself be worth a lot of money. Hell, it could be worth a lot of money even if SRC *wasn't* successful. We placed as few restrictions as possible on the salespeople who'd be coming in. We wanted to offer them all the opportunities in the world. They could sell whatever they liked to whomever they liked and reap tremendous rewards in the process. The one condition was that they had to take responsibility for themselves. I didn't want them blaming me if this thing failed. Each of us had to be responsible for our own livelihood. That was the deal.

I had a sense of the kind of salespeople we wanted, and I also had some particular individuals in mind. Three of them I'd met through Harvester, and one was a neighbor of mine in Springfield. They were all extremely successful, not to mention gainfully employed. I called each of them up and gave my pitch. I said, "Look, we'll push a lot of business through you, and if you guys want to, you can sell other people's products to customers we don't even have a relationship with. We won't hold you back. The idea is to build a real business here, a manufacturer's rep firm, and we'll finance it. You'll earn commissions on your sales, and we'll split the ownership with you. If you guys do what you're capable of, you stand to make a fortune."

It wasn't even a hard sell. They all wanted in. So I set up a meeting at a nice hotel in Wisconsin. I told them we'd take three days to get to know one another and iron out the details of the agreement. Then we'd get going.

I was thrilled. I thought we'd found our salvation. With a sales team like this one, we could run circles around Dresser and open up all kinds of new markets. At the same time, we'd be giving our new superstars the opportunity of a lifetime. Between them they had an awesome amount of experience, connections, and talent. It was inconceivable to me that they couldn't find a way to make RSC successful on a grand scale and make themselves wealthy in the process.

In fact, I thought that RSC had a better shot than SRC. We were still in the survival stage, after all, and it was by no means certain that we'd last long enough to get out of it. In the meantime, equity wasn't going to play much of a role. For one thing, most people didn't have any stock yet; we hadn't had time to launch the ESOP. As for the shareholders, there might have been three or four people who were really tuned in to the opportunity we had. Equity may have raised them to another level. Nobody else, however, gave it a second thought. Building wealth just didn't seem all that important when we were still struggling to save our jobs.

RSC was a different ball game. Its owner-employees had none of our baggage to weigh them down. We'd gone out of our way to make sure they'd be able to operate on their own. Yes, SRC had a right of first refusal on any business they came up with, but they wouldn't have to depend on us for their success. They could develop other product lines, other customers, other market segments, other industries. They could do whatever they liked. It was all gravy to us; we owned 60 percent of RSC's stock. We weren't about to prevent the RSC guys from pursuing any good, solid business opportunity. And if SRC went under, they could carry on by themselves.

Frankly, I didn't see what could stop them. There was nothing in their way. They didn't have to worry about any of the things that were keeping us from moving forward. They could be successful out of the box.

In doing so, moreover, they'd validate my dream. I saw RSC as the first real chance we'd had to witness that dream in action, to find out what you could do with a company of owners. It was as nice, as clean, and as simple an experiment as you could ask for. You'd be dealing with four intelligent, well-educated, hard-driving, highly motivated individuals, each with a wealth of hands-on business experience. They didn't need any of the training in basic business concepts that you'd have to give, say, the people on the shop floor. Hell, these guys knew more than we did.

What's more, they all had an equal stake in the outcome, or at least the equity portion of it, and so you wouldn't run into the kind of envy I'd encountered when I divided up the SRC stock. There would be differences in the sales commissions they earned, of course, but they were used to dealing with that type of inequality.

Most important, they could start out with a clean slate and a clear road in front of them. What could possibly go wrong?

As it turned out, just about everything.

Who's in Charge Here?

The problems began to surface about an hour or so into our first meeting. We were sitting around a small table in a room at the Marriott Hotel in Racine, Wisconsin, and you could choke on the tension in the air.

Dennis Sheppard and I had flown up from Springfield with one of the RSC people, my neighbor Bill, who had experience selling to small businesses. Joe, who'd been a star salesman at International Harvester, had come in from Chicago. The other two members of the team, Ralph and Doug, both lived in Racine, where they'd worked for Modine Manufacturing, a maker of radiators and other vehicle components. They'd met us at the hotel.

I gave them all a little pep talk. I wanted them to focus on the opportunity they had. Each of them was so talented, and their talents were so diverse and complementary. I told them there was no limit to what they could accomplish once they came together as a team.

They wanted to know who was going to be the boss.

I said, Ralph's going to be president, but you're all going to be owners. You'll be working for yourselves. You need to be a team of entrepreneurs. You can build this thing into something awesome, a really dynamite organization, if you just keep your eyes on the Big Picture.

They wanted to know what their sales territories were going to be.

I said, Don't worry about it! You can work that stuff out among yourselves later. What you should be doing now is trying to understand what each of you brings to the party. Then you can figure out how to make the most of your individual strengths and really blow this sucker out of the water.

They wanted to define their job responsibilities.

No matter what I said, they kept going back to the operational details. Joe came on strong, arguing that he should get various plum territories in the Midwest, where he had a lot of contacts. Wait a second, said the others. Does that mean we can't sell in those areas? We've been selling there for years, for chrissakes. Hey, it's a big country. We can't all be tripping over each other. Well, who's running the show here? Didn't Jack say Ralph was president?

So it went. I could see that the pressure was getting to Ralph, who clearly was going to have his hands full. Finally, we decided to take a break and go to lunch.

There was a restaurant off the hotel lobby called the Peppertree

Lounge. We found a table behind a small grove of plastic plants. As we were taking our seats, Ralph suddenly slumped to the floor. I grabbed for him. He was out cold. I thought he was dead.

He wasn't dead, in fact, but he'd had a major heart attack. He lay there unconscious. We shouted for help, and people came running. Did anybody know CPR? Nobody knew CPR. Someone called an ambulance. There was total chaos and a feeling of utter helplessness. I telephoned Ralph's wife and told her to get over to the hospital right away. I didn't know what was going to happen, but I feared the worst. I was scared. We were all scared.

In the end, thank God, Ralph recovered, and he's alive and well today. RSC was not as fortunate.

Old Habits Die Hard

In my opinion, it never really became a business. Even after Ralph returned, it was just a bunch of individuals, each doing his own thing and competing against the others. They seemed oblivious to the opportunity that was staring them in the face. No matter how much we talked about the Big Picture and the need to work together, they couldn't get over all the habits they'd learned growing up as employees in traditionally run companies. They'd been trained to follow a job description that said you should generate as many sales as possible and not worry about anything else. To look out for number one and regard your colleagues as rivals. To focus on the size of your paycheck and the title on your business card.

And they couldn't stop. Right up to the end, they were fighting over who was going to be president, who was going to work for whom, who was going to get which territories, and what exactly a territory was anyway.

Joe was the worst offender because he was the most aggressive. He wanted everything. Not that he didn't pull his weight. On the contrary, he worked his butt off, and he lived up to his advance billing as a superstar salesman from the old school. The guy was just born to sell.

He went to see everybody—Greyhound, General Motors, Thermo King, White Engine, Deutz-Allis, Ingersoll-Rand, Clark Equipment, you name it. He'd force his way into the purchasing department, and he wouldn't leave until he got what he came for. He was driving our engineering people crazy, because he would agree to whatever a potential customer wanted. He'd promise that we could deliver a given quantity of something at such and such a time, and meanwhile we'd never laid eyes on the product before, to say nothing about knowing how to remanufacture it or what to charge. Mike Carrigan, our head of operations, who had to come up with the price quotes, was going out of his mind. I helped him out as much as I could, staying late at night, breaking down products for potential customers, trying to put together bills of materials and quotes. It was murder. We just couldn't keep up with Joe. We were quoting for him all the time.

But the guy delivered.

The others didn't do badly either. Like Joe, Doug went after big manufacturers, including J. I. Case, which was based in Racine and eventually became one of our largest customers. As for Bill, he focused on the Dresser dealers and was able to peddle a fair amount of material to them.

Together they brought a ton of business into SRC. Joe delivered Thermo King, which is still a major account for us, and General Motors, which turned out to be huge. In our third year, GM accounted for $11 million in sales, 36 percent of our business. In our fourth year, it passed Harvester—which by then had become Navistar*—as our largest customer, with $19 million in sales, or 50 percent of our business at the time.

What the RSC people didn't do was to take advantage of the opportunity we'd given them. Instead of figuring out how to build the value of this business in which each of them was a 10 percent shareholder, they fought over territories and titles. When they didn't get their way, they complained to me, but I wasn't about to come in and solve their problems.

---

* A number of companies have changed their names during the course of our journey. International Harvester became Navistar in 1986 and then International in 2000. J. I. Case became Case Corp. and then CNH Global, N.A., in 1999. To avoid confusing readers, we'll refer to International as Navistar for the remainder of the book, and we'll call CNH Global simply Case.

Besides, I didn't know what I could do. I couldn't make them think like owners. I couldn't force them to act like members of a team. I had no idea how to deal with all the egos involved. They were all intensely competitive in the worst sense. They were always worrying about what someone else was doing. To me, the RSC guys were among the smartest, best-educated, most-talented business practitioners I'd ever met, and yet they couldn't figure out how to work together on the most basic issues, let alone grab the brass ring we'd offered them.

So RSC went into the tank, and with it, our dream of creating a fabulous, low-cost manufacturers' rep firm that was going to solve our sales problems and make its owner-employees rich. In the end, they simply couldn't overcome the obstacle of the way they did business in the past.

They'd had all the tools they'd needed—a shareholders' agreement, a supply agreement with SRC, individual contracts, you name it. The deal was fair all around and easily understandable. Everybody was protected.

It didn't help. They couldn't put aside their rivalries and personal grievances and figure out how to play like a team. Although they were owners, they had no idea what it meant to think and act like owners, and so they blew an incredible opportunity.

Just how big was that opportunity? Under the terms we'd agreed upon, RSC was entitled to 5 percent of any sales to any customer SRC didn't already have when the deal was signed. Over the years, we lived up to both the letter and the spirit of that agreement. And we would have continued to honor it. All the RSC people had to do was to get along with one another and hold the organization together. If they had, RSC would today have net pretax earnings of more than $1.5 million a year and would be worth somewhere in the vicinity $9 million.

The Ripple Effect

The experiment with RSC played itself out over two or three years, although it didn't take me that long to realize it had failed. That was a disappointment, for sure, but I can't say I was focusing at the time on the lost opportunity. Mainly I was worried about the effect our experiment was having on the rest of the company.

After fourteen months of RSC, our engineering department was totally decimated. The people there were worn as thin as paper, and we stood a risk of destroying from within, which we'd promised ourselves we wouldn't do. People were fighting with one another. People were mad at one another. It wasn't fun.

And RSC was the cause, no question. It tore us apart—because we couldn't turn it off. After losing Dresser, we'd been desperate to get every piece of business we could lay our hands on. Along came the RSC guys, bringing in wheelbarrows of stuff. That was great, except that we could never live up to their expectations. They kept screaming at us that we were letting customers down by not moving fast enough. Where were the damn quotes? Why weren't we giving customers what they'd been promised? How could we build a business if we couldn't deliver on time?

Inside SRC, the engineering people were flipping out under the pressure. You can't imagine the amount of work involved in figuring out the bill of materials and costing out the remanufacturing process for literally hundreds of products. Some of our key managers were stretched to the breaking point, and we'd begun to take out our frustrations on one another.

And the situation just kept getting worse. As it did, I and the other managers felt increasingly inadequate, which made it hard to lead. You have to be confident to run a business. You can't walk around feeling like a loser. If you do, you transmit that sense to everybody else in the organization. It becomes extremely difficult to generate the commitment and enthusiasm you need because you can't pump yourself up. Image counts in business. As a leader, it's important to come across as strong, healthy, optimistic. That's hard when you have a bleeding ulcer that's sapping all your energy.

So our sales were rising, but parts of the company were coming apart at the seams. For them, at least, our dream seemed very hollow. Here we'd launched RSC as a company of owners, and they'd torn each other apart. Now we ran the risk that they'd wind up taking some of us down with them.

What Went Wrong

The whole experience gave me a lot to think about. I kept asking myself, How could RSC have gone so wrong? I mean, these guys were the best. If they'd come in for interviews, you'd have hired them on the spot. Even if you could have afforded anybody you wanted, they were the ones you'd have chosen. You simply couldn't find people with better qualifications.

So what had happened? We'd done all we could to set them up to succeed. We'd given them a fabulous short-term compensation program. We'd given them a fabulous long-term equity program. We'd financed their business. We'd done everything, and we'd done it with the best intentions and the loftiest goals. Yet, for some reason, they couldn't see those goals. They were looking too hard at the next sale.

What had kept the RSC people from going for the real pot of gold? Why didn't they see how successful they could be if they just focused on increasing the value of their stock?

Commissions were a big part of the problem. The closer I looked, moreover, the more convinced I became that the drawbacks were built in. I hadn't seen that in the beginning. To me, commissions were simply a way of rewarding salespeople for their individual performances, which seemed fair. Besides, I thought I could use the promise of sales commissions to attract the RSC guys to our new venture. They were all on salary in their previous jobs. My pitch was that, by joining RSC, they'd make more money in the short term through commissions and more money in the long term through stock.

Commissions Encourage Short-Term Thinking

As it turned out, however, the commissions were too powerful. People were so focused on competing with one another to make as much money as possible right now that they never took in how much more money they could make down the road if they worked together. In effect, the incentive of commissions overwhelmed the incentive of the stock. By packaging the two together, we inadvertently created a culture that undermined our ability to achieve our primary goal.

Commissions Discourage Teamwork

The hallmark of that culture was an intense individualism, which got in the way of teamwork. I should have expected that, I suppose. When you pay people a sales commission, you're giving them a powerful reason to make sales their first priority, and selling is a solitary activity. It's hard enough for salespeople to think about the greater good or the long-term reward under any circumstances. It's almost impossible when their entire compensation is based on what they sell today.

Individualism Is the Enemy of Performance

The effect is to encourage salespeople to focus on themselves, and so you get individualism, which is the enemy of performance—unless maybe you have a one-person business. Phil Jackson, the former coach of the Chicago Bulls, used to beat that message into Michael Jordan. "What will make you a superstar," he said, "is not being the star." That is so true, and Jordan knew it. When he was questioned about his loyalty to Jackson, he said, "He taught me to let other people have the sunshine."

At RSC, it appeared that no one wanted to let anyone else have the sunshine, and the commissions just reinforced the behavior. They held people back, kept RSC from fulfilling its potential.

In addition, the commissions created huge problems inside SRC. The RSC guys were so single-minded in pursuit of the sale that they were oblivious to the pain they were inflicting on the rest of us. As an organization, they didn't care about the long-term health of our company. Sometimes it seemed as though they didn't see us at all. They didn't take in how much we all were depending on one another to develop strong relationships with customers that would last well into the future. At times the RSC guys seemed to regard us simply as an obstacle keeping them from getting their commission check as quickly as they would have liked.

That was ridiculous, of course. We needed them, but they also needed us. Although we'd set them up to be able to survive on their own, they clearly stood to benefit from our success, just as we stood to benefit from theirs. So, like it or not, they were on the same team as our engineering department—and yet they came close to destroying it.

The experience convinced me that our salespeople had to be integrated into the company. By giving the RSC guys their own business and putting them on commission, we'd wound up creating a monster that nearly ate us alive. In the future, we wanted to be sure that the salespeople understood their responsibilities to the rest of the company, and vice versa.

But there's a curious thing about business, *real* business, as it's practiced in the real world. You often have difficult experiences, and learn important lessons, and yet when you look back, you realize that you wouldn't necessarily have done much differently. I can't say, for example, that we were wrong to have launched RSC in the first place, or that under the same circumstances I wouldn't do it again. Yes, the experience showed us the dangers of commissions, but without commissions we probably wouldn't have been able to sign these guys up to begin with. And, although they drove us crazy, the sales they brought in not only kept us alive in the early days but wound up fueling our growth for the first five years we were in business.

In retrospect, we could have saved ourselves a good deal of anguish had we set up the commission structure differently. For one thing, we should have based the commissions on gross margins rather than sales, which would have forced the RSC guys to think about the cost of producing the stuff they brought in. In addition, we probably should have limited the commission part of their compensation to sales of products that had already been researched, designed, engineered, and produced.

That's what hurt us most: The RSC guys were constantly bringing in new programs, and it nearly killed us. Instead of selling the water pump we already made, they were forcing us to engineer a totally different water pump. As a result, we were always falling short. We were constantly late, and so we walked around with a tremendous feeling of inadequacy.

That feeling had devastating effects inside the company. People had no self-esteem. They didn't see themselves as winners. We couldn't generate a sense of pride, because we always had one foot in the hole.

And yet, as crazy as RSC's sales were making us, we felt we couldn't afford to turn them down. After losing Dresser, we lived in constant fear that we wouldn't have the cash we needed to survive. So we accepted all the jobs the RSC guys brought in, even though we didn't have to under the terms of our agreement. We'd anticipated the possibility that they might generate more business than we could handle. What we hadn't anticipated was the difficulty of getting everybody to work together—or the price we'd have to pay to find that out.

Dreams Matter

I'd assumed that ownership would overcome whatever problems the RSC guys might encounter. But it didn't, and so I learned another lesson, the most important one of the whole RSC episode—namely, that it wasn't enough to share equity. Ownership, by itself, doesn't give you an edge. Because people don't get it, even smart people.

That was a revelation. For the first time, I began to see just how tough it was going to be to build this company of owners we wanted. Handing out stock wasn't enough. Somehow we had to develop a process that would teach people what ownership is all about—why equity is worth having, what it takes to increase its value, how the different pieces fit together, the role of teamwork, the importance of focusing on the greater good.

It was a lesson that many other companies have learned. They share equity with the best of intentions but soon discover that it either has no effect or produces unintended consequences. I remember reading about an Indiana company called South Bend Lathe that set up an ESOP in the 1970s, hoping to motivate employees. Instead the move raised false expectations, and management failed to provide the necessary ownership education. As a result, the experiment fell apart in bitterness and rancor.

Or consider United Airlines, which introduced employee ownership with great fanfare in 1994, expecting to generate a new spirit of cooperation between labor and management—only to find that the same old conflicts kept resurfacing. Even companies like Phelps County Bank in

Rolla, Missouri, and Stone Construction Equipment in Honeoye, New York, which are now role models of employee ownership, floundered around for several years before figuring out how to make it work.

To one degree or another, we all made the same mistake. Like them, I hadn't understood the need to prepare the soil and create an environment in which ownership could flourish. I'd assumed you could go straight from point A to point B—that you just gave people a piece of the action, and everything took care of itself. I didn't realize how deeply buried the habits of the past are. People go to work in traditional businesses and learn traditional ways of thinking and acting, which become habits over time. You can't change those habits overnight. You can't change them by logic and rational discourse. Sometimes you can't even change them by appealing to self-interest. You can change them only by developing a process, by repetition—in effect, by replacing employee habits with owner habits.

With RSC, I saw what we were up against: the training of the industrial society. I saw the long-term effects of growing up with the modular style of management, which teaches you to look at everything through your job description. These four guys had all been in business for a long time, and they had plenty of experience. The problem was, they'd been working for someone else, someone with goals and values different from the ones we were trying to promote.

The result was that they couldn't understand ownership. They seemed more interested in competing with one another than with our real competitors. I felt they put their personal priorities higher than the company's long-term interests.

So I learned that, with many people, even experienced businesspeople, you have to start all over again. You have to show them a different way of thinking about the business and their role in it. You have to set up an educational process that's going to allow everyone to learn together. And that meant making big changes in the organizational structure, the relationships between people, the paths of communication, the whole concept of responsibilities and duties and goals.

7

What's in a Game?

Open-book management is one of those terms you think you understand as soon as you hear it. I myself didn't hear it until 1990, when *Inc.* magazine published an article called "The Open-Book Managers" and included SRC as one of the prime examples. Now, more than ten years later, I'm still not sure we're all talking about the same thing when we use the phrase.

Some people, I think, simply mean the practice of sharing financial information with employees, which is fine as far as it goes. At SRC, we, too, were open with our numbers from the beginning, but I don't consider what we did back then open-book *management.* You aren't using the financial information to manage, after all, if people aren't learning from it and don't know what to do with it. For that to happen, they need to know something about business.

Other people see open-book management as little more than a collection of motivational techniques. They think it's all about getting line employees to work harder. Some companies may use it for that purpose, but it wasn't what I had in mind. Not that I have anything against cheerleading. It's important to create an environment in which people really want to win, and there's nothing wrong with using whatever works to make everyone feel like a member of the team, to generate team spirit—pom-poms, banners, balloons, fireworks, celebrations, whatever. I love all that stuff.

But you can go only so far with motivational techniques. Maybe you'll encourage people to work harder or to be more productive, but you won't get them to think and act like owners. At best, you'll wind up with more enthusiastic employees—which isn't bad. It just wasn't what I was after. What's more, it doesn't have much to do with creating a culture of ownership.

"Reality Is Something You Have to Teach People"

A culture, any culture, is based on relationships and values. So when you set out to create a particular type of culture, it's important to be clear about the values you want to promote and the kind of relationships you want to foster.

I wanted a company of independent people, independent thinkers. I didn't want paternalism. I wanted people to be motivated because they saw the opportunity they had, not because I'd tricked them into doing what I wanted, or what was good for me. We were giving them a tremendous opportunity in the form of ownership. I wanted them to make the most of it by taking responsibility for themselves instead of counting on someone else to look after them.

And I didn't see any reason why we shouldn't all take responsibility for ourselves. We were there for the same reasons. I might be the boss, but my circumstances weren't much different from anyone else's. I also had to work for a living. I also had a family to feed. I also wanted some financial security, and ownership was the only way I knew of to get it. That was reality, and it was a great motivator for me. I figured it would be a great motivator for other people as well.

The question was, Did they understand reality? By the end of our first year in business, I had to admit that the answer was probably "no." It was becoming clear to me that reality was something you had to teach people. It wasn't enough to give them ownership. You had to show them what it means, what they could do with it.

OWNERSHIP RULE #7

Ownership needs to be taught.

That was the number-one lesson of the RSC experiment. As wonderful as a business design might be, it won't produce a company of owners, or a culture of ownership, all by itself. If people don't recognize the opportunity they have to create some financial security for themselves and for one another, they won't be motivated by it.

To be sure, we were neither the first company nor the last to run into this obstacle. Sooner or later, it rises up to block the way of every company that shares equity. If you want stock to have the desired effect, you have to help people make the transition from employee to owner. You have to teach them the meaning of economic value—what it is, where it comes from, how they can create it. You have to make them understand how the market looks at companies, what actually makes a business worth owning. You have to introduce them to the language of business, demystify it for them, show them the logic of profit, explain the whole scorekeeping system that businesspeople use.

I actually had a sense of what people needed to know thanks to the education I'd received during the two years I'd been out on the road, trying to raise money to buy the factory. I'd learned so much from my meetings with investors. I'd found out firsthand how the outside world evaluates a company like ours. The investors made no bones about telling me their view of our strengths and weaknesses—and what a shock it had been.

Investors, I discovered, didn't care how we ran the business. They weren't interested in our management philosophy. They wanted schmozzle, as Stan Golder had said. I realized that if we knew how to create schmozzle we could generate all that wealth for ourselves. We wouldn't have to let outsiders have it. We could do for our own people what the money guys get other people to do for them.

That is, in fact, a good way to play the business game. You find out how smart people value a business, and then you use that knowledge to increase the value of your own business. In effect, you match and align what you do inside the company with what investors are looking for. And you can do it with your own employees as the investors, provided they understand the game and know how to play it. That means, for openers, that you all have to be working from the same set of scorecards—the ones that investors use.

Our people knew nothing about that way of keeping score. During our years with Harvester, we'd had dozens of scorecards—for dress, for safety, for housekeeping, for quality, for whatever. What we hadn't had were the financial scorecards, and those were the only ones the investors I met with cared about. I thought, "Hey, if these scorecards mean so much, shouldn't we all be looking at them?"

The Origins of the Great Game of Business

So I was already beginning to think about the need for business training by the time we finished our search for financing. There's nothing like getting rejected forty or fifty times to drive home some valuable lessons. It's sort of like failing the same course again and again. As long as you keep taking it, sooner or later you're going to figure out what you need to know.

The question was, How could I share what I'd learned with everybody else? Like most companies—especially small, struggling start-ups—SRC had neither the time nor the money to put our entire workforce through courses in business and ownership. Besides, my instincts and experience told me that formal training wasn't going to be all that effective in any event. What were we going to do, anyway—teach people accounting? Most people don't want to learn accounting. For that matter, most people aren't terribly eager to learn about business and ownership either, partly because they think it's beyond them.

On the other hand, I knew that almost everybody liked a good game, and I'd learned at Harvester that games could be an effective means of both teaching and managing. As a young manager at Harvester's Melrose Park plant in the 1970s, I'd had great success setting up games around the performance targets I was given. Back then, you weren't supposed to share that kind of information with employees—which made no sense to me. I not only gave my people all the information I received, but I organized competitions with other departments to see how well we could do on our goals. The result was that we blew them away.

So naturally I began thinking about using a game to teach people what they needed to know about creating economic value. Yes, we had some pressing needs as a business, and there were some critical financial goals we had to meet, but maybe we could figure out how to bring a bit of fun into the process. Maybe we could set up a game around hitting the goals. In order to win, people would have to learn about financial concepts, and we'd be there to teach them. *In effect, we'd trick people into learning.* Over time, they'd begin to understand the larger opportunity they had as owners, and then they'd motivate themselves to take advantage of it.

There was another factor that came into play as well. Aside from wanting to teach people about ownership, we also needed to introduce some predictability and common sense into our lives. By the beginning of our second year, we'd had our fill of crisis management. You can go only so long in survival mode, racing around like maniacs, trying to deal with every problem that comes along, before you sit down and ask yourself, "How are we ever going to get beyond this?"

Part of the answer, we knew, involved coming up with some new management processes. We were burned out on the daily meetings we'd been having ever since we lost the Dresser account. What we needed were fewer meetings and more efficient ones. But how could we move to, say, weekly meetings without getting in trouble? We still couldn't afford a $10,000 surprise. We had to develop tools to make sure that, even though we weren't meeting every day, we didn't lose control of the situation.

In doing so, we were dealing with the same questions every business has to address: how to plan, forecast, communicate, and so on. The difference was that we didn't like the typical answers. I was determined not to replicate the divisions and conflicts that I believed were built into traditional management practices. I didn't want the kind of compartmentalization that encouraged everybody except the top two or three people to focus on a narrow set of accountabilities. We certainly couldn't build an ownership culture that way, and we might well not succeed as a business. We'd run the risk of destroying ourselves from within, as so many companies were in the process of doing. Somehow we had to find ways of operating that would allow us all to see what was happening throughout the business, share in the risks and rewards, and learn together as we went along.

How to Launch a Management System

Those were the specific circumstances that led us to begin developing the Great Game of Business. Looking back now, I realize that, from the start, we were looking for management processes—mechanisms—that would serve the two critical purposes I mentioned in the first chapter:

1. provide informal business training to people throughout the organization; and
2. keep us all focused on the goal of building the kind of company we wanted.

We wanted to engage the minds of our employees, knowing that their hearts would follow. Not that any of us understood the implications and ramifications of developing such a system. In the beginning, we didn't even think of it as a system. Nevertheless, we wound up following the path that hundreds of other companies have since taken in starting their own journeys toward a culture of ownership.

The process was, and is, fairly straightforward:

- You begin by setting up a game around hitting a critical number—that is, a performance target that will address your greatest weakness as an organization.

- Next, you do everything you can to educate people about the target—what it is, why it's important, how each person can contribute to achieving it.
- You also encourage people to give their own spin to the game and work with them to develop additional mechanisms (scoreboards, scorecards, huddles, and so on) that can help them win.
- They win; everybody celebrates; and you do it again, and again, and again—steadily refining the process, adding new mechanisms, looking for ways to improve the system.

There are numerous variations on that theme. There are also many other ways to get started. Some companies begin with business literacy training. Others have people read books or articles and then hold discussion groups around the company. Still other companies start by tracking one or two critical numbers on scoreboards (a practice that almost always produces immediate improvement in the number by 15 percent to 30 percent).

But most companies I know have begun with some kind of game, as we did. In fact, our experience is a pretty good example of the way the process works.

First, we identified our critical number, which was easy. After a year in business, our financed debt still totaled $7.2 million and cast a shadow over everything we did. We decided we'd shoot for reducing our financed debt by $3 million in the coming year. It was a goal that everybody could understand and get behind, since meeting it would greatly increase the job security of us all.

We also set a target of $2.2 million in pretax profit for the year. Hitting that one would ensure that (a) we didn't sacrifice profitability to meet the debt-reduction goal; (b) we'd have enough cash to pay whatever bonuses we earned; and (c) we'd be able to get people focused on learning about the income statement and its relationship to the balance sheet.

The next step was to come up with a set of rewards for winning the game. We figured that, if we actually hit the two goals, we could afford to pay $300,000 in bonuses, which amounted to about 8 percent of our

WHY WE CALL IT A GAME

The Great Game of Business was originally a phrase I used in an effort to make business a little less intimidating to people. I wanted them to see business the way I saw business. I wanted them to realize that it didn't have to be an instrument of exploitation, or a tool of greed, and you didn't need an MBA to understand it.

Some people outside the company later took offense at the phrase. They thought we were trivializing business by referring to it as a game. Well, there's a grain of truth to that objection. While I didn't mean to trivialize business, I was certainly trying to demystify it, knock it off its pedestal. I wanted to break down the walls of hype and nonsense that make business an elite sport for the select few and keep everybody else in the dark and out of the money.

And I wasn't telling people anything that wasn't true. Business *is* a game, after all. I'm not saying that it's *like* a game. I mean it's a game *as a form of human activity*. It's not an art or a science. It's a competitive undertaking, with rules, ways of keeping score, elements of luck and talent, winners and losers, and all of the other characteristics of games. What's more, it can be as exciting, as challenging, as interesting, and as much fun as any game you can think of—provided, that is, you understand what's going on.

The difference, of course, is that the stakes are higher. You're playing for your livelihood, for your family's welfare, for the future. You play for the jobs of the people you work with. You play for your customers and your customers' customers, and for the health of both your community and theirs.

And you play for money—potentially lots of money. As we all know, people who play the business game well can make a fortune at it. Okay, so some of them get greedy and keep the winnings to themselves. But I wanted people to understand that business doesn't have to work that way. There was no reason you couldn't set up a company so that everybody could play the game together and share the rewards. Then the game of business would truly be great, in the full meaning of the word.

annual payroll. So that was the pot. Each of us would be playing for a potential bonus of 8 percent of our pay.

Of course, there was always the possibility that we'd do well but fall short of the highest target on one of the goals. In that case, we decided, the fair thing would be to pay out a portion of the bonus pool. So we divided the pool between the two goals. (In later years, we went a step further and set different levels of payout depending on how well we did on each goal.)

We also realized that it was important to keep everybody involved in the game throughout the year. So we decided to have specific targets—and potential bonuses—for each quarter. To avoid the possibility of a letdown after a lackluster quarter, however, and to keep the focus on the annual goal, we set up the game to make sure the stakes kept rising as the year went along. In the first quarter, 10 percent of the annual bonus pool would be up for grabs; in the second, another 20 percent; in the third, another 30 percent; and in the last quarter, the remaining 40 percent. (Hence, the 10-20-30-40 bonus plan.)

What's more, any part of the bonus we didn't earn in one quarter would be added to the pot in the next quarter. So even if we fell short in the first three quarters, we could still come back and win it all at the end of the year.

That was the game. There were enough twists in the rules that it wouldn't be boring, but it wasn't so complicated that people wouldn't get it. We decided to call the program "Skip-The-Praise-Give-Us-The Raise" (or STP-GUTR, pronounced "Stop-Gooter"). It was a way of telling people that, much as we wanted to pay them more money, the company couldn't afford any raises unless we hit certain targets. Just to make sure everybody got the message, we put together a chart showing how to translate the payout levels into individual bonuses.

Winning the game became our entire focus for the next twelve months—which was just sound business. After all, if we came even close to hitting the targets, most of our other problems would take care of themselves. I suppose that's one test of a good bonus program.

In addition, I think you send a terrible message about responsibility if you put out a bonus program and then don't do everything in your power to help people earn the bonus. We'd done that once, in our first year, and the results had been disastrous. Everyone had blamed someone else for the program's failure. No one took responsibility for anything. The only positive outcome had been that we'd learned how *not* to do a bonus program in the future.

I was determined that we wouldn't repeat the mistake this time, and the other managers felt the same way. The entire team worked overtime to make sure people understood the game and the goals and knew what they had to do to win. In the process, we all became teachers, especially those of us with a somewhat better grasp of the numbers.

For example, I put our standard cost accountant, Doug Rothert, in charge of production, which came as a shock to him since he had no experience in manufacturing. I told him not to worry: His job was to teach finance to the people in the plant. He began conducting almost daily tutorials with individual supervisors, going through work orders, showing how the numbers flowed back to the income statement and how the income statement flowed into the balance sheet. The supervisors then went out and did the same thing with the hourly people.

Meanwhile, the other managers ran training sessions of their own, and we talked up the game at every chance we got. Our CFO, Dan McCoy, would regularly go on the public address system to give updates on the score. At the end of each quarter, we'd hold a series of informational meetings throughout the company to review the results with all of the employees.

Adding Mechanisms

So the bonus program became a powerful mechanism for informal business training. At the same time, moreover, it served as the catalyst for developing a whole series of other mechanisms that became crucial elements of our management system.

The *weekly huddle process*, for example, grew out of our need to stay

DEALING WITH DOUBTERS

There are always doubters when you introduce a new system, and the Great Game of Business is no exception. One of my doubters was a key manager and close associate, Mike Carrigan, our head of operations, who was extremely skeptical about the value of teaching the financials. "Why do we need all of these numbers?" he'd say. "That guy grinding crankshafts doesn't give a damn, and frankly neither do I. You got a job, you go out and do the job. You don't need to know all of this other crap. It's management's job to worry about the numbers. Let's let people do whatever the hell they're good at. I'm good at making parts. Let me make parts."

I obviously disagreed, but I couldn't just dismiss what he was saying or ignore his doubts. He might turn out to be right, after all. Even if he wasn't, I needed his cooperation, however reluctant, as well as that of all the other people who shared his doubts but weren't speaking up.

So I sometimes found myself having to camouflage what I was doing as standard operating procedure. I'd be surprised, for example, if more than a handful of people viewed our bonus plan as a way to learn about the debt-equity ratio or the charge-out rate. And when they were getting the weekly updates on the numbers, or making their weekly forecasts, most people didn't notice how comfortable they were becoming with income statements, variances, margins, and the like—including Carrigan, by the way, who became as financially literate as anyone on my staff.

At our sales and marketing meetings, we asked the salespeople to give us in-depth reports on our competitors, including financial ratios, wages, market share, and so on. The salespeople saw the reports as a job requirement. I saw them as an invaluable learning tool.

But even the doubters accepted the mechanisms because they worked on both levels. They really did help us to reduce the chaos, hit our goals, and operate the company more efficiently—at the same time as they were giving us all the business education we needed.

on top of the numbers and keep everyone informed about our progress in the game. Early on, we began holding weekly meetings at which the department managers would report their numbers for the prior week. With that we could put together a rough income statement, which gave us an indication of how we were doing on the profit goal. The managers would then take the information back to their departments and fill in the people who hadn't been at the meeting. The front-line supervisors would do the same with people on the shop floor.

We soon found, moreover, that it wasn't enough to get the prior week's numbers. We needed to know what was coming up. So each week we began having the managers forecast what they expected their month-end numbers to be. We could then compare the forecast with the plan to see how we thought we were doing in the game—and later compare the forecast with the actual result to see how much control we had of the numbers. That practice evolved into the mechanism known as *forward-looking financials.*

The STP-GUTR game was also the catalyst for our *high-involvement planning* mechanism, whereby we get people throughout the company involved in our budgeting process. I realized that, as long as I and the other senior managers could control the bonus line, we could afford to delegate the planning function. If the budgets we got back were out of line—as they sometimes were—we could use the bonus as an incentive for people to do better. That was far preferable to the usual practice of tearing the budgets apart, which pretty much guarantees that people feel little responsibility for achieving the plan.

Then there were the *sales-and-marketing meetings*, which we held twice a year to review how we'd done on our earlier sales projections and to present detailed forecasts of our sales in the months ahead. The format of meetings changed dramatically over time, for reasons I'll explain in the next chapter. As they changed, we developed still more mechanisms having to do with the form of the sales forecasts, the market research behind them, and the information we wanted them to include—notably, in-depth customer appraisals.

In fact, every mechanism we came up with evolved over time, as did the entire management system. We tinkered with it constantly, and we still do. I don't think anyone who develops a management system ever stops tinkering with it. You're always looking for ways to refine and improve it, and you're always having to adapt it to changing conditions.

So creating such a system is not a simple, straightforward, step-by-step process, although we're sometimes led to believe otherwise. That's a problem with most management theories and books (including, I suppose, the one we wrote in 1992). On paper, the concept sounds great. Then people try to implement it, and they run smack into reality. They think they must be doing something wrong. In fact, they're just going through the same difficulties everyone faces, including the people who came up with the concept in the first place. Why? Because reality is different for every company, and what works is going to be different as well.

You run into a similar problem in describing a company's evolution, which always looks a lot neater, better planned, and more logical in retrospect than it does at the time. That's partly because you forget about the uncertainty that surrounds every decision, the difficulty of weighing all the intangibles, the confusion that comes from trying to deal with a hundred different issues at once. Soldiers talk about "the cloud of battle." There's a cloud of business, too, but the memory of it fades as time goes by.

So when you go back and try to explain how you got here from there, you don't mention all the guesswork and instinct that were involved, all the false starts and blind alleys. You focus instead on the step-by-step logic of your actions, which inevitably makes the process seem a lot smoother and more rational than it actually was.

Learning to Love the Variances

In our case, there was plenty of chaos, but there was also a definite logic to the way we built the structure of our management system, and we were probably a little more methodical than most people. We were manufacturers, after all, and we had a manufacturing mentality. We went about developing the management system more or less the same way we would have developed any other process. Our approach was to:

- identify a function
- define a process for carrying out the function
- figure out how to quantify the key elements of the process
- measure the results at regular intervals
- focus on the deviations and the variances
- tweak the process until we got the results we wanted

In 1996, for example, we came up with a new mechanism, *semi-annual employee morale surveys*. The function, in this case, was to get regular feedback from employees that we could use to improve morale throughout the organization. We'd spent years searching for ways to do that. We'd tried suggestion boxes. We'd taken polls from time to time. We had tons of meetings, large and small. It all helped. But I wanted objective benchmarks we could use to measure and improve the quality of life in the company, and I couldn't figure out how to get them.

Then one day we were asked to take part in a national survey on employee job satisfaction being conducted by the Gallup Organization. Gallup, it seemed, had put together a questionnaire it was using to measure how employees felt about various aspects of job satisfaction. Not only did we agree to participate, but we borrowed the concept and created our own morale survey, which became the process for carrying out the function we had in mind.

The initial survey consisted of fourteen questions, such as "Have you received praise or recognition for your work?" and "Do you feel this company is promoting your long-term security?" Twelve of the questions called for people to respond on a scale of 1 to 5, with a high score indicating full satisfaction. (The other two questions required a yes-or-no answer.) We could then calculate the percentage of neutral or positive responses to each question and get a rough measure of the way people felt. Of course, each score was important mainly in relation to other scores. For example, we could compare responses people in one facility gave to the different questions, and we could look at the responses to the same question in different facilities. By repeating the survey every six months, moreover, we could see whether the scores were moving up or down.

So we had a way of quantifying morale, and we could measure the results at regular intervals. The next step was to focus on the deviations and variances so that we could figure out how to improve the process—and the company—as we went along. We learned, for example, that the answer to the first question ("Does your supervisor care about you as a person?') was a reliable predictor of responses to the other thirteen. We also learned that the answer to the question "Do you feel you have a chance to become a leader?" was a great measure of our training and succession planning programs. What's more, the percentage of people who answered "yes" to "Are you looking for another job?" was the same as our turnover rate—proving that the best way to forecast employee retention is to ask people if they're planning to leave.

But above all we learned it was possible to improve scores significantly by digging into the reasons for negative responses. We set up employee focus groups throughout the company to do just that. They discovered a lot of little problems we hadn't been aware of and could easily fix, as well as some big problems we needed to pay attention to. Meanwhile, we used the variances to continually refine the process, figuring out, for example, when and where we should have people fill out the surveys so that we'd get unbiased responses.

In the end, we wound up creating a mechanism that no one in the company can imagine living without.

The variances play a critical role in the development of all such mechanisms. I'm talking about the variances from the plan, the variances from the ideal, the variances from the way we want things to be. The whole idea behind our approach is to find a way of identifying and measuring the variances, so that we can then go in and fix whatever was causing them.

When you follow such a method, you can deal with whatever reality you're facing. The variances serve as your guide. I'm a great admirer of

W. Edwards Deming, who often noted the tendency of managers to blame people for problems, although the fault almost always lies in the processes that people are following. Without variances, however, it's easy to fall into the blame game. They're an indispensable tool for looking at the processes behind the people. Indeed, managing by variance has been a cornerstone of the system we developed. It's the means by which we force ourselves to keep learning and improving.

A lot of people don't get that part of the formula. They hate deviations and variances, which they regard as signs of failure. Thus, for example, companies get into the habit of changing their annual plan midway through the year, because they want to make the variances disappear. And the variances *do* disappear—but the underlying problems that caused them remain.

If you want to make your management system better, you have to learn to love the variances, which doesn't come naturally. It's easier when you have a culture built around openness and continuous learning. You come to realize that you need the variances. They're clues that can help you understand what's wrong with your management system, your processes, your model. They point you toward the changes that will make you stronger. They show you what you have to do differently, so that you don't keep having the same problems and making the same mistakes year after year after year.

Good Results

Of course, the proof of any management system is in the pudding, and our pudding began to taste very good as people got into playing the Great Game of Business. In the first STP-GUTR program, we wound up hitting 100 percent of the debt reduction goal and 70 percent of the profit goal and paid out $291,000 in bonuses (an average of $1,500 per person). The next year we came up with two new goals—debt-to-equity ratio and net profit before tax—and paid out another $420,000 in bonuses (an average of $1,450 per person).

In the process, the company turned around. We finished our second year with a pretax profit of $691,000 on sales of $24 million, reversing the first year's loss of $60,000 on sales of $16 million. By then, we'd reduced our financed debt from the $8.9 million we'd had in the middle of 1983 to $2.5 million. We'd completely paid off our note to International Harvester. We'd also renegotiated our loan with the bank.

Within the company, morale was sky-high. Our management system, and the educational process within it, was beginning to generate a powerful strain of the psychic ownership I talked about in the first chapter. People really did feel as though they owned the company, even though they were just beginning to get acquainted with equity.

In fact, it wasn't until the beginning of our second year that we mailed out the first annual ESOP certificates to the 121 people in the plan. At the same time, we sent letters to the other 85 employees explaining why they were not yet eligible and when they could expect to receive certificates of their own.

That was the first tangible evidence people had of their equity stake. Not that we'd left any doubt before then that everyone was going to be a shareholder. We'd been talking up stock ownership since day one. We'd also gone ahead and set up the plan, putting in 10,000 shares of SRC stock, and held elections for ESOP representatives. We couldn't actually send out the certificates, however, until we'd figured out exactly who was eligible to receive shares (based on hours of service) and how much each participant was entitled to (based on compensation).

In the meantime, we did everything we could to generate enthusiasm for stock ownership. We ran articles in the company newsletter. We talked about how the stock was valued. We explained how people could have a direct influence on the price per share by reducing debt, increasing profits, and doing all the things we were trying to accomplish through the STP-GUTR game.

Yet I can't say people were overjoyed about the ESOP, even after they got the certificates. By then, we'd been talking about it for so long that the novelty had worn off. We also had to position it as a retirement program, since it was going to take eleven years to become fully vested and we didn't expect most participants to cash out until they retired at age sixty-five. That's a hard sell with a workforce whose average age is about thirty.

Despite our efforts, most people just didn't get it at first. They weren't sure whether to believe us or not when we talked about the opportunity that equity-sharing gave them. Some of the hourly people later told me they thought it was a management trick. It's not for nothing that Missouri is called the "show-me" state.

But attitudes began to change as people saw the value of their ESOP stakes grow. There was a lag in the reaction because of the time it took to do the formal stock valuation. With an ESOP in a privately owned company, you don't actually find out how much you've increased the stock value during the course of a fiscal year until long after the year has ended (in our case, about five months). When the results were finally announced, however, everyone sat up and took notice.

Recall that our stock price at the buyout had been 10 cents a share. After the first year, the value rose to 62 cents per share—a feat we accomplished just by surviving. That's when we introduced the Great Game of Business, and the company began to hum. At the end of our second year, the stock soared to $4.02 a share and then rocketed up to $8.46 a share after the third year. The following year, sales climbed another 26 percent, while profits rose to $1.6 million—and the stock price hit $15.60, a 15,500 percent increase in just four years.

We were helped, of course, by a recovering economy and falling interest rates. We also got a big boost from the RSC guys, who'd landed a huge contract with General Motors and then another with J. I. Case*, which had bought Harvester's agricultural equipment division. None of that would have made a difference, however, if we hadn't come up with a system to bring order out of chaos and get us all focused on driving toward the same goals.

Those were glory days. There was almost a feeling of euphoria around the company. We were putting a lot of our pretax earnings into

* Now known as CNH Global, N.A.

the ESOP, which helped the company's cash flow and allowed us to broaden the ownership base significantly. The typical ESOP stake rose from about $50 at the beginning of 1984 to about $23,000 in the middle of 1986—a lot of money in a city where the average price of a home was $40,000. For many employees, the ESOP was suddenly the most valuable asset they owned.

Best of all, people were beginning to get it. They understood the game. They could watch the whole process of wealth creation unfold before their eyes. Instead of thirteen owners, we had 240 owners, and we could all see how every person and every department was contributing to the success of the company, and how the success of the company was driving the value of the stock. It was great. It was a gas. We were working together, having fun together, making money together, growing together—just as we'd hoped we would when we'd started our journey.

And what a journey it was turning out to be. No longer were we slashing our way through jungles. Now we were driving along a beautiful highway in perfect weather, in a convertible with the top down and the engine purring. I couldn't imagine how the ride could get any better.

Of course, when things can't get better, they often get worse. As it turned out, we were already heading for our next pothole.

FIELD NOTES

Lessons from Companies with an Ownership Culture

Charlton & Hill, Ltd., Lethbridge, Alberta

A successful ownership culture produces fundamental, long-term changes in behavior. You get those changes by eliminating the barriers that have traditionally kept people from understanding the realities of the marketplace. In the old paradigm, companies set performance standards for employees and then questioned whether or not they could meet them. In the new paradigm, employees get their performance standards from the market.

That happens quite literally at Charlton & Hill, Ltd., in Lethbridge, Alberta, which does roofing, HVAC (heating, ventilation, and air conditioning), metal fabrication, and welding. The company began playing the Game in 1996 and saw sales increase 159 percent in the next four years, while profits rose more than 300 percent.

At one point, the members of the HVAC business unit decided, as part of their high-involvement planning process, to analyze their major competitor by reconstructing its income statement. To come up with sales, they counted the number of tradesmen the competitor employed. To figure out payroll, the guys had their spouses call up the competitor to inquire about salaries, benefits, and so on. To estimate other expenses, they counted company vehicles, calculated the building's square footage, determined the size of the office staff, and so on.

Finally, the leader of the Charlton & Hill group called up a manufacturer who, he knew, had seen the competitor's financials. "I realize you can't tell us any confidential information, but how close are we?" he asked and gave the group's estimates of the competitor's sales and profit.

"You're damn close," the manufacturer replied.

Best of all, the group determined that the competitor was significantly leaner than Charlton & Hill was in some areas—and recommended a number of ways to save money and boost profitability.

8

You Can't Trust Success

There's a common mistake people make when they're setting out on their first business venture. They think all they have to do is survive. They figure that, if they can just get beyond the survival stage, they'll be home free.

In fact, they don't even realize that there are any stages beyond survival. I've learned that a company has to go through at least three stages to reach its full potential: the survival stage, the growth stage, and the maturity stage. But you're not aware of them starting out. You think there's just survival, followed by success or failure. That's it. That's all you have to worry about.

So you're not ready for what lies ahead—even if you've been warned. "You won't know what real problems are until you're successful," Dennis Sheppard had said at one of our first meetings. I didn't doubt him. I fully expected that we'd run into some new challenges on the other side of the hill. But I had to find out for myself exactly what the challenges were.

As it turned out, the growth stage brought a whole slew of them, but two in particular stand out in my mind, mainly because of what they taught us about ownership, business, and the consequences of human frailty. We learned how behavior can change when a company takes off and the stock value soars. We discovered how various forms of blindness can set in, posing threats you can't imagine when you're starting out.

In one case, we wound up dealing with issues that any company with partners might run into. It was a serious crisis, and it led to a lot of sleepless nights, but thanks to our shareholders' agreement, it didn't imperil the business. The other challenge was more dangerous. It involved a different kind of blindness, one that affected all of us and, I suspect, everybody else who experiences the exhilaration of growth for the first time. That challenge came perilously close to costing us our dream.

The Dark Side of Equity

Looking back, I realize that equity didn't play much of a role in our company until the stock value began to rise. That's usually the case. When you're just starting out, after all, everybody is in the same boat, paddling like crazy. No matter how tough things get, no matter what disagreements may arise, there's a feeling of all-for-one-and-one-for-all. You're bound together by the struggle. The stock isn't an important factor because it isn't worth anything.

But then it starts to have value, and people react differently to the change. I thought we were promoting positive behavior by sharing equity—and, by and large, we were—but sometimes you also get negative behavior. If it comes from people who should know better, people with a high level of authority and an equity stake to match, you've got a big problem on your hands. You'll find yourself refereeing fights between partners, dealing with bad morale, facing questions about your own leadership and commitment to your values. You may even wind up struggling to save your dream.

And that, for me, was a revelation.

We had a few people who let ownership go to their heads, but no one got as carried away as Dan McCoy, our CFO and the second-largest shareholder in the company. As the stock value rose, he became increasingly overbearing. He made no bones about telling people they were lucky to be working in his company. In McCoy's eyes, he and I were the founders, and we were damn nice to let everyone else have a piece of the action. He pretty much came right out and said it.

Worse, he acted accordingly. He treated the company as his own private property and the other employees as hired hands. I tried to rein him in, as did some of the other managers, but there was nothing we could do. He felt entitled to say what he wanted, go where he wanted, and act how he wanted. He was the owner, and owners have special privileges.

As time went along, I began to see the broad impact his behavior was having on the company. He was giving ownership a bad name. His ownership style was utterly incompatible with the one I was trying to promote. I wanted participative ownership. I wanted to use ownership to drive innovation and creativity. I was looking for a kind of ownership that people could feel proud of, not embarrassed by. Above all, I didn't want ownership being used to make people feel subservient, and McCoy's style did exactly that. He was placing himself above everybody else.

I didn't believe that style of ownership was sustainable over the long run. It certainly wouldn't have worked for us. It would have undermined everything we were trying to do with the Great Game of Business (which McCoy, ironically, had played a major role in setting up). Here we were trying to get people to think and act like owners, and McCoy, by his behavior, was telling people, in effect, "This company is mine, mine, mine." I felt it was exactly the wrong message to be sending. To build an ownership culture, the message has to be "It's ours, ours, ours."

Playing the Owner Card

All of which forced me to do a lot of thinking about ownership. I was particularly struck by the reaction that certain shareholders provoked in other employees. You could see not only fury, but a flash of recognition in their eyes—as if the shareholders' behavior confirmed something the employees already knew.

It began to dawn on me that most people hate owners. I hadn't realized that before. I'd thought it would be easy for us all to be owners together, even though we might have different amounts of equity. I had no idea of the depth of animosity that exists toward owners as a class.

Not that I had trouble seeing where the animosity comes from. Many owners bring it on themselves. The most successful know how to park their sense of entitlement at the door, but a lot of owners can't resist putting it in a person's face. Sometimes they do it symbolically—with the car they drive or the liberties they take. Other times it comes across in the way they speak and act. One way or another, they make it clear that they're different. They flaunt their wealth and status and power.

That's what I call "playing the owner card."

I've seen it happen over and over again at SRC. In the middle of a discussion, a major shareholder will say, "Well, as an owner, I think . . . ," and a chill runs down the spines of the other people in the room. Their antennas and their horns come out, and they get into a fighting mood. It's incredible to see the reaction, and it's very consistent. It happens whenever you hear that one phrase—because it makes people feel helpless. They feel as though they've suddenly been reduced to nothing.

And that's the intention. That's why someone plays the owner card in the first place.

It's a bad habit, and it always has negative effects. For one thing, people become very passive when the owner card is played. They may be angry, but they don't fight back. Instead they clam up. They shut down. They just obey. You don't get any creativity from them, any engagement. They do what they're told to do and nothing more. So they don't learn.

Beyond that, the behavior tends to feed on itself. A guy who needs to assert his ownership almost always goes further. He begins to take certain things for granted. He imagines he has certain rights and privileges as an owner. He thinks he's entitled to play by his own rules. Maybe he starts believing it's okay to charge personal items to his expense account. Or he has a right to give the company's products away to people he wants to impress. Or he can treat employees any way that he likes.

That way of thinking comes straight out of our business culture. We tend to expect that owners will use a company for self-gratification, not just because they have the legal right, but because so many of them do. It's the cliché, the stereotype. It's celebrated in the media, enshrined in books and movies, embedded in the language. If you've got it, flaunt it.

But there are consequences for acting out the part. You erect barriers between yourself and everybody else in the company. You undermine your stature and your ability to lead. You create an environment in which people are constantly holding back.

I can readily understand how owners fall into that trap—especially those who are very successful, who've built a certain amount of wealth. Sooner or later, you want to spend some of it. You feel like acquiring some of the nice things that are your reward for working hard and taking risks. As soon as you do, however, you notice that people are looking at you differently. They don't think, "Well, he had nothing, and he earned it." They just look at the fact that you have it and they don't.

You feel that envy, that resentment, and it's easy to get cynical. There's a natural tendency to cut yourself off from people. You think, "Well, screw you if you feel that way. That's tough. I earned it. If you want some, go get your own." But that attitude comes back to haunt you. You wind up feeding the resentment and the anger, and you pay a price both in your company and in society.

I think owners could avoid the problem—or at least minimize it—if they could just see how they look and hear how they sound. What people resent is not wealth or ownership per se. It's the flaunting of wealth and ownership. It's the feeling of being excluded. If you don't want people to have that feeling, you need to recognize the messages you may be sending unconsciously by the type of car you drive and the way you talk.

And it's especially important to recognize those messages when you're trying to build a culture of ownership. You can't have unity of purpose if there are class divisions in your company. The idea is to have one class, a class of owners, but that means selling people on the concept of ownership.

OWNERSHIP RULE #8

You build an ownership culture by breaking down walls.

You have to show people that ownership means opportunity, not exclusion. You have to convince them that, with ownership, they can go as far as their talent, their will, and their energy can carry them. They won't be blocked by class distinctions, by bogus barriers, by somebody else's decision to keep them out of the club.

We can all learn something from Sam Walton, the founder of Wal-Mart, in this regard. Here you had the most successful owner of his time, the richest man in the world, and yet he was almost universally loved and respected. Why? Because he was plugged into reality. He understood what ordinary people were thinking and feeling. And so he was able to sell the concept of ownership to his own employees and to people all over the world. He got rid of the class distinctions by putting stock in everyone's hand and also by being careful about the symbols. He didn't divide his company into owners and nonowners. He created a picture of owners as one class—the class that you wanted to be in.

That's essential if you want to create an ownership culture, but it involves presenting ownership in a new light. You have to challenge the popular image of the owner as lord of the manor. I saw an owner as a common person, a player among people. To me, owners do not hitch up their spurs and ride higher than the crowd. They don't stand over anyone. They don't let ownership go to their head. They show respect, and they receive it. Yes, some people in a company may have more shares than others, but you want everyone to understand that the organization is being guided, not by the narrow interests of the largest shareholders, but by a commitment to doing the right thing at the right time for the majority of people who are going to be affected.

So how do you deal with a major shareholder whose behavior is actively undermining what you're trying to do?

That's probably every CEO's worst nightmare, not to mention the great fear that stops many entrepreneurs from sharing equity in the first place. The good news is that those people take themselves out. The more they play the owner card, the more isolated they become. It's only a matter of time before everyone realizes they have to go. As long as you have a good shareholders' agreement and a sensible, supportive board of directors, you have nothing to worry about.

McCoy's case was perhaps a little more difficult than most, partly because he occupied such a critical management position. As the CFO, he was our primary liaison with the bank, which still loomed large in our lives. Beyond that, he was a big part of SRC, one of the reasons the company existed. Not only had he played a major role in getting us started, but he'd helped to keep us alive during the most treacherous part of our journey. Some people believe we wouldn't have survived the first year without him. They could be right.

I put off taking action as long as I could, but his behavior created so much resentment that I finally decided I had to move. Right before one of our board meetings, I asked him for his resignation. He requested an opportunity to present his case to the board and the other major shareholders. I agreed.

I called the group together and explained that I'd asked McCoy to resign, and why. He made his own statement and left the room. In the discussion that followed, not a single person rose to his defense or voiced any interest in having him stick around. He was gone by evening. It was a sad day, but so it always goes.

Not So Fast, Kowalski

As stressful as it can be to deal with unruly shareholders, there's a far more insidious danger for companies that get past the hardships of the start-up period and begin shooting up the growth curve. It's very easy for success—or rather the illusion of success—to go to your head.

The farther you've come, the bigger the risk. You look back and see what you've survived, and you think you must truly be blessed. By the grace of God, you've made it, and now you're experienced businesspeople. You're battle-hardened. You've learned from your mistakes and know how to grow a business. All you have to do is go out and execute.

Meanwhile, you're doing pretty well by the standard measures. The company is profitable. Morale is high. Sales are going up nicely. Cash may be a little tight, but that's normal in a growing company. You can get the capital you need, and you have more business opportunities than you can handle. Life is good.

To make matters worse, you may be hearing from other people how great you are. It's in the growth phase that the media start paying attention to a company. Everybody loves a success story, and to all outward appearances that's what your company is.

Not that everyone is so easily seduced. Some people are paranoid by nature. Too much success makes them nervous. They search for vulnerabilities. They try hard to think of everything that can go wrong. But even for people like that—and I'm one of them—there's a tendency to focus on the fire that's already burned you once before. You evaluate your weaknesses by looking at the kinds of problems you've had in the past. What you don't see are the dangers lurking out there with which you've had no direct experience, and those are the ones that always get you.

That was exactly the situation we found ourselves in, and we didn't know it. I doubt you ever do. When I looked around the company, I didn't see any major vulnerabilities. We knew we had to be diversified, and we thought we were. Experience had taught us the danger of depending on one wobbly customer. Now, instead of one customer, we had four, each signed up to a long-term contract. Our largest customer was General Motors, accounting for 50 percent of our sales, and what could ever happen to GM? As for International Harvester, which had changed its name to Navistar, it was looking healthier than it had in years.

We thought we were pretty well insulated from the ups and downs of the business cycle as well. Our sales were spread out among several market segments, each of which tended to do well in a different phase of the cycle. When the economy was strong, our heavy-duty division would go full blast, supplying engines and engine components for the farm, construction, and truck sectors. Automotive, on the other hand, would tend to lag, since people were more likely to buy new cars than fix up their old ones. Then again, if the economy went bad, the situation was reversed.

So what weaknesses did we have? For one thing, our products would eventually become obsolete; we needed to keep developing new product lines. For another, we were dependent on our customers (the OEMs, or original equipment manufacturers) for distribution, and we knew from the Dresser episode how vulnerable that made us. I'd have felt a lot better if we had our own distribution network.

But I couldn't see much else to be concerned about. I figured we could maintain an annual growth rate of 20 percent for at least the next five years. If we needed capital to finance the growth, we'd go public—or maybe we'd be acquired. Either way, I'd be happy as long as we could still provide our employees with job security and our shareholders with a good return.

In the midst of all this optimism, SRC was "discovered." A reporter from *Inc.* magazine came to visit, and the next thing we knew, our smiling faces were on newsstands all over the country. I was stunned, and so were the other managers. I'd read articles in *Inc.* about some of the great entrepreneurial companies of our time. It blew my mind to see our little engine-remanufacturing business on the cover of the same magazine.

Evidently the article struck a nerve with *Inc.*'s readers. We began receiving dozens of queries from people who wanted to come see for themselves how we played the Great Game of Business. We told callers that they were more than welcome to visit us in Springfield and sit in on our weekly staff meeting, but we didn't have anything to give them beyond what was in the article. They came anyway.

The presence of visitors made for some odd staff meetings. There were times when we had so many guests we could hardly squeeze all of our own people into the room. What concerned me most, however, was the effect our sudden notoriety was having on some of our managers. A few of them began to dress more formally. They walked and talked differently and seemed to find it harder to make decisions.

But reality was getting ready to give us all a good, hard whack on the side of the head.

It came in the form of a telephone call from General Motors. GM, it turned out, didn't need nearly as many remanufactured diesel automotive engines as we'd signed up to produce. Out of the blue the company had settled a class action suit over alleged defects in the original engines, which meant it had no use for all the remanufactured ones it had ordered. We were told to stop sending engines immediately.

The cuts were devastating. Overnight, we'd lose 17 percent of the sales we'd been counting on for the coming year and, with them, the cash to employ 20 percent of our workforce. We had a whole factory geared up to assemble the type of engine GM wanted—a 5.7-liter diesel engine used in certain Oldsmobile models. We'd bought and equipped the plant specifically to accommodate GM's needs. We had a signed contract that called for us to deliver thousands of engines per year through 1989, and we'd hired and trained a hundred employees to do only that. What were we supposed to do with them now?

We pleaded with GM to reconsider. I myself made an ungodly number of trips to Detroit—to no avail. GM had its own priorities, and they didn't include protecting our employees from layoffs. The best we could do was to win a delay. Instead of beginning the cuts immediately, GM gave us ninety days. We also persuaded GM to purchase the inventory. But we still had to figure out what to do about those jobs.

You could argue, I suppose, that the situation was unfair, that we were victims, that GM should have given us more warning, but I couldn't honestly make such excuses. Business doesn't work that way. The buck has to stop somewhere, and I believe it should stop with management. Who else can you hold accountable? Who else has the power to do what's necessary to protect employees' job security?

Much as I might have wanted to blame someone else, I knew in my heart that the responsibility was mine. As the CEO, my job was to make sure we'd anticipated such threats and developed contingency plans to deal with them. In that, I'd failed miserably. We'd been oblivious to the danger. We had no fallback position—no big customer waiting in the wings, no new product lines ready to get up and running, no other business we could quickly start. We were at a total loss. We'd blown it. Unless we came up with something fast, moreover, the price of our mistakes would be paid, not by me and the other managers, but by the employees in the automotive division—people whom we'd recruited to come work for us, who'd done everything we'd asked of them, who depended on us for their livelihood, and who were in no way responsible for the situation we now faced.

That, I realized, would be unfair, and we'd sworn from the start that we wouldn't engage in that type of unfairness. We weren't going to treat people as disposable assets we could let go whenever we ran into trouble.

So we had an excruciating choice to make. We could keep the people employed, remain true to our principles, and take an enormous risk with the company. Or we could protect the company, do the layoff, and negate everything we'd been trying to accomplish from the day we'd launched the business. There was no middle ground.

We did a lot of soul-searching and, in the end, decided not to have the layoff. Instead we converted the factory and began remanufacturing a full range of gasoline automobile engines—an extraordinarily complex and difficult undertaking. It was like starting a whole new business, only worse, much worse. We were taking an operation set up to accommodate eleven products and revamping it to accommodate 400 products, and we had to do it in three months.

Somehow we pulled it off and kept everyone employed, although we never got the factory working as it should. It struggled for twelve years before we finally found someone else to take it over.

But the experience of the GM cutback taught me some absolutely critical lessons about business. It forced me to go back and reexamine the entire way I'd been thinking about our company and its future. I suddenly saw how arrogant we'd become. We'd been living with illusions. We'd been blind to our weaknesses.

We'd told ourselves, for example, that we were diversified, that we had viable businesses in four or five different market segments—including automotive, where we thought we were doing great. Wasn't our automotive division making a lot of money and generating a lot of cash?

But, in fact, we were hardly diversified at all, and automotive was far from being a viable business—as any objective observer could have told us. There's an acid test you can use to figure out whether or not a business is truly viable: Would anybody want to buy it from you? In retrospect, it was clear that our automotive division couldn't have passed the test. Who would pay for a business with one customer that could cancel its contract at any moment? Minus the GM account, we didn't even have an automotive business. We had some real estate, some equipment, and some people—that's all. Without a track record, without a history of earning profits by making various products and dealing with various customers, the division wasn't worth anything in the market. Buyers would have no good reason to believe they'd get a decent return on whatever money they invested—and so they wouldn't invest.

It had been arrogant for us to think otherwise. When I looked back, moreover, I realized we'd been arrogant in other ways as well. We'd taken for granted our ability to keep growing indefinitely. We'd assumed General Motors and all of our other customers would be around forever. It had never occurred to us that any of them might leave, least of all GM.

Nor had we looked objectively at our ability to raise capital. We'd been confident that we could go public if we wanted to, or find outside investors, or do a merger, but could we really? And, if so, on what terms? Was there, in fact, any part of our business we could sell if we had to? What did we have to offer?

It was appalling how naive we'd been. We'd taken so many things for granted. We'd had a little taste of success, and it had gone straight to our heads—as it always does. If you're lucky, however, something will come along and snap you back to reality before you make a blunder that puts you out of business. At the time, it will seem like a calamity. Years later, however, you'll look back on it and thank your lucky stars that it came along when it did.

The GM cutback turned out to be a watershed event for us. Afterward we could never again be complacent about the future. We lost any illusions we had about the world we operated in. It was a place filled not only with opportunities, but with all kinds of hidden perils, some of which you could sniff out, some of which would spring up and hit you out of the blue, and we couldn't forget it.

To avoid experiencing a comparable surprise in the future, we looked for ways to protect ourselves. We developed a kind of creative paranoia, questioning every assumption, constantly searching for holes in our expectations, asking ourselves what might go wrong and what we'd do if it did. It was very similar to the "what-if" process we'd used in putting together our shareholders' agreement (see Chapter 3), but we kept adding new wrinkles as we went along.

We changed our entire planning process, for example, putting more emphasis on the need for contingencies and trapdoors. We wouldn't accept a sales forecast anymore without knowing what contingency plans were in the pipeline. Over time, we streamlined the process. We began to insist that each business unit go into the year with contingencies equal to 15 percent of its projected sales for the year. The unit had to include the contingencies in the forecast it presented to the rest of the company and tell us the stage of development each one was in.

But perhaps the biggest change came in another area. The GM episode forced us to get serious about a critical issue we hadn't paid much attention to before. It was something else that we thought we had covered. When we took a close look at it, however, we realized we had no idea how to handle it.

Dealing with that issue became the focus of our lives for the next fifteen years. It affected the whole way we went about building the business. It presented us with problems that baffled us, frustrated us, motivated us, and drove us. In the process, we became much better businesspeople. We learned what it really takes to succeed under capitalism, and we began to develop the routines and disciplines you need to spread that knowledge throughout an organization.

And yet, oddly enough, it was an issue that very few people think about when they start out in business. We certainly didn't. In the end, one of our employees had to bring the matter to our attention.

FIELD NOTES

Lessons from Companies with an Ownership Culture

Kacey Fine Furniture, Denver, Colorado

Any company can look good in a booming economy. The true test of a culture comes when the chips are down.

A case in point is Kacey Fine Furniture, a prominent Denver-based retailer that began playing the Great Game of Business in 1992. During the next eight years, the company's sales increased 168 percent, from $17.5 million to $47 million, while profits climbed more than 1,500 percent. In that same period, its workforce grew from 96 to 197 people, and the number of showrooms from four to seven.

But then, in the spring of 2001, the economic slowdown hit Denver, and sales began to plummet. By the start of the company's fiscal year, on June 1, it was clear that, whatever was happening in the economy at large, Kacey's corner of it was already in recession. When owners Leslie and Sam Fishbein presented the annual forecast to the rest of the company, they said there was a strong possibility that sales could drop by as much as 16 percent in the coming year.

Everybody understood what that meant: Jobs were in jeopardy. Immediately people began coming up with ideas for reducing costs and increasing productivity. Hourly employees voluntarily cut back their schedules from forty-five to thirty-five hours per week. Some people offered to take unpaid vacations. Departments figured out ways to operate more efficiently. The display department, for example, decided it wasn't necessary to replace three people who had left. By rearranging the workload, six people could do the job that ten people had been doing before, leaving one person free for other duties.

At the same time, the attrition rate increased, thereby reducing the need for job cuts, and the employees who left were those who had never bought into Kacey's culture in the first place. Every company has those people, the cynics and doubters who go through life unable to recognize the value of what they have. Yet they often wind up making a contribution in spite of themselves—by leaving when the going gets tough.

As it was, Kacey reduced its monthly break-even point from $3.6 million to $3.1 million in just two months—a savings of $6 million a year, or about 15 percent of its annual budget. Most important, the employees were heavily involved in making the cuts, so the effect was not to cripple morale, as is often the case. On the contrary, morale was higher than ever.

9

The Little Secret of Ownership

I can't recall the exact time and place, but it must have been within a few months of McCoy's departure. We were having one of the big meetings we held from time to time to discuss major issues facing us.

There are certain issues we always look at—customer service, quality, and so on—but we undoubtedly spent a part of the meeting talking about the increase in our equity value, which was dramatic enough to be attracting a lot of attention throughout the company. The price of a share had already gone from 10 cents to $8.46 and was well on its way to $15.60. A typical ESOP stake was worth about $23,000, enough to make anyone sit up and take notice. Suddenly, there was a tremendous interest in equity—what it was, where it came from, how you could increase it, what you could get for it when you left the company.

I could see that our people were learning fast, and I suspected that our settlement with McCoy had accelerated the process. Here was a guy who'd put up $17,000 and was walking away two and a half years later with $660,000. That was more money than any of us had ever seen in our lives, more money than we'd ever dreamed of having.

That's a general rule, by the way. People don't really start to learn about equity until their stake is worth enough to make a difference in their standard of living. Up to that point, ownership is an abstract concept. It sounds nice, but people don't really appreciate its ability to change their lives. Not that you can't teach about the operational aspects of business, as we were doing through the Great Game of Business, but ownership becomes real to people only when they have an equity stake with substantial value. At that point, they start to learn fast.

In any case, we'd been talking about cash and where it goes, and I was probably giving my usual explanation. When I'm trying to demystify cash flow for people, I generally tell them that there are only seven buckets you can put cash into: inventory, receivables, fixed assets, compensation, paying off debt, buying back stock, and taxes. I may have said something about cash being tied up in connecting rods and engine cores.

One of our hourly guys sat there, listening to me, and when I finished, he raised his hand. He said he was very happy to have stock in the ESOP, especially when he saw the value of his holdings shooting up. He was also interested in everything I had to say about the cash. He understood that most of it was going back into the company, except for what was being used to pay off our bank debt or to buy back McCoy's stock.

There was one thing he wondered about, however. A lot of us were about the same age, and there was a good chance we'd be retiring about the same time. Where was the money going to come from to purchase the stock of all the other shareholders? "Okay, so we've got a lot of cash tied up in connecting rods," he said. "We can't eat connecting rods."

Now, that was a great question. It was absolutely the right question to be asking at that time, and I should have been proud and happy to get it. That's why we were teaching and coaching and playing the Great Game of Business. We wanted people to see how they made a difference, how they each contributed to the ultimate outcome. We wanted them to care about profit and cash and equity, to make connections between the work they did every day and the stake they'd take home at the end. This guy was looking at the Big Picture and thinking about the future, and that's what it's all about.

So I should have been happy, right?

In fact, I was thrown for a loss. *I didn't have an answer. I hadn't given any thought to how we were going to cash everybody out.* I didn't even know what the numbers were. Given the average age of employees, we probably weren't going to face the situation for another twenty years or so, and by then . . . well, yes, by then the numbers could be fairly large. How *were* we going to pay everybody when the time came—especially if a lot of people wound up leaving together? It was a damn good question.

Somehow I'd lost sight of the final stage of our dream, the part when everybody walks away with a fair share of the wealth that's been created. You wonder afterward how you can miss something like that, but it's actually very easy. Being in business only three years and fighting to survive and struggling with all the operational challenges, the subject of an exit strategy never even crossed my mind. I just assumed we had it covered, and we did—on paper. What I didn't see was the amount of cash it was going to take to live up to our obligations. By our very success, we were building a mountain of contingent liabilities. Now that I was forced to look at the mountain, I realized that, if it continued to grow, it would someday be as high as Mt. Everest.

I couldn't ignore that mountain. It represented a lot of promises we'd made. Until we had a plan for keeping them, I was stuck. I couldn't leave. How could I take my money out if I didn't have confidence that other people would get theirs? We'd all created the wealth together. We all needed to be able to leave with our fair share of it. For my sake as well as theirs, I had to make sure we had a way for them to cash out when they were ready.

Knowing what I had to do didn't solve the problem, however. On the contrary, the more I thought about it, the more complicated it seemed. Should we be trying to build up our cash reserves? Should we be thinking about selling the company at some point? Should we be investigating the possibility of going public? And what about succession? Even if we had a plan for cashing people out, how could I leave before I'd found someone to replace me? Wasn't it my responsibility as CEO to

A LESSON IN EQUITY

There are certain rites of passage you go through along the way to understanding equity, and one of the most important begins the day you buy out a major shareholder for the first time. Before then, you're an equity virgin. Whatever equity value you create is all on paper. You don't really appreciate the power of equity until you're faced with the prospect of spending a large amount of cash to buy back someone's stock.

I was stunned when I realized it would cost us $660,000 to cash out McCoy. I was afraid we couldn't afford it. I also felt a twinge of envy. I remember asking myself, "Will he turn out to be the lucky one?" That's a common reaction. You can't help wondering whether the person who's leaving is getting out while the getting is good. Even if you're confident about the future, there's a little voice that says, "Maybe there won't be anything left for anyone else."

In fact, McCoy's stock was a bargain for the remaining shareholders. By repurchasing his shares and retiring them to treasury, we got an automatic increase in the value of our shares, just because the pie was being divided into fewer slices. Moreover, we bought back McCoy's 170,000 shares when they were still relatively cheap. Today, they'd be worth $14 million, instead of $660,000. Back in 1985, however, I could think only about the cash going out the door, and so I couldn't see what a good deal we were getting.

I had a similar reaction in 1989, when another major shareholder, Lee Shroyer, announced that he wanted to sell his entire stake back to the company. As a senior manager, he'd been cut in for 8½ percent of the equity at the time of the buyout, and that stock was worth about $1 million six years later. Now Shroyer wanted to get his money out—even though he had no intention of leaving SRC.

I was very angry with him. I thought he was deserting us at a crucial point in our journey, and the other remaining members of the original thirteen felt the same way. We took his decision as a slap in the face. On the other hand, we realized it would send a terrible message to everyone else if we didn't agree to buy back his stock. We'd be telling people, in effect, that we didn't have confidence in the company's future. So we agreed to buy back Shroyer's stock, again following the formula in the shareholders' agreement, but we were so furious that we refused to invite him to the dinner we gave on the tenth anniversary of the buyout for all the original shareholders who were still with the company.

In retrospect, I find our reaction interesting. It shows how hard it can be to break out of the survival mentality. We were still in it even after ten very successful years of business.

Of course, you need that mentality when you're starting out. Otherwise you're liable to wind up dead. You learn certain habits out of necessity, and they stay with you. You think about operational needs. You become obsessed with cash flow. You get so focused on it that—faced with the opportunity to buy out a major shareholder—you're overwhelmed with feelings of fear and envy. Why? Because you're thinking about surviving, and you don't understand the equity game.

It's a lot like what happens when you go out to buy your first home. You're terrified that you won't be able to afford the mortgage payments. You forget that your income is going up, that your interest payments are tax deductible, that property values are on the rise. So you don't look at the purchase as an investment but as a risk.

We didn't know enough to realize that McCoy's stock was actually a bargain, and we still didn't get it four years later, when we had to cash out Shroyer. We didn't realize that he was doing the rest of us a big favor. We should have been grateful to him, or maybe sorry for him. Instead we were angry and jealous.

Eventually, however, we came around. We cashed out one shareholder for $1.2 million in 1995, and another for $2.2 million in 1997, and nobody said a word. By then, we'd learned to recognize a bargain when we saw one.

Sort of. Some feelings are difficult to shed. When we bought out the second guy, in 1997, I knew it was a good deal for me and all of the other shareholders. I knew the company could afford the expense. I knew it was a win-win situation all around. But once again that nagging little thought came back. "Is he the lucky one? Is there going to be anything left for the rest of us?"

come up with a successor? For that matter, how were we going to replace the other people when they left? Would the company go on, or would it die?

OWNERSHIP RULE #9

Getting out is harder than getting in.

And so, step by step, I came to grips with the big issue that almost all entrepreneurs, chief executives, and company owners have to eventually face: How do you leave with a clean conscience? It's an issue I've been working on for the past fifteen years, and I haven't finished. When I mention my problem to seasoned business veterans—especially people who run companies they've founded—I usually get a knowing smile in return. It's our little secret. It's what no one tells you when you go into business.

How to Avoid the Founder's Trap: Start Early

Succession is, of course, an issue that sooner or later confronts every business and every business leader. The bigger the company and the stronger the culture, the more attention the issue gets. Witness all the drama surrounding Jack Welch's retirement from General Electric.

In such situations, the concern is that the next generation of leaders won't sustain the culture, and the company will therefore lose its competitive edge. That's an acute concern in companies with strong ownership cultures, especially if it's the founder who's leaving, as we saw when Sam Walton turned over the reins at Wal-Mart and as we're seeing now with Herb Kelleher's exit from Southwest Airlines. Subsequently, the anxiety may diminish somewhat as people gain more confidence in the staying power of the culture and realize that it is not dependent on any one individual. Both Harley-Davidson and Herman Miller have been through several successions, and their cultures are as strong as ever.

But all those companies have an advantage over most of the rest of us when it comes to transferring leadership. For one thing, they're publicly traded, so they have a mechanism in place to cash out major shareholders. In addition, the companies are under so much scrutiny from the public equity markets and the media that they're forced to confront the succession issue while there's still time to deal with it.

Companies with venture backing also pay a lot of attention to exit strategies, but they represent a tiny percentage of the total number of businesses started each year. Having an exit strategy and getting out with a clean conscience, moreover, are two different things. Sad to say, most venture-backed entrepreneurs don't last long enough to worry about succession.

It's a different story in the vast majority of companies that are neither venture-backed nor publicly traded. Getting out is, in fact, the furthest thing from most people's mind when they launch a business. If the subject comes up at all, they figure they'll deal with it when the time comes. They say, "We'll sell the company" or "We'll go public." Unless they have outside investors, they don't address the tough issues like valuation or buyout formulas, which is a huge mistake.

But if you've ever participated in a start-up, you know how easy it can be to make that mistake. In the beginning, you're too worried about staying alive to be concerned about getting out. You think only about what it will take to build a viable company. You get used to viewing the business from the inside out—not as an objective observer, but as a player, an operator. You're constantly thinking about what you need to do to stay in the game.

Even after you get beyond the survival stage, those habits stay with you. You see the business as an unfolding drama, a story that you're writing as you go along. You don't think much, if at all, about the end of the story. You figure you'll wait until it comes and let yourself be surprised.

If you own all of the stock, or if all of it is in your family, there isn't much pressure to change the way you think about your business. Chances are, your whole identity is centered around the company. It's your baby. You can hardly imagine life without it. You figure you'll be there forever, or maybe pass the business along to your children. In any case, you don't seriously contemplate leaving—which affects your decisions in ways you probably don't even notice.

You may, for example, develop a subtle bias against experimenting, innovating, pushing the business in new directions. In particular, you may shy away from diversifying. Why? Because you prefer to stick with what you know, with what's worked for you in the past. Most people tend to be somewhat risk averse as it is, and they get a lot of encouragement to "stick to the knitting." It's supposedly a tried-and-true strategy.

And you may be successful with it. I've seen many good businesspeople who focus on doing one thing extraordinarily well, and who make a ton of money in the process. They don't even give a thought to diversifying. Why should they?

In fact, there's only one reason to do it: because you're thinking about the future. You know that the good times aren't going to last forever, and you have to be prepared. Fear leads you to diversify, and fear can be a great motivator. To be an entrepreneur, to innovate, you can't be comfortable. You have to be afraid of something. Our fear was that we wouldn't be able to pay off these people when the time came, that we wouldn't be able to deliver on our promises.

You don't have that pressure if you own all the stock. You're not faced with the prospect of having a lot of shareholders thinking you let them down. You have one thing to worry about: making sure you have the cash you need to survive.

In that situation, there's a natural tendency to protect the present rather than position yourself for the future. You develop a whole rationale around staying in your core business, being really good at a few things. You keep all your eggs in one basket, and then you watch that basket, as Mark Twain said. That's what I mean by protecting the present, and you can be very successful at it. I know companies that have done very well without diversifying, without thinking about the future.

But the owner can't die.

And that's the whole problem. It takes time to figure out how to leave with a clean conscience. It takes time to develop a realistic exit strategy. It takes time to come up with choices you'll feel good about as you're walking out the door. If you don't start early enough, you might inadvertently wind up digging a hole for yourself, and most people do. The vast majority of privately owned businesses turn out to be unsellable. But even if people can find a buyer, they rarely get the kind of terms they want unless they've spent a lot of time laying the groundwork in advance.

I'm talking here about entrepreneurs, founders, people who've built companies or inherited family businesses and who want to do the right thing when they leave. Most successful entrepreneurs I know fall into that category. They're very fair individuals, who recognize the contributions of their employees, acknowledge the sweat equity they've put in, and want to make sure everybody gets a fair share of rewards.

Listen, sooner or later, we all leave the businesses we've built. Some of us may have to be carried out, but we're gone just the same. Most people, I'm sure, would prefer having time to enjoy the wealth they've generated, and there's nothing wrong with that. Nor is there any reason you can't enjoy it without any second thoughts or regrets, knowing that you've taken good care of the people who helped get you there—provided you start planning far enough in advance. You have to create that opportunity for yourself. If you wait too long, you'll wind up with limited options. There's a good chance you'll simply run out of time.

I go back to the observation of Harold Geneen: "You read a book from the beginning to the end. You run a business the opposite way. You start with the end, and then you do everything you must to reach it." It's one of the best pieces of business advice I've ever received, particularly when it comes to getting out.

I was fortunate to get an early start on the problem, thanks to a question from an employee.

Sizing Up the Problem

That's actually one advantage employee-owned companies have over single-owner businesses: There's really no avoiding the issue. One way or another, it gets put on the table at a relatively early stage, whether you want it there or not.

I doubt, in fact, that anybody is happy to see it. By the time the problem is big enough to notice, it looks as scary as all get out, particularly if you've been sharing equity from the beginning and seen a significant increase in the value of your stock.

In our case, for example, there were 297 members of the ESOP by the end of our fourth year in business, and their average age was about 32. I knew that our stock value wouldn't keep doubling every year, but even if it rose at a more modest rate of, say, 10 percent to 15 percent a year, the price would double every five to eight years. It wasn't unreasonable to expect we could be looking at a stock price of $200—and a total ESOP liability of $64 million—by the time the bulk of our current employees were hitting retirement age of 60 in the vicinity of year 2015. Assuming normal attrition rates and the usual five-year buyout provision for ESOPs, that translated into an annual expense of about $15 million—just for our current employees.

And what about the people who owned stock directly in the company? After buying out McCoy, we still had 830,000 shares between us. At $8.46 per share, the liability to the original shareholders came to $7 million; at $15.60, the number was $13 million. If we had the same number of shares outstanding in 2015—and if we did, in fact, manage to hit a stock price of $200—the total would be $166 million, on top of the $64 million we owed to members of the ESOP.

Let me tell you, when you see those kinds of numbers, your knees start to quiver. The $100,000 in equity we started out with was peanuts by comparison. We could lose it, and we'd all survive. But owing millions of dollars to your fellow employees is another story, especially if you know the number could be in the tens of millions of dollars later on.

What's more, you can't forget about the company's other needs. Looking into the future, I could see tremendous competition for cash. While we were buying shareholders out, people were still going to want machine tools. Inventories would be growing. Receivables would be rising. Somebody would ask for a new building. Somebody else would argue for acquiring another business. What if we decided to start a new subsidiary? How would we pay for developing new product lines? There was no end to the demands we were likely to face.

And what about replacing the people who would be leaving? Most of the major shareholders had told me they planned to retire in three to five years. Money aside, we didn't have replacements for them. We hadn't had time to develop our own talent, and so we'd have to look outside. Could we find the right people? Could we afford them if we did?

For that matter, could we afford to pay the shareholders what we owed them? Even with the ten-year buyout provision in our shareholders' agreement, we could be looking at an annual payment of $20 million to $24 million. The prospect scared the living daylights out of me. I didn't know where we'd get the money to pay these guys—unless we borrowed it, which would put us right back to square one.

The more I thought about it, the queasier I became. And here was the kicker: The problems would only get worse as we became more successful. I thought, "Wow, this is like quicksand. The better you do, the bigger the pie, the more cash you need to get out. How are we ever going to get on top of this thing?"

Our situation may have been a little more complicated than most, but we certainly weren't the only ESOP company ever to find ourselves in such a predicament. There's more or less a standard routine for dealing with it. The first step is to get an accurate assessment of your liabilities. You do that by hiring an actuary, who does a study based on certain assumptions about the growth of the company, the future contributions to the ESOP, the rise in the value of the stock. The actuary looks at the composition of the workforce and makes some guesses about who's going to stick around and when they're going to retire. Then the numbers are run through a computer, and you get an estimate of what you should be setting aside every year to cover your future shareholder obligations.

The hard part comes next: figuring out how you're going to deal with the situation. In my experience, there are three typical reactions. Some companies go into denial, thinking the problems will either go away or take care of themselves over time. We tried that—it doesn't work.

Other companies panic. Sometimes they shut down the ESOP, pay people off, and forget about building a company of owners. Alternatively, they freeze the program, so as to limit the size of the future liability, and try to manage from there. Either way, they wind up sacrificing a major part of their dream.

But most ESOP companies bite the bullet and start putting aside enough cash to make sure everybody can be taken care of when the time comes. That's not the only option, of course. You can also work toward a sale of the business, figuring you'll use the proceeds to cash out the members of the ESOP. Or you can see about taking the company public, which opens up a variety of possibilities—and a number of pitfalls as well (as we'll talk about in Chapter 10). If you intend to remain private and independent, however, the standard, prescribed method of meeting your long-term ESOP obligations is to build up a cash reserve large enough to deal with them.

Unfortunately, there are a couple of problems with that approach. First, it doesn't always work very well. Typically, a company puts the cash into the ESOP, whose trustees then have to figure out what to do with it. They have a fiduciary responsibility to the ESOP members, who are counting on getting the money they've been promised when they retire. So what happens? The cash goes into very conservative investments—certificates of deposit, U.S. Treasury bills and notes, municipal bonds, and the like—that tend to be safe and stable. They may not lose value over time, but they aren't going to increase in value very quickly either. If the company's stock appreciates faster than the value of the reserve, you're going to come up short despite your best intentions.

The cash-reserve approach has a second drawback, however, that bothered us even more than the first one. We didn't like the idea of limiting our growth by giving our cash to someone else instead of putting it back to work in SRC.

That's what you do when you take cash out of a company. You're making an important choice. You're deciding not to invest in your own company and your own people. A company needs cash to grow, particularly a capital-intensive business like ours. There was simply no way we could build up a cash reserve large enough to cover our equity obligations without slowing down our growth and thinning out our business.

But what happens when you don't grow? For one thing, you stop creating opportunities for employees. The chances for promotion dry up. People get stuck in the same job year after year. They don't learn. They don't expand their horizons. Pretty soon, they realize they're not going anywhere, and the best ones leave. Meanwhile, you start looking at the money you're putting aside, and you realize you're squandering it. You aren't earning the kind of returns you should be getting as a business.

We played out the scenario and concluded that the strategy of building up cash wasn't going to work for us. If our people didn't have a chance to make more money, take on new challenges, move forward in their careers, we'd die from attrition. There had to be a better way to deal with the challenge of getting out, we decided. We just had to find it.

GETTING MORE BANG FOR YOUR EQUITY BUCK

An ESOP can help you in more ways than is commonly realized, but you discover them only by going out and playing the game. Until we tried it, for example, we had no idea of all the benefits that could come from using the stock of departing shareholders to fund the ESOP.

Let's say that we bought back McCoy's stock at $4 per share, put it in the company treasury, and let it sit there for a few years. At some point, we could decide to sell it to another shareholder. Assuming we've been doing a good job with the business, the stock would now be worth more—say, $16 per share. If we sold it at that price, we'd have a net cash inflow of $12 per share, and we'd see an increase in our book value (that is, assets minus liabilities).

Now let's say we wanted to put $500,000 into the ESOP one year. That total is deducted from pretax earnings. Assuming a tax rate of 40 percent, we'd wind up with an additional $200,000 in cash—the amount of money that would otherwise have gone to the tax collector.

Take this a step further. Suppose that, before the ESOP contribution, we have pretax earnings of $3 million. If we don't have an ESOP—or if we decide not to fund it—we'll pay 40 percent of the $3 million, or $1.2 million, in taxes and have current-year retained earnings of $1.8 million, and our book value would increase by that amount. Instead we make the $500,000 ESOP contribution, reducing our taxable income to $2.5 million, of which we pay $1 million (40 percent) to the government. So now our current-year retained earnings are $1.5 million.

But wait. We decide to make the ESOP contribution with $100,000 in cash and $400,000 of the stock we have in the company treasury from the buyout of McCoy. That is, it's worth $400,000 at the current price. We actually bought it from McCoy for $100,000. So there's an increase in book value of $300,000.

Here's what's happened. First, we've increased the value of the ESOP by $500,000, which means all of our employees now have a bigger piece of the pie. They see their wealth increasing, and they get excited. They understand how they'll benefit by doing what's necessary to make the company successful.

Second, we have an additional $200,000 in cash we wouldn't have had otherwise, courtesy of the tax code. Granted, we put $100,000 of it into the ESOP, but that still leaves us with $100,000 we can use to buy equipment, pay bonuses, retire debt, start subsidiaries, whatever.

Third, our debt-to-equity ratio will improve, and it will improve even more if we use the additional $100,000 in cash to pay off debt. So now we're in a better position to borrow money if we have to. The bankers will look at our history and say, "Wow, this is a great company. They just keep making money and strengthening their balance sheet."

You can't learn those tricks without trying. You pick them up as you go along. We didn't plan on using McCoy's stock to fund the ESOP. It was an opportunity we stumbled across. As a result, McCoy wound up fueling the ESOP for several years.

10

Crossing the Great Divide

You often hear how companies have to "cross the threshold to professional management" once they get beyond a certain size and stage of development. The implication is usually that you do it by changing leaders—that is, by getting rid of the entrepreneurial founders and replacing them with professional managers. Maybe that's because most of these theories come out of business schools and consulting firms.

There are hundreds of individuals, however, who make the transition successfully on their own, and some of them have names that are familiar to us all: Gates, Walton, Ford, Hewlett and Packard, Galvin, Watson, Marriott, and so on. They all built companies in which they played critically important roles—but the companies weren't dependent on them for survival. They each made sure the business could go on without them. It had a value of its own.

I don't mean to compare SRC to those companies, or myself to those great business leaders, but I have to believe that they underwent something similar to the process we've been going through for the past fifteen years, ever since we got serious about getting out. In fact, I think you need to go through some such process, or your company will never grow beyond a certain point, and you'll wind up being trapped in it. You may make money while you're running it, but you'll have a tough time figuring out how to leave.

There's an interesting paradox here. In order to build a great company, a company that will endure, you have to imagine getting out. You have to think about turning your business over to someone else. Many people find that hard to do, and so did we. After all, we'd put our hearts and souls into building SRC. How could we contemplate selling it, say, to a group of investors or another company? Back then, we had no idea that the discipline of planning for the future—saying to ourselves, "What are our responsibilities and how will we meet them?"—would unleash the creativity and innovation we needed to find an altogether different way out of our dilemma.

The Road to the Next Level

When you think about it, there are only three ways to get out of any business of any type and size, and two of them aren't very appealing.

First, you can decide simply to close the company down: sell your assets, pay off your debts, and go out of business. That's really your only good option if the business itself isn't salable, and it won't be unless it can survive without you. If you're the owner of such a business, and you're planning to retire, you may have no choice but to get out as gracefully as possible. If your assets happen to be very valuable—say, you own an oil well or an important patent—you could do all right. Otherwise you're out of luck.

Unfortunately, a graceful exit is not always possible. If you can't make ends meet, your creditors will take you to court in an attempt to make you pay your bills. Under the U.S. bankruptcy laws, you'll have an opportunity to come up with a plan for paying them off while you keep the business going. If you fail, however, the assets will be seized and sold, with the proceeds going to cover your debts. That's another way to get out, but not one that anybody is likely to choose voluntarily.

The third way to get out is to sell the stock to people who intend to keep the business running after you've left. The buyer could be another individual, a company, an investment group, your employees or partners, or even a bunch of strangers you've never met (if you decide to take your company public). Whoever the buyers may be, what they're buying is the opportunity to own your business. Why? Because they think they can earn a return on their investment. The bigger the return they expect, the more they're willing to pay for your stock.

So the goal is to make sure, first, that your business is salable and, second, that when you do sell you can get the best price for your stock. You have to achieve both parts of the goal if you want to leave someday and take with you the full value of what you've created.

And how do you achieve the goal? By making your company better, stronger, able to stand on its own. If you want to maximize the company's value, you have to practice the fundamentals of good business. You have to figure out what it really takes to succeed under capitalism.

I have to admit that we discovered that connection by sheer luck. We didn't see it for a long time. We just had this enormous problem of the contingent liabilities to shareholders, and in the course of addressing it, we stumbled across a process that took our business to a whole different level.

The process began as soon as we realized how much cash we were going to need in the coming years. Naturally, we started thinking about ways to raise it. One obvious possibility was to bring in outside investors at some point—through a private placement, a public offering, an outright sale of the business, or whatever. So we asked ourselves the logical questions. Who would buy our stock? Why would they buy it? How much might it be worth to them? What would it take to get them to pay a higher price?

Just by asking those questions, you're forced to look at your business in a different light. You can no longer think only in terms of what you might want to do with the company. You have to ask yourself what somebody else might want to do with it, what would make it an attractive investment.

That change in perspective had far-reaching implications for us, as I'm sure it does for every company. Previously we'd focused all of our attention on the operational side of the business. How can we survive? How can we reduce our debt? How can we become more efficient? How should we handle the various aspects of running a company day to day, week to week, month to month, year to year?

Now, in contemplating the possibility that we might want to sell all or part of the company someday, we began focusing on the choices we had about different ways of growing. If we went in the wrong direction, the company might not be worth anything when it came time to sell. Then again, if we made the right moves, it could be worth a lot.

That was a revelation. Oddly enough, it was the same revelation I'd had during my search for money to buy the factory, but in the course of getting through the survival stage, I'd lost sight of the lesson the investors had taught me.

OWNERSHIP RULE #10

To maximize equity value, you have to think strategically.

The value of a business depends on much more than having efficient production, great customer service, on-time delivery, and all the other things you think about from an operational standpoint. You have to start looking at the business strategically if you're going to increase its equity value. You have to think about improving its position in the marketplace.

So we began looking for ways to improve our position, to make ourselves more attractive to investors, and we wound up reinventing our business. That wasn't what we set out to do, however. At the time, we were thinking only about trying to increase the number of options we'd have when we reached the point of having to cash out a large number of shareholders, and when we ourselves decided to leave.

Increasing our options became, in fact, the goal of the entire process. The whole idea was to make sure we'd have more choices tomorrow than we had today. When you have that goal, it turns out, many good things start to happen. For openers, you're forced to think long-term, to think like an investor. Instead of looking at your business from the inside out, you develop the habit of looking at it from the outside in, the way you would if you were considering whether or not to buy it.

You also spend a lot of time thinking about the future—about what could go wrong and what could go right. You learn to protect yourself against the surprises of the market by having contingency plans and trapdoors. You become acutely aware of your vulnerabilities and search for ways to eliminate them. At the same time, you're on the lookout for new opportunities. You develop the courage to innovate, to take calculated risks, to make the investments today that will pay off down the road and provide the funds you need to cash people out.

As time goes along, moreover, you realize that you can institutionalize the process of expanding your options. How? By building innovation and entrepreneurship into your management system. You come up with new disciplines, new routines that will get a wider circle of people involved in developing the contingency plans, searching for the opportunities, looking to the future, thinking ahead.

You also start looking around for people to help you take advantage of the opportunities when you find them, and who better but your own employees? So you begin moving people up, finding replacements, developing succession plans, creating opportunities for people to grow inside the business. As they grow and take on new responsibilities, you suddenly discover that you have a whole new range of options available to you.

The result is that, step by step, your business moves to another level. You begin to gain more control over your destiny. You're no longer a frail ship being pushed around on the ocean by winds and currents you can't even see. You have a destination. You have a strategy. You know where you're going, and you have a much better chance of getting there. Surprises will still come along and knock you off course, but you'll be able to recover quickly and continue on your journey. You have the tools you need to guide you to your port of call.

Learning to Think Differently

Now, that's a long and complex transition. Obviously, no company can make it simply by reorganizing itself or hiring a new CEO. Something else has to happen. There needs to be a fundamental change in the way people think about the business and its future. You can accomplish such a change only by going through an elaborate process of self-education, starting with the people at the top.

It's a process, moreover, that isn't necessarily organized or structured. It wasn't in our case, at any rate, and I'm not sure it can be. Mainly it involved a lot of talking, studying, brainstorming, getting outside opinions, debating, asking ourselves "Why?" and "What if?" We looked high and low for answers to our questions, and the search went on for years. To some extent, it's still going on today. You really can't stop searching until you've reached your destination, whatever that may be.

Why? Because, in business, unforeseen opportunities are always coming along. So, for that matter, are unforeseen problems. You can best protect yourselves and the people who are depending on you by creating as many options for raising cash as you can think of.

With that in mind, we focused on figuring out what those options might be. We did that by continually asking ourselves four key questions:

- What is this company really worth?
- What are our weaknesses?
- What would make us more attractive to a buyer or investor?
- What can we do to give ourselves more options in the future?

Then we debated the answers until we were blue in the face. We had a couple of people who would never accept any answer we came up with. One guy thought his mission in life was to prove the rest of us wrong, and occasionally he succeeded. That was the atmosphere—challenging everything, debating everything, trying to figure out which way to go.

It could be annoying at times, but overall it was healthy. It forced us to be objective, which is the hardest part of this process. You can't succeed at it if you're not objective, and it's difficult to be objective about a company you've poured your heart into. It's particularly difficult if the company appears to be doing well.

In the wake of the GM cutback, however, we were acutely aware of the perils of complacency. We realized we had to ask ourselves tough questions and insist on honest answers. What is a strong business, anyway, and how do we fall short? Do we have good cash flow compared to other companies? Do we have proprietary products? Do we have special knowledge that can't be obtained anywhere else? Are we sufficiently diversified? How does our return on equity compare to the rest of the industry? And so forth and so on.

We also brought in outsiders to challenge us. One of the shareholders didn't like the way our appraiser was valuing the business, and so he went out and found someone with a different approach, who came in and made a presentation. We didn't change appraisers, but we learned a lot about valuation methods. I regularly had investment bankers visit us and tell us what they saw as our strengths and weaknesses—especially the factors that would count against us if we ever decided to go public. From time to time, we'd get calls from potential investors or acquirers. We told them we weren't interested in doing a deal, but I made sure I learned as much as I could from them before sending them away. In addition, I began serving on various boards and encouraged other people to do the same. Many of us became active in business and industry organizations.

Those kinds of activities are all part of the educational process. They all help you to begin looking at your company from the outside in. You need to use every tool available to see yourselves objectively. You need to strip away all the things you think are great about your company and view it with the cold eye of someone who has no attachments to the people, no sentimental memories, no love for the culture. Then you can decide what you're going to do based on an objective assessment of your strengths and weaknesses.

Of course, there are other factors you have to take into account before actually settling on a particular strategy. I'm not suggesting that you compromise your principles in order to make your stock more attractive, or to give yourself more options for cashing out. Then again, it's important to know if your principles are hurting your stock value—so that you can figure out what to do about it.

Why Businesses Get Bought and Sold

When you embark on such a process, you soon come up against one of those basic questions of business that sound simple enough but often prove exasperatingly difficult to answer—namely, why do people buy companies, anyway? What are the factors that make a particular enterprise attractive to an investor or an acquirer?

It turns out that companies are bought for a limited number of reasons—five, to be exact. We discovered all five in the course of our search for exit options, but I wasn't really aware of them until my friend Sam Kaplan laid them out for me. Sam has bought and sold upward of fifty businesses in his career, either on his own or with partners. I was attending a workshop he was giving on the subject. In almost all acquisitions, he noted, the buyer is looking for one of the following things:

1. market share
2. earnings
3. cash flow
4. strategic advantage
5. some sort of synergy

You might ask, What about specific assets? Suppose a company has proprietary technology, say, or a state-of-the-art manufacturing facility. Aren't those things valuable in themselves? The answer is: Not necessarily. People need a reason for buying something. They don't usually acquire an asset simply for the satisfaction of owning it. They buy it because they believe it will allow them to improve their earnings, cash flow, or whatever.

By the way, a sixth criterion for acquisition has emerged in recent years. I know of businesses that have been bought, not for the traditional reasons, but because the acquirers want the company's "human capital"—that is, its people. The trend will no doubt wax and wane as the economy goes up and down, but the long-term demographics pretty much ensure that the competition for talent will intensify in the years ahead. So you might want to add "people" to the list.

In any case, if you're planning to sell your company at some point, or to bring in outside investors, you need to consider, first, how well it measures up in terms of those five (or six) criteria and, second, whether you want to grow the business with an eye toward strengthening it in one or more of those areas, thereby making it a more attractive investment (or acquisition) in the future.

That takes time and persistence. The answers are seldom obvious on the surface. Nor can you rely on the strategic advice of business gurus, or follow blindly the strategies adopted by other companies.

We faced a choice, for example, between diversification and building market share. Jack Welch, the legendary CEO of General Electric, has a theory that you should always be the number-one or number-two player in a market. You can question whether or not he actually lives by that philosophy—the companies that GE Capital invests in certainly don't—but he's such a great businessman that a lot of people have adopted his policy as gospel.

We gave it a lot of thought as well. One strategy, after all, would be to strive for market dominance in our various niches. Maybe we could position SRC to make it attractive to buyers looking for market share. We were strong in the truck engine remanufacturing market. We were also good at dealing with certain OEMs (original equipment manufacturers). Should we follow our strengths? Should we strive to be the market leader in every niche we entered? Or should we worry less about being the leader and more about being diversified?

We tried to think the issues through objectively. What happens, we asked, when a company dominates a market and the market goes to hell? You have to lay people off, right? What other choice would you have if you'd put all of your eggs in that one basket?

That was a problem for us, as we'd discovered with the GM cutback. We didn't like using people as the cushion against bad times. Layoffs can destroy an ownership culture. How? By undermining the mutual trust that holds it together and by introducing fear into the workplace. Yes, a layoff is sometimes unavoidable, but we thought it should be the last resort. It was better, we figured, to have a job with the number-three company than to be unemployed with number one.

We also wondered about the effect on our valuation if we focused on building market share and wound up being concentrated in one or two markets. Chances are, we'd find ourselves competing against publicly held companies. As a result, our value would likely depend on how those public companies were being viewed at the time, how analysts thought the industry was doing. You could have a really good company, the industry leader, but your stock price would suffer if you happened to be in a lousy market or a lousy industry.

We drew two conclusions from all this. First, it isn't always wise to focus on building market share. Second, you should never accept what any business genius tells you without questioning it. It's no doubt fine to seek market dominance as long as you're in a lot of niches and can move people between them. If you're competing in relatively few markets, however, you have to be careful. Jack Welch's philosophy could get a company like ours into serious trouble.

We went through a similar process with the other criteria. Should we try to build up our earnings? Given our narrow margins, we'd have to grow a tremendous amount before they would be substantial enough to look good to a buyer. And where would we get the cash we'd need to finance that kind of growth? We'd probably have to borrow heavily, which would not only hurt our balance sheet but put jobs at risk.

If we decided to focus on earnings, moreover, we'd probably feel pressure to do a lot of things that might later come back to haunt us—for example, scale back the Great Game of Business. We invested in training and other activities that cost us money in the short run but paid off down the road. A couple of our managers argued that we could boost our earnings by reducing our Great Game expenses, but I didn't think we could make those cuts without losing our competitive edge.

Besides, I didn't believe our OEM customers would let us increase our profit margins in any event. If they thought we were making too much money, they'd force us to cut our prices. They had that kind of clout.

When we looked at cash flow, the picture was even grimmer. Cash flow was our greatest weakness. It was the first thing prospective investors and buyers would look at—and they'd gag. Inventories were eating us up. Receivables were eating us up. We were getting killed by all of the engine cores that kept coming back, absorbing our cash. As long as we stayed in remanufacturing, anyone looking for cash flow wouldn't touch us with a ten-foot pole.

So what kind of strategic advantage could we offer another company? In theory, a distributor might buy us to have its own manufacturing facility, but that seemed like a long shot. It was even more unlikely that a manufacturer would buy us for strategic reasons, since we didn't have our own distribution system. Unless we could build or acquire one, the strategic option didn't look too promising, either.

That left the synergy option. Did we have specific assets or attributes we could offer another company, allowing the two of us to achieve things together that neither one of us could achieve on our own? Maybe, I decided. There were some remanufacturers around that we could approach at some point about a merger. What SRC would bring to the party was tremendous knowledge of our industry and market niche, our principal form of intellectual capital. We also had a top-notch workforce, trained in the business skills required to succeed in a highly competitive business environment. Combine all that with another remanufacturer's knowledge of its industry and market niche, and the two of us might find that we both had a whole range of interesting new possibilities.

On the other hand, we couldn't hang our hopes for getting out on such a prospect. For one thing, we had no reason to believe another company would be interested in a merger. Even if we could pull it off, it was unclear how many of us would then be able to leave. Our continued participation might well be a condition of the deal.

Questions, Questions

That's pretty much how this process goes. You look at each of the possible options, turn it around and upside down, and try to figure out whether or not it's worth pursuing. At the same time, you have to ask yourself a number of other questions about issues you could face down the road, depending on the exit strategy you decide to pursue. For example:

- *Can you go back to being an employee after you've been out on your own?* I had my doubts. The longer you work in your own business, the more independent you become. You learn new habits of thinking and acting, and it becomes difficult to return to the old ones. I had to wonder, for example, whether any of us could get used to working in a big company again—calling into headquarters every day, fighting for resources, dealing with corporate politics, waiting endlessly for decisions, and so on. Did we even want to entertain the possibility?

- *Are you willing to let go of the culture you've built?* That's hard, particularly if you've put a lot of care and effort into building it. We were arrogant enough to think we'd created a pretty good place to work. We wondered about our ability to find new owners who shared our values—or to predict in advance how they'd react to the inevitable challenges they'd face. Everybody talks the language of empowerment these days. The question is, How do people respond when they don't get the kind of performance they'd hoped for and so they're not earning the returns they'd expected?

- *Do you really want the kind of life you're choosing?* Businesspeople have a tendency to focus on doing the deal and to forget about the life that comes along with it. I'm thinking especially about entrepreneurs who take their companies public. It's easy to underestimate how different your life will be after the public offering. You wake up the next day with a whole new set of variables and responsibilities. Your flexibility is limited by your stock price, and your stock price is often subject to factors beyond your control. If investors get nervous about interest rates, or what's happening in Afghanistan, you can lose half of the wealth you've created overnight and suddenly find yourself coping with bad morale, shareholder lawsuits, cash shortages, the whole bit. I saw nothing appealing about subjecting ourselves to those kinds of pressures.

WHAT ABOUT GOING PUBLIC?

Entrepreneurs contemplating an initial public offering tend to focus on the money they hope to raise, but aside from a lot of cash, the principal by-product of an IPO is a tremendous increase in your responsibilities. When you sell your stock to the public, you wind up with other people's life savings. Yes, some stock market investors are speculators, but most of the money you get will come directly or indirectly from people who've given you their savings because they think you can make it grow.

We considered the possibility of going public, and we always left that avenue open. The closer I looked at it, however, the more reluctant I was to travel down it, mainly because I didn't feel ready to take on those additional responsibilities.

Some of my problems were personal, I admit. I had nightmares of investors calling me every day and grilling me about their stock, asking me what I was doing with their money, how I was spending their savings. I thought I'd be dealing with them all the time, which seemed like sheer torture. If the stock ever took a dive, I'd feel guilty as hell, which was the last thing I needed. Here I was, trying to figure out how to get out with a clean conscience. Why would I take on more guilt by going public?

Besides, I thought there was something illogical about asking outside people to invest their savings in our company. We didn't want to run the company for their benefit. We were running it for the benefit of the people who worked here. Those were the shareholders I was willing to be responsible to—the ones who had earned their stock. I didn't want to be worrying that some people might lose their homes because of our decisions. I wanted to make it possible for people to buy homes.

Nor did I want to be pressured into changing our philosophy of benevolence toward employees. I could well imagine how our obligations to outside shareholders might conflict with our obligations to inside shareholders. Investors generally don't care about preserving a company's culture. They don't have much patience, either. I was afraid they'd take a critical look at SRC and want us to fix things that looked broken to them but not to us.

We had many practices, for example, that hurt our earnings. We carried extra people in overhead. We put a big emphasis on teaching business skills. We also bent over backward to avoid layoffs, and we kept product lines running that might not look good at the moment but could give us a payoff in five years. Although some of our programs didn't work out, the ones that did were critical to the future of the company. I thought we'd feel pressure to dump them if we went public.

You need to think about those things before doing an IPO. I know quite a few CEOs who wish they had. Not that there's anything inherently wrong with going public, but it's important to be ready.

So when *are* you ready for the public market? I think it's when your company has enough financial savvy and discipline to allow you to protect your culture. No one complains about the crazy way that Southwest Airlines goes about making money and having fun. With the kind of performance its people turn in year after year, investors are happy to go along for the ride.

So you go through this process of questioning, evaluating, searching. In the meantime, of course, the business isn't standing still. While you're out there trying to find the right growth strategy, the company is growing. Sooner or later you run into a whole other series of questions that have to do with the process of growth itself.

There were three issues in particular that we focused on:

- *How can you grow without getting too big?* We worried, for example, about the size of our factories. We believed that, once you have more than, say, four hundred people working in a facility, you lose something important—the intimacy, the family feeling, the sense of all-for-one-and-one-for-all. A lot of us had worked in big factories. I'd spent ten years at International Harvester's plant in Melrose Park, Illinois, which was the size of a small city and had the problems to match. We knew what happened when a factory got too big. We'd seen the anger that develops, the barriers that go up, the divisions and the bad communications that seemed to be an inevitable consequence of size. We wanted to make sure we didn't have those problems if we could avoid them.

• *How do you keep creating new opportunities for people?* Companies, like people, can experience hardening of the arteries. People get stuck in jobs and stop growing. We faced a challenge with our supervisors and middle managers, for example. Many of them were already earning as much as they could in their present positions, and they had no place to go because the people above them were all the same age and not yet ready to retire.

I'd seen the same problem at Melrose Park. There, too, all of the senior managers had been about the same age. As a result, the company had lost a whole generation of young people who'd looked around and decided they had no chance to move up until the older generation retired. I didn't want that to happen to us—not after all we'd done to train these people in the Great Game of Business. The last thing I wanted to do was to lose them. But where could they go?

• *How do you foster ongoing innovation and creativity?* It's all well and good to talk about growth strategies and exit strategies, but as a practical matter, how do you sustain your momentum over a long period of time? How do you make sure you're going to have the products of tomorrow when you need them? Looking around SRC, I didn't see anything we were doing that would lead us to them. We were inwardly focused. When we talked about innovation and creativity, we looked only at ways of improving what we were already doing—refining the processes we were using, becoming more efficient, doing more of the same but doing it better. We didn't think about breaking out into new areas. If we were going to be successful over the long haul, I realized, we had to come up with mechanisms to ensure that we were always developing new things, coming up with new ideas, going off in new directions.

You wrestle with those kinds of questions at the same time that you're trying to figure out where you should take the company from the standpoint of cashing out. It can all get very complicated, not to mention frustrating. There were times when I felt as though we were going down a series of blind alleys. None of the options we talked about seemed very inviting. I didn't know what we were going to do.

The Secret of the Chinese Firecracker Factory

There's an old saying that, when the student is ready, the teacher appears. One of my teachers turned out to be a guy from Springfield named Mike Ingram, who's a wholesaler of fireworks. I ran into him one day at a restaurant, and he told me a story that hit me like a Roman candle. I'm not sure I knew at the time why I found it so fascinating, or how we might use it, but I sensed immediately that it held one of the keys we needed to get ourselves out of our trap.

Ingram had recently returned from a buying trip to China, which was just beginning to open itself up to trade with the United States. Conditions were very harsh. There were all kinds of currency problems, language problems, transportation problems, you name it, and Ingram was full of stories from his trip. He talked about buying a rug and about the difficulties of converting dollars into Chinese money. Mainly, however, he talked about his visit to one of the big fireworks manufacturers, with which he wanted to cut a deal.

The manufacturer, he said, was located in a remote region of the country, and there was no easy way to get there. From Beijing, he'd taken a rickety airplane to a distant city, where he'd picked up a guide and set off by truck to the fireworks factory. After driving for several hours, they'd come to the base of a hill. The guide had told Ingram that the factory was on the other side.

I guess he was pretty excited that he'd finally found it. He talked about the anticipation he'd felt as they drove up the hill. Then a weird expression came over his face. When they reached the top, he said, all he could see was a village with hundreds of little huts.

"Where's the factory?" he'd asked his guide.

"Down there," the guide had said, pointing to the village.

Ingram didn't understand. "The fireworks company," he said. "Where do they make the fireworks?"

"Down there, down there," said the guide.

Ingram still didn't get it. "I mean, the factory. I only see huts."

"The huts are the factory," said the guide. "They put two workers in each hut. If one hut blows up, it doesn't destroy the whole village."

I don't know what lesson Ingram took out of the story, but for me it set bells ringing and lightbulbs flashing. In the weeks and months that followed, I couldn't get it out of my mind. That may have been when I started to think of our company as a village. Weren't we protecting a village, just like the fireworks manufacturer? Maybe we could break our village into huts as well. Maybe we could put a limited number of people in every hut. Maybe we could use the huts to diversify in a way that would add to the value of the company.

There was something about the story that resonated with me. We'd been focusing so much on growth, talking endlessly about strategies for growing the company, and you tend to assume that a company can't grow without getting big. Yet Ingram's fireworks manufacturer had figured out how to grow and stay small. Couldn't we do the same? Couldn't we grow by starting other businesses? Weren't there real advantages to operating on a smaller scale?

It began to dawn on me that we could use the model of the Chinese fireworks factory to address all of the growth issues we'd been struggling with. I thought, "Man, if we go with this concept, we can provide career opportunities for people. We can let them create their own business plans. They'll innovate away in their individual huts, and we'll limit our risk. We'll balance cash flow and earnings. We'll create our own orchestra, with everyone singing off the same song sheet. And the song sheet will be our philosophy, the Great Game of Business. We'll center the whole thing around our culture."

The more I thought about it, the better I liked it. There was, however, one piece of the puzzle I hadn't yet put together with the others. We were talking about starting businesses, after all, and start-ups don't generate cash—they absorb it. So how, I wondered, was the Chinese firecracker factory going to help us solve the problem of all the contingent liabilities to shareholders?

The answer, it turned out, was right under my nose.

FIELD NOTES

Lessons from Companies with an Ownership Culture

Daryl Flood Warehouse & Movers, Carrolton, Texas

One of the more frustrating challenges in business has to do with getting people to see their impact on such critical issues as speeding up collections, reducing the average days outstanding of receivables, and improving cash flow. The common wisdom holds that most people don't understand such issues and wouldn't care about them if they did. In an ownership culture, everybody can make a difference.

Consider Daryl Flood Warehouse & Movers, in Carrolton, Texas, which is one of the two or three largest companies in the Allied Van Lines network and ranks within the top 10 percent by size in the industry as a whole. The company specializes in corporate and household relocation, with 90 percent of its business coming from national accounts with the likes of EDS, Compaq Computer, Hewlett-Packard, and Southwest Airlines.

Flood began playing the Great Game of Business in the mid-1990s and saw its revenue almost triple from $16 million in 1995 to $45 million in 2000. Profitability also grew dramatically at first, from 1.8 percent in 1996 to more than 5 percent in 1998, but then slid back under the pressure of relentless growth. Even more worrisome, the company became sloppy with cash. At the end of 2000—on the eve of a recession—Flood found itself with $1.5 million in receivables that hadn't been collected in more than ninety days.

"It was right out of the book," said Steve Weatherford, vice president of finance and human resources. "I think it's the ninth higher law of business: 'If nobody pays attention, people stop caring.'"

For the next year, cash became the focus of the entire Flood workforce, and all the mechanisms of the Game came into play. The message was clear: In a bad economy, cash flow is a matter of life or death. To emphasize the importance of the campaign, Weatherford made one employee the credit and collections czar and gave her a staff of three people. Together, they mobilized the rest of the company.

Everyone got into the action. The salespeople were enlisted to coax speedier payments out of customers and discovered that invoices were often being sent to the wrong office. A new form was developed to correct the problem. At weekly huddles, someone would report on collections and average days outstanding of receivables. A "notorious top five" list of the five largest late-paying customers was presented. After the huddles came the "chalk talks" with the front-line employees, including the blue-collar guys who move furniture all over the country. How could they affect cash? Happy customers tend to pay their bills on time. A scratch on a dining-room table could delay a receivable, the movers realized. Then again, if Flood scored well on customer-satisfaction surveys, its cash situation was more likely to improve.

And it did. By the end of August, the over-ninety-days portion of Flood's receivables had declined from $1.5 million to $400,000—a drop of more than $1 million in eight months. Meanwhile, the customer-service scores were the best they'd been in five years. Most important, Flood's cash flow was beating all projections, despite a dismal economy that led sales and profits to fall short of the plan.

11

The True Profit of Business

Sooner or later, if you're lucky, you discover the true profit of business, but it takes a while. You start out thinking there's only one way to make a profit in business: by running your company well, by keeping your costs down and your sales up. You spend years trying to perfect your processes, squeeze out the waste, improve productivity, and so on, and you think you're doing well if you earn 5 percent after taxes. Then you start a business with a $1,000 investment and wake up one day to find that you could sell it for millions of dollars.

OWNERSHIP RULE #11

You create wealth by building companies, not by selling products and services.

That's what I mean by the true profit of business. If I sell you a pen, I can make a penny. If I sell you the pen company, I can make $10 million. When you play the game of business at the highest level, you understand that the company is your product, not the pen.

Once you make that leap, your whole perspective on business changes. For openers, you realize that there's a lot more money to be made in building and selling companies than in building and selling products. So you start searching for opportunities to start other businesses. What do you find? They're all around you. There are more than you can handle. You can't believe you haven't noticed them before.

What you need at that point is a formula that allows you to take advantage of the opportunities, preferably with resources you already have. If you can start businesses with your own people, with a minimum of capital, and with high probability of success, the world becomes your oyster. You gain an extraordinary degree of control over your destiny. You can grow in whatever direction you choose.

We discovered such a formula, and it became our principal mechanism not only for growing the company but for expanding our future exit options. At the time, however, we weren't looking for a formula. We didn't even know that one existed. We were mainly trying to solve a problem we were having with an engine component known as an oil cooler.

A Problem of Innovation

On the surface, the problem was about nothing more than the tendency of certain critical engine components to break down over time. Every used diesel engine—or core—we brought in came with an oil cooler whose function was to keep the engine from overheating. Unfortunately, most of the coolers leaked so badly we had to replace them, which was costing us a lot of money. That was the immediate problem.

In fact, however, the oil cooler problem was a symptom of a much larger problem—namely, our growing inability to innovate internally. I was convinced that we wouldn't have had an oil cooler problem if we were still as resourceful and as hungry as we'd been in our early days. We'd have already fixed it. How? By coming up with a process to remanufacture the coolers that came with the cores. Those coolers cost us about $50 each, as part of the price of the core. Every time we threw one away, we replaced it with a brand-new cooler at about $100 a crack. All told, we were spending more than $275,000 a year on an item that I believed should have been costing us about $60,000, and the money was coming straight out of our profits.

The situation was driving me crazy. I kept asking our engineers to come up with a remanufacturing process for the coolers, and they kept telling me they were too busy. They didn't have time. They had too many other things to do that were more pressing.

And it wasn't only the oil coolers that upset me. There was a whole mess of components we were buying because we couldn't remanufacture the ones that came in with the cores. So why couldn't I get anyone to focus on the problem?

Mike Carrigan, our vice president of manufacturing, told me I was wasting my energy. We weren't capable of coming up with those kinds of remanufacturing processes anymore. We'd grown too big and bureaucratic. We'd lost our entrepreneurial edge. Besides, he didn't think that, given our overhead, we could make money on oil coolers. It wouldn't work.

I didn't buy it. I thought there had to be a way. Other people could remanufacture oil coolers, so why couldn't we? I believed we simply weren't trying hard enough. We were looking for excuses. Finally, I got so exasperated, I said, "Screw it. Let's settle this thing once and for all. We'll take the damn oil coolers out of our factory, set up an independent company, and give it the oil cooler business. We'll bring people in from the outside to run the operation and let them fix the problem for us."

I was determined to show that we could dramatically cut our oil cooler costs if someone just made it a priority, and I was willing to put my money where my mouth was. So a small group of us got together and started a business, Engines Plus, to remanufacture oil coolers for SRC.

But while the oil cooler problem was the immediate impetus behind the new business, I have to admit that I also had another motive for starting it. I wanted to answer a question I was extremely curious about. The question was, Could we do with another start-up what we'd done with SRC? I wanted to see if we could generate wealth—and do it quickly—by harnessing the power of leverage.

The Power of Leverage

Leverage is a concept that experienced businesspeople take for granted but the rest of us have a hard time learning. It is, indeed, the foundation on which the entire venture capital industry has been built. The whole idea can be boiled down to a simple rule of thumb: The more debt and the less equity you use in financing a start-up, the greater will be the rise in the value of the stock if you're successful.

That's actually just a matter of arithmetic. Let's say you need $100,000 to get a business up and running, and you can afford to invest only $10,000 of your own money. If someone else puts up the other $90,000 in the form of equity, the company will start with a book value of $100,000. (For the sake of this example, we'll assume that everyone agrees to value the company at book, which can be measured as equity investment plus retained earnings.)

With your financing in hand, you go out, work hard, make a profit, and reinvest all of the earnings in the business. Suppose you have retained earnings of $125,000 per year for four years—that is, $500,000 in total. At the end of the period, your company has a book value (equity investment plus retained earnings) of $600,000, or an increase of 500 percent over your initial investment. If your stock was worth $1 per share when you started, it's worth $6 per share after four years.

But what if you'd borrowed the additional $90,000 instead of getting it in the form of equity? You'd have the same amount of retained earnings after four years, $500,000, but your book value would go from $10,000 to $510,000. That's an increase of *5,000 percent* over your initial investment. Your stock price would rocket from $1 to $51. You'd be eight and a half times as rich after four years as you'd be if you hadn't used the leverage of debt to get started.

The same principle holds true whatever method of valuation you use. The smaller the equity base you start with, the bigger will be the jump in equity value when you get the business up and running.

We had, of course, already seen a dramatic demonstration of this principle with SRC, but that had been an accident. At the time, we were just trying to get the company started any way we could, and the deal we wound up with was the best one available. We certainly weren't looking to get a bigger bang for our buck. The astronomical rise in our stock price—15,500 percent in four years—had come as a total shock.

But once I saw what had happened, I couldn't help wondering if we could do it again. There was no logical reason we couldn't. To me, it looked as though the same formula would work in any business. Why not give it a try?

So when we sat down to design Engines Plus, our new oil cooler company, we deliberately applied the leverage principle. Five of us put up $1,000 of our own money as an equity investment, paying 10 cents per share for a total of 10,000 shares. Then we arranged a $50,000 line of credit from SRC. Engines Plus thus began with a 50-to-1 debt-to-equity ratio—not quite as steep as SRC's, but close.

It's important to understand that the new business was an experiment. We didn't know for sure that the people we brought in would be able to develop a process for remanufacturing oil coolers, or that the coolers they produced would meet SRC's specifications. We certainly didn't know whether they could run the business profitably. As for the power of leverage, it was a theory. We had no idea what problems we might encounter when we tried to apply it in practice.

Because Engines Plus was an experiment, and because experiments often fail, we made sure that there wouldn't be any negative repercussions for SRC. We didn't take people out of SRC to work on it. We didn't use SRC facilities or equipment. We'd didn't put SRC funds at risk. If things fell apart, SRC would be able to recover whatever working capital it had advanced either from the assets of the business or from the partners. We wanted this to be a separate deal.

What we didn't expect was that the experiment would be so successful so soon. Within three years, the value of our Engines Plus stock had risen about 13,000 percent from $.10 per share to more than $13 per share. By then, we no longer had any doubts about the power of leverage. Doing it once might have been a fluke. Doing it twice was a pattern. As it turned out, however, we'd done much more than prove a theory. In the course of building Engines Plus, we'd accomplished three other things as well:

- First, we'd discovered a formula we could use to start businesses over and over again at minimal risk to SRC.
- Second, we'd learned how to identify the businesses we could start—and realized there were more opportunities lying around than we'd ever imagined.
- Third, and most important, we'd come up with the strategy we'd been searching for. We finally had a way to grow the company that would give us all kinds of options for raising the cash we'd need to buy out shareholders when the time came.

The Ingredients of a Successful Spin-Off

Businesses begin with people. It's an obvious point, but it's worth mentioning anyway because it's so easy to forget. Nothing happens in business—no start-up ever gets started—unless someone wants to go somewhere and sees the company as a way to get there.

So if you want to start businesses, you need to think first about who's going to run them. We had a whole slew of bright, young managers at SRC who were itching for a new challenge, and they came to play a critical role in our growth strategy once we got around to formulating it. With Engines Plus, however, we went outside the company, mainly because we wanted to insulate SRC from our little experiment. Then again, it didn't hurt that we already had a candidate in mind to run the new venture.

Let me say a few words here about the qualities I look for in choosing general managers of our spin-off businesses. There are two broad criteria that I use, and they reflect my own business priorities. I measure our success as a business in terms of (1) the retention of employees and (2) the growth of the company—by which I mean the growth of our people as well as our growth in sales, earnings, stock value, and the other financial yardsticks. Accordingly, I tend to evaluate potential general managers by their ability to help us in both of those areas.

I look closely at the track records of candidates. How good are they at building and holding on to a team? Do they have a strong network? Do they know how to find the people they need? I also look at the candidates' grasp of contingency planning, which I consider crucial to the long-term health of any company. Do they truly understand the what-ifs of business? I don't care so much whether a person has been in sales, engineering, finance, operations, or whatever, but I do like to see a record of growth. I want managers who can get people working together and make things happen.

By those criteria, Eric Paulsen measured up well. He was a vice president of Aaron's Automotive, a Springfield-based remanufacturer of automotive transmissions and parts and a strong competitor of ours. There he'd built and managed a wholesale distribution system, with seven warehouse locations around the country. So he had a good track record, with experience in accounting and in sales and marketing. He also had a network of contacts he could call on, including a number of loyal employees who would follow him wherever he went.

Aside from meeting my general criteria, Paulsen brought something else to the party—namely, his experience in setting up distribution systems. I thought we needed one. Since losing the GM account, our automotive division had been remanufacturing engines and engine components for a wide variety of makes and models of cars. We found ourselves in a whole new business—one that was intensely competitive, moreover, with thin margins. We still hadn't figured out how to make money in it. Part of the answer, I thought, might be to cut out the wholesalers and distribute the parts ourselves.

Paulsen could help us do that, but I had to find the right place for him. He'd already turned down a purchasing job I'd offered him, which he considered a step backward. What he really wanted was to run his own business.

So, naturally, his name came to mind as we began thinking about Engines Plus, and his experience in automotive parts distribution fit right in. We realized that the new business was going to have to diversify very soon after it got started. We hadn't forgotten the lesson of the GM episode. Engines Plus might be able to get up and running with one product (oil coolers) and one customer (SRC), but it wouldn't be a real business, with real value, until it diversified. How better to diversify than by getting into the distribution of automotive engines?

A plan quickly took shape. We'd set Paulsen up in business, give him a significant equity stake, and put him in touch with people who could help him develop a process for remanufacturing oil coolers. As soon as he had a process, he could focus on producing as many coolers as possible. He wouldn't have to worry about selling them. SRC would gladly buy them all. The price was bound to be a fraction of what we were currently paying.

Of course, the new company would need cash to get started, and we could help out there as well. First, we could provide oil cooler cores on consignment, thereby allowing Paulsen to obtain most of his raw materials without actually spending any money on them. In addition, we could set up a line of credit with SRC at minimal risk. After all, the start-up would have a guaranteed market for its products, at least its initial ones, and so it should be able to begin generating cash flow fairly quickly. The cash could be used to pay off the debt and finance the development of new products and new markets. Even there we could help—by supplying Paulsen with the automotive engines and components he needed to begin developing a wholesale distribution network.

The plan seemed so perfect we had to wonder whether we were missing something important, but we weren't, as it turned out. Although we didn't realize it at the time, we were actually creating a model we could use to start any number of businesses in the future. All the elements were there:

1. Find a customer who has a specific need and is willing to pay to get the need taken care of. I call that the *cash-flow generator*. In this case, it was SRC, which needed to stop wasting money on new oil coolers.
2. Come up with a product that's going to meet the need and that you can begin selling immediately. You're going to have overhead expenses as soon as you start the business: salaries, rent, electricity, telephone, and so on. You need to be producing something you can use to cover those expenses—or absorb them, as we say in manufacturing. I call that element the *overhead absorber*. In the case of Engines Plus, it was a line of remanufactured oil coolers.

3. Once you put together a cash-flow generator and an overhead absorber, you have the most important thing a start-up needs: *guaranteed cash flow*. As a result, the business is immediately viable, meaning that it can support itself on the cash it's generating internally. It doesn't have to rely on outside sources of capital to stay afloat.
4. So you can get the business up and running, but the equity isn't worth much as long as the company's cash flow comes from one source. Hence the next step: Build the value through *diversification*.

It was a formula we could use again and again—if it worked, that is. Back in 1987, when we launched Engines Plus, we still weren't sure that it would.

Designing Engines Plus

In late August, Mike Carrigan and I had dinner with Paulsen and sketched out our plan. He loved it. He couldn't wait to get started. There were, however, some things we needed to take care of first. To begin with, we had to come up with an ownership structure and a shareholders' agreement. In other words, we had to design the business.

It is, in fact, as important to have a good design for a subsidiary or a spin-off as it is to have one for any other business. We knew that from experience. The mistakes we'd made in designing RSC, our manufacturer's rep firm, had contributed not only to its eventual demise but also to the pain and suffering we went through along the way. On the other hand, our design of SRC had been a major factor behind our success.

In the case of Engines Plus, we began with some numbers. Our best guess was that the company would need about $50,000 to get off the ground. We wanted to provide most of the financing in the form of debt, mainly to see whether or not we could harness the power of leverage. Paulsen would need some cash up front, but not much—maybe $7,000. The rest he could receive over time. As for the participants, we decided to limit the group to five people, each of whom had some role to play in the start-up, as well as some degree of accountability if the business failed. In addition to Paulsen, the investors would be our chief financial officer, Marty Callison; our head of manufacturing, Carrigan; our attorney and board member, Dennis Sheppard; and me. We'd all put up our own money and personally assume all liabilities in case Engines Plus went under.

With that in mind, we worked out a deal. The five of us would invest a total of $1,000, and SRC would lend Engines Plus $50,000 in the form of a note. Paulsen would receive $6,000 immediately and draw down the other $44,000 as he needed to. The equity portion would consist of 10,000 shares valued at 10 cents per share. Paulsen would invest $250 and receive 25 percent of the stock. Carrigan, Callison, and I would each put up $220 and receive 22 percent of the stock. Sheppard would purchase the remaining 9 percent for $90.

In other words, the SRC officers—Carrigan, Callison, Sheppard, and I—would own 75 percent of the stock. That turned out to be a more important number than I realized. Why? Because we intended to sell our stock to SRC if Engines Plus was successful. So SRC would ultimately get our 75 percent stake, which posed a problem. If your company owns less than 80 percent of the stock of a subsidiary, you can't take out your share of the cash without paying taxes on it. As a result, those earnings wind up being taxed twice—first at the subsidiary, then at the parent company. We'd have divided the stock differently if we'd thought about that at the time.

The need to guard against a potential conflict of interest also led us to adopt two different methods of valuing the stock—one for Paulsen, and one for the rest of us. The value of the stock owned by the SRC officers was the price at which SRC could buy it. We set that price at one-half of book value, which we defined as assets minus liabilities. Considering that book value is essentially the liquidation value of a business, SRC would be getting a great deal, as we intended. (That's a matter of law, by the way. Under the so-called corporate opportunity doctrine, you have to follow some fairly rigid guidelines in taking advantage of any business opportunity that comes your way in the course of conducting a company's business. Otherwise you open yourself to various forms of litigation.)

Paulsen's stock value was another matter. We wanted to give him a powerful incentive to operate on a shoestring, keep the company lean, and plow all of the cash back into the business. That's how you create equity value in a start-up—by focusing single-mindedly on building up your assets and paying down your debt. You do that, in turn, by maximizing your retained earnings, which means resisting the temptation to take cash out in the form of salaries, or bonuses, or unnecessary luxuries.

We wanted Paulsen to be watching every nickel, and so we set the value of his stock at two times book. In other words, his stock price would rise fifty cents (25 percent of two dollars) for every dollar he invested in the company, either by increasing its assets or reducing its liabilities.

You might wonder why we didn't go with an annual valuation at Engines Plus, as we had at SRC. In fact, we included a provision that allowed us to do one. As a practical matter, however, it didn't make much sense to spend, say, $9,000 doing a valuation of a company we were starting for $1,000. Moreover, there was no compelling reason to do a formal valuation since we weren't setting up an ESOP at Engines Plus.

I might add that we subsequently changed Paulsen's stock valuation formula—after Engines Plus was more or less established. In March 1991, we amended the shareholders' agreement so that the stock would be valued at two times book *plus* a multiple of earnings. Up to that point, we hadn't been very concerned about earnings. You expect a start-up to run at a loss as it struggles to get off the ground. But that changes once it's up and running. If an established company has no earnings, its real value goes down, even though its book value may be unchanged. We needed to make sure the formula reflected reality.

That's a point worth bearing in mind if you decide to go down the equity-sharing route. Unless the company is publicly owned (in which case the market sets the value) or has a formal valuation done at regular intervals, you may have to change your methodology from time to time.

Happiness Is a Plan That Works

In putting together our plan, we'd drawn on everything we'd learned during our first five years in business. Unlike some of our earlier experiments, this one unfolded about as smoothly as any of us could have hoped.

Motivation was certainly not a problem. Paulsen threw himself into the start-up even before we'd finished the plan. His first challenge was to come up with a remanufacturing process—a tough job for someone who had no technical training, had never worked with engines, and didn't know an oil cooler from a thermos bottle. So we teamed him up with one of our best engineers, Al Fabbri, and sent them to Joplin, Missouri, to meet a guy we'd heard was already working on the problem.

Leo Lema had been an engineer at Modine Manufacturing, one of the major producers of oil coolers. After his retirement, he'd set up a small repair business, Heatexchanger Specialties, in a shop next to his house in Joplin, where he fixed radiators, oil coolers, and various other gizmos for anyone who managed to track him down. Having worked on oil coolers at Modine, he knew them inside and out, and he already had a process for repairing ones that leaked.

The leaks typically occurred inside the oil cooler, which is a 20-inch-long metal cylinder with caps at each end. Oil is pumped in and out at one end, and water at the other. The water flows through ninety-four thin copper tubes, thereby reducing the temperature of the oil that is running through the cooler. Over time, the vibration of the engine can cause some of the copper tubes to spring leaks. Fortunately, however, the coolers had been designed with excess cooling capacity. As a result, you could plug as many as four of the ninety-four tubes, and the cooler would still meet specifications.

Lema had his own method of repairing leaky coolers and bringing them up to spec. He agreed to teach Paulsen and Fabbri what he knew and work with them on developing a remanufacturing process. Meanwhile, Paulsen would start looking for used coolers that could be repaired, and he'd send all of the work to Lema for the first six weeks or so—until Engines Plus had its own shop up and running. That way, Lema would be compensated without Paulsen having to spend any of his precious cash.

Obviously, he had gotten the message.

Indeed, Paulsen displayed many of the entrepreneurial qualities I thought we were in danger of losing at SRC. He was resourceful. He was creative. He operated on the edge. He did all of the things you do when you're getting by on pocket change and know you're doomed if you run out of cash. Instead of spending money to solve problems, he relied on his own ingenuity and that of two or three friends he'd brought in to help out—just like any bootstrapping entrepreneur.

The business couldn't even start, for example, until they could get some worktables for the shop they'd leased. The place was utterly barren. So Paulsen and his buddies looked around and found some heavy crates GM had used to ship engines. They cut out the saddle for the engine, came up with square metal tubes to use as legs, added a top, and they were in business.

Then there was the oven they needed to dry the rebuilt coolers before checking them for leaks. Industrial drying equipment, it turned out, could cost as much as $10,000. But Paulsen had an idea. He'd worked in restaurants as a kid. He decided to look up a company that sold used restaurant supplies. There he found a pizza oven with just the right dimensions. Two full rows of oil coolers—about twenty altogether—could fit perfectly inside the oven, and they came out as dry as overcooked pizza crust. He bought the oven for $200.

Bit by bit, the business came together. It happened so fast we could hardly believe it. In February 1988, its third month in existence, Engines Plus shipped 350 to 400 rebuilt oil coolers to SRC. I'd spent two years trying in vain to get our people at SRC to focus on developing a process for remanufacturing oil coolers. Paulsen and his people had come up with one in a matter of weeks.

By the time the bugs had been worked out, Engines Plus was able to remanufacture those oil coolers for a fraction of what we'd been paying. SRC took all that Paulsen and his people could produce, and the numbers kept climbing. Within a year or so, production leveled off at about 1,000 oil coolers per month, providing a very substantial annual savings to SRC.

Meanwhile, Paulsen had begun his diversification program, ordering automotive engines from our factory in Willow Springs, Missouri, and marketing them by direct mail. By the end of 1989, he was selling between thirty and forty engines per month, at $800 each, and trying to develop an engine-installation business on the side. But a much bigger opportunity had presented itself that quickly transformed our experiment with oil coolers into a serious business proposition.

One of our major customers, Case, had a joint venture with Cummins Engine under which the two companies manufactured and sold a couple of powerful engines used in agricultural equipment. Case's president of parts operations, Robert Nardelli (now president and CEO of Home Depot), was looking for opportunities to sell more of the engines. He also wanted to give the people he worked with a lesson in entrepreneurship, showing them how a large company could be innovative and move fast. He came up with the idea of incorporating the engines into a new line of stationary power units, which farmers would use to pump water for irrigation. Through one of our salespeople, he inquired whether SRC would be interested in manufacturing the power units as a subcontractor to Case.

It was a nice offer, but we couldn't see where we'd do the work. The power units didn't really fit in with our main businesses. So we put the Case people in touch with Paulsen, who listened to their proposal and signed up on the spot. He told me later he was too stupid to be scared. After looking at some power units made by other companies, he put together a quote, which the Case people accepted. They came back with a design of the unit they wanted. "Can you do it?" they asked.

"Sure," he said.

There was just one problem. The Case people wanted him to exhibit a prototype based on the design at their big annual trade fair in Kansas City on November 1. Paulsen found out about it in the middle of September, and he knew immediately he was in trouble. Neither he nor any of his people had ever built a prototype before. They had no experience with metal fabrication. They knew nothing about making power units.

Nevertheless, they somehow managed to pull a prototype together in time for the trade fair. Paulsen's buddies Daren and Doug Whipple stayed up the whole night before, drying the paint with handheld hair dryers. When Paulsen returned from Kansas City three days later, he had orders for 200 power units, which Case would buy from him for $5,000 each—$1 million in sales of a product that had never been tested, that he wasn't even sure would work.

It was one of those classic entrepreneurial situations. Even if the product passed muster, Paulsen didn't have a factory large enough to make the power units. For that matter, he didn't have machine tools, a workforce, raw materials, and whatever else might be required. Worst of all, he didn't begin to have enough cash to finance the power unit business—either now or in the future. The Case people were talking about ordering 800 units in the first year, 1,200 in the second, and 2,000 the year after that. If those numbers were realistic (they weren't, but we didn't know it), Engines Plus's annual sales could grow from less than $1 million to more than $11 million in three years. Where would the cash come from to pay for that kind of growth?

The answer, it turned out, was Case.

When we sat down to negotiate with the Case people, we told them that, as much as we wanted to do the deal, we couldn't go forward unless they could give us favorable terms. Engines Plus simply wasn't in a position to carry the full burden of financing the business, particularly since Case wanted us to buy the engines from the joint venture. We weren't getting them on consignment. That made a lot of sense for Case, but none at all for Engines Plus—unless, of course, it didn't have to pay for the engines until long after it had been paid for the power units.

The Case people wanted to know what we had in mind. We proposed a deal under which Case would pay Engines Plus in thirty days, and Engines Plus wouldn't have to pay Case for ninety days. That way, Case would get what it wanted: the opportunity to record the sale of the engines as soon as they were shipped. And Engines Plus would get what it had to have: net positive cash flow for sixty days.

That was, in fact, the arrangement we agreed upon, and it was a very good deal for Engines Plus. At a production level of sixty-six power units per month, the sixty-day lag time was like getting an interest-free loan of $800,000 for the entire length of the contract. As a result, Engines Plus—which had already paid off its note to SRC—was able to grow for the next seven years without taking on any significant bank debt.

I can honestly say that such a proposal would never have crossed our minds a few years before. We must have learned something after all.

The Future Opens Up

As it turned out, the Case deal was a turning point, not only for Engines Plus but for SRC. The implications of the deal began to dawn on me sometime during the fall of 1989, when I sat down to look at Engines Plus's stock value and did some quick calculations on the potential impact of the new line of business.

The numbers took my breath away. Even without the power unit order, the value of Engines Plus had grown dramatically. Under the formula we were using—two times book value—Paulsen's $250 investment was now worth more than $32,000. In twenty-six months, the price of his stock had risen from 10 cents to $13 per share. With the first order of 200 power units, the company was certain to double in size during the next year. It was thus altogether likely that, by the end of its third year in business, a share of Engines Plus's stock would be worth $40 at the agreed value—and Paulsen's stake would have grown to $100,000.

I had two immediate reactions to those numbers. The first was: "*Holy shit, it works.*" We really could harness the power of leverage. It wasn't just a theory, and it wasn't a matter of luck. It was something you could actually build into a start-up's business plan.

My second reaction was: "*We gotta get out.*" Even at one-half of book value, the stock I'd bought for $220 was already worth $14,000, an increase of more than 6,000 percent over what I'd paid. Altogether, the stock owned by Carrigan, Callison, Sheppard, and me was worth $50,000. That's what it would cost SRC to buy us out before the launch of the new power unit line. If Case's optimistic projections proved accurate, the price tag could conceivably rise to $300,000 in another year.

We all agreed that we couldn't wait. We had to sell right away—when the greatest risk was behind us, the major payoff lay ahead, and the stock was still a bargain. So, on February 1, 1990, the four of us sold our stock to SRC, which became the 75-percent owner of Engines Plus.

But the stock transfer was only the beginning—because Engines Plus had clearly changed. It was no longer simply an experiment, nor even just a clever way for SRC to save a lot of money on oil coolers. With the Case deal, Engines Plus had become a real business, capable of standing on its own, generating a significant amount of cash flow from a mix of products and a mix of customers, both of which could be expanded in the future.

That change had enormous implications. To begin with, it meant that Engines Plus could be sold. We could probably find a buyer right away if we had to. We could certainly find one in the future if we did a halfway decent job of developing the business. By then, the company might well be worth a lot of money. It was by no means inconceivable that, in a few years, SRC could sell its stake for $2 million, $3 million, maybe even as much as $5 million.

And how much might SRC itself be worth in a few years? What would our shareholder liabilities be at that time—$20 million? $30 million? If so, Engines Plus could be one of our contingency plans for taking care of shareholders. We could sell our stake and use the money to pay off the people who were cashing out of SRC.

The realization hit me like a thunderbolt. That was it! We'd finally found the solution we'd been searching for! If we'd done it once, why couldn't we do it again and again? Why couldn't we keep on starting businesses, using the same formula that had worked so well with Engines Plus? We could put together cash-flow generators and overhead absorbers, get the businesses up and running, diversify them, and build them up. Then, if we needed cash to buy out shareholders, we could sell our equity stake. Maybe the subsidiary's managers would do a leveraged buyout. Maybe we'd arrange an acquisition by another company. Maybe we'd take the subsidiary public. The point is, we'd have all kinds of options. We could decide what we wanted to do when the time came.

In the process, we'd be moving our game to another level, taking advantage of the true profit of business. SRC would be far more valuable as a collection of businesses that could be sold separately than it would be as a single entity that had to be sold in one lump. The principle is the same one that corporate raiders use when they take over a big company—divide it up, and auction off the individual pieces. If you have several profitable businesses and a few losers, you can make more money by selling the profitable ones individually than you can by selling the whole package—because the losers detract from the value of the winners. Of course, a lot of people usually get hurt when corporate raiders apply the principle. By standing the principle on its head, we could use it to create value for our employee-shareholders and ensure that they'd be able to cash out when the time came.

Meanwhile, we had a growth strategy we could follow indefinitely. We could grow just like the Chinese firecracker factory—getting big by staying small. We could divide up into huts. We could take our best young managers and let them build their own businesses from scratch. They'd get a new challenge, an opportunity to learn and grow, and SRC would get all kinds of benefits. We'd keep our factories small. We'd give line employees a chance to move up. We'd reduce our overhead without downsizing, without laying anyone off, and we'd make ourselves more competitive in the process. Through the subsidiaries, we could experiment and innovate constantly, at minimal risk. If one of the huts exploded on us, the rest of the village would be safe. Unlike the firecracker manufacturer, moreover, we wouldn't lose the people. We could bring them out and set them up in another hut.

I could see our future opening up before us. It was as if a great cloud had lifted. We were back on the road to building the kind of a business we'd been dreaming about for eight years. We'd found the missing piece of the puzzle. At last we had a strategy for getting out.

Now we just had to implement it.

12

A Question of Stewardship

When you build a business, you create a community. You may not know you're doing it. You may not want to do it. But, like it or not, you wind up with one. It just happens. You wake up one day and discover that your company is not only a business but a sort of ecosystem, a society in which people are spending a significant part of their lives.

Of course, people have different ideas about the kind of the community they want in their company. I'd always had a pretty clear picture of the one I hoped we'd create at SRC. I wanted it to operate according to certain principles of fairness that we'd all grown up with and that I thought we all shared. And I had high expectations. In my mind's eye, this community was going to be a perfect place. As time went along, I realized that perfection was not possible here on earth, but I still wanted to build a society that was reasonably just and fair, one in which we'd all have opportunities to improve our lives, raise our standard of living, and no one would be held back by arbitrary barriers. It would be a society based on mutual trust and respect, as well as mutual responsibility. Yes, we'd have different roles, but everybody would be valued. We'd have the sort of relationships at work that we've come to expect in the rest of our lives. People would be treated neither as children to be coddled nor as disposable assets, but as adults and citizens.

In the beginning, I thought it would be easy to establish such a community and run a company according to those values, but it turned out to be extremely difficult—mainly because of all the threats we faced, threats we could never have imagined before we were actually in business. There were the threats from our lenders, threats from competitors, threats from our customers and suppliers, threats from the economy, from regulators, from outside lawsuits, even from some of our own people. There were all kinds of threats, and we found ourselves in a constant battle to defend the community against them.

What's important, we learned, is to find the right balance. Almost every move you make, after all, affects the business as well as the community. How do you do what's right for both? The key, we discovered, is to make sure that the members of the community are also businesspeople—that they know what's going on, understand their roles, and benefit from the results. You can't have mutual responsibility without mutual advantage. Our community and our company were built around both.

We learned a tremendous amount by taking this approach. We learned about the need to diversify. We learned about the importance of having contingency plans. We learned to develop the habit of trapdoor thinking—always running through the what-ifs, focusing on the things that could go wrong and what to do about them. We engaged in "creative paranoia" even before Andrew Grove of Intel popularized the concept in his book *Only the Paranoid Survive*. We were constantly trying to figure out where the next threat might come from and how we could deal with it, preferably before it became a real problem.

There was, fortunately, a bright side to the process. As we learned how to defend and expand the community, we also created wealth. The threats gave us an extraordinary education in business by forcing us to figure out new ways to deal with them, and the better businesspeople we became, the more wealth we created, which was exactly how we thought it should work. We believed we could have both the financial rewards of business and a strong, healthy community to live in, and we couldn't see anything in capitalism that would stop us.

In business, however, you eventually have to ask: Where does this all end? When do I get to take my wealth and leave? That's presumably why you care about creating wealth in the first place.

When you have an employee-owned business, moreover, getting out *has* to be one of your goals. Otherwise your company will become a prison and a hoax. It will be a prison if people have no other choice but to keep working for the rest of their lives. It will be a hoax if you can't deliver on the promises you've made, if your employees can never actually lay hands on the money they've earned.

My responsibility as the CEO was to make sure that SRC didn't become either prison or hoax, which meant finding a way to cash everybody out. I'd be letting the whole community down if I didn't. Not that I was driven only by my sense of duty to the other shareholders. I, too, wanted to be able to move on at some point, and I couldn't go anywhere until we had a mechanism in place that would guarantee people would be paid when the time came.

Without such a mechanism, we'd make a mockery of everything we'd accomplished. Why? Because communities are built around rules. The rules may be explicit or implied, but they're understood and accepted by everybody. They provide the glue that holds the community together, and you can't violate them without doing a tremendous amount of damage.

We'd built our community around a common understanding that we'd all share whatever wealth we created. That was our bargain, and our people had lived up to their end of it. I could never walk away from SRC until I knew for certain that I'd lived up to my end of it as well—that we were all going to get our fair share of the rewards, that no one was going to leave the table hungry.

So I was very excited in early 1990 as our new strategy came together, and I began to see clearly how we could get where I knew we had to go.

The Plan

The idea in a nutshell was to take the lessons of our experiment with Engines Plus and blow them out to the whole company. We'd start new businesses as fast as we could, recruiting people from our heavy-duty and automotive divisions to run them. Meanwhile, we'd decentralize the rest of SRC. The automotive operation would get its own name—Sequel was the one we eventually came up with—and would be set up as a separate entity. It would no longer share functions with the heavy-duty division (which held on to the name SRC, although internally we called it "Heavy-Duty"). They would both operate as independent businesses, as would the new companies we were launching. We'd establish a small central office to do the deals, develop the strategy, manage the finances, oversee the company, and so on, but the emphasis was on decentralization. We wanted to turn SRC into a diversified collection of enterprises, a sort of miniconglomerate, as well as an ongoing business incubator.

At the time, I expected that we'd eventually sell all the businesses—ideally to their managers and employees. Our intention was to bring at least some of the managers in as part owners of the new companies from the beginning. People who were leaving for a start-up would cash out of the ESOP and invest the money in the new business, thereby getting a chance to take advantage of the early rise in the equity value. If they subsequently acquired the business, they could then releverage it and do the same thing we'd done with SRC—that is, buy the business with debt, pay it off out of earnings, and send the stock price soaring. Meanwhile, they could continue to spread the wealth by giving their employees the same chance to participate that we'd given them.

That's how I imagined things would work out, at any rate. We eventually wound up taking a different path, for reasons I'll explain in the next chapter. Back then, however, I was mainly concerned with building businesses that we could sell someday to raise the cash we'd need to pay shareholders. How would we sell them? Whom would we sell them to? Would we sell them individually or as a package? I couldn't answer any of those questions, and I didn't think we had to. I wanted to keep an open mind. It was too soon to worry about the specifics. Who could say how circumstances might change? My guess was that we'd split SRC into pieces that could be sold separately, but I didn't think we should rule out any possibility. When the time came, we'd do what was best for the people involved. That's how we'd always operated, and I saw no reason to stop now.

Building-to-Last Versus Building-to-Sell

There is, I admit, a paradox here, and I'm sure other companies run into it as well. You work extremely hard to build a community you feel good about, but then—in order to fulfill your commitments to its members—you have to contemplate breaking up the business that's made it possible. Why wouldn't you instead try to preserve the community and the business? Shouldn't you be striving to build your company to last?

Those are good questions, and my answer today would be different from the one I'd have given you ten years ago. The truth is, I'd never assumed we were building a company for the ages. I would have considered it arrogant to suppose we could. To be sure, I was proud of what we'd done, and I would no doubt have felt a sense of loss if SRC disappeared, but we weren't in business to create an institution. We were in business to help a bunch of people get through life.

That assumption lay at the heart of our dream. The whole idea had been to build a business that made our lives better, rather than one that was constantly sacrificing people to a supposedly higher goal. I was wary of putting the company up on some kind of pedestal. Our commitments weren't to the company, after all, but to one another.

Not that we wouldn't lose people now and then. We'd already lost a few. And, yes, we'd all have to make some sacrifices along the way. Life is often tough. Business can be hard. Markets are unforgiving. That's just reality. As long as we were all willing to face reality, however, we could figure out what we had to do—both individually and collectively—to protect ourselves and generate the rewards we were all going to share.

In the process, we'd learn and grow. We'd meet challenges and overcome them. We'd raise our families, help our communities, struggle and sweat, have fun and make money. And when we'd had enough, when we were ready for something else, we could take what we'd earned and go.

That was the goal. We weren't building a monument. We wanted to have rich, happy, fulfilling lives. I did, at any rate, and I assumed others felt the same way. SRC was just a means to help us get what we wanted, fulfill our individual aspirations. Whether it survived as a freestanding business over the long run—indeed, whether it survived at all—didn't matter as long as we achieved the goal.

And I thought our new strategy would allow us to achieve it.

How? By making our stock liquid. By providing us with a compass we could use to grow in a way that would both make SRC more attractive to prospective investors and give us a broad array of options and choices for generating the cash we'd need to buy out shareholders.

It's important to note, however, that we couldn't succeed without building both the business and the community in the meantime. Even though our long-term intention might be to break up SRC and sell the parts, for now we had to work on strengthening all aspects of the company. That's how we'd make our stock more attractive and expand the range of choices we'd have in the future.

So, oddly enough, our strategy for getting out was just what we would have needed if we were instead going to build an enduring company, but I didn't think about that at the time. I was focusing on how we could make our stock more liquid.

Five Imperatives of a Mature Business

So what exactly does it take to move a company up the ladder of durability—to go from what I call the growth stage to the maturity stage? I believe you need to improve the business in at least five respects, and I could see us doing all five in the course of turning SRC into a decentralized collection of companies growing start-up by start-up.

Not that our strategy was necessarily better than anyone else's. There are a lot of ways to grow, and there are a lot of companies that successfully manage the transition from a small business dependent on a few individuals to one with the potential to endure. But all of those companies have something in common. They not only get bigger as they grow—they strengthen themselves in the process, and they do it in the following ways:

1. **Diversification.** No company can last unless it protects itself against the surprises of the market, and diversification is still the best form of protection anyone has come up with. To be sure, you have to begin by identifying your vulnerabilities (through some version of the process we described back in Chapter 10). Once you know what they are, however, the best way to address them is usually to diversify.

Our growth strategy turned out to be ideally suited for diversification. We'd figured out early on, for example, that we had a cash-flow problem, mainly because remanufacturing absorbs so much cash. We decided to tackle the problem by launching high-cash-flow businesses outside of remanufacturing. At the same time, we used our knowledge of the industry to diversify into new types of remanufacturing—with different products, different customers, different market segments.

The new businesses provided us with contingencies in case anything happened to the mother ship, Heavy-Duty, which had a major vulnerability: Almost 50 percent of its sales were with one customer, Navistar. While we had a good relationship with Navistar, we knew from the GM experience how fast circumstances could change. It was important for Heavy-Duty itself to diversify to protect the jobs of the people who worked there. In the meantime, we could use the other companies as a kind of safety net. If disaster struck, we could avoid layoffs by placing people from Heavy-Duty in the subsidiaries or by bringing work in from the subs.

2. **Innovation and entrepreneurship.** Beyond diversification, every business is under pressure these days to reinvent itself constantly, if only to keep up with changes in the competitive environment. To stay ahead of the curve, you have to institutionalize the process of innovation, so that it happens continuously and automatically, and you have to come up with entrepreneurial mechanisms that allow you to turn innovations into business successes.

We knew that we'd have to innovate like crazy if we were going to create entities we could sell someday, and we could see from Engines Plus how much faster and more effectively we could innovate if we set up subsidiaries to develop specific products. We'd also seen how resourceful people can be when they're operating on a shoestring. At Engines Plus, there was a spirit of entrepreneurship that's almost impossible to foster in a large organization with an abundance of resources. That spirit took hold because the people at Engines Plus really were in business for themselves.

So there was every reason to grow by following the Engines Plus example. This led us to adopt what later became a hot trend among big manufacturers—namely, the concept of "focus factories," whereby you set up factories around specific product lines. Of course, we gave the concept our own spin, running the factories as separate companies operated by employees who were also owners and businesspeople.

3. **Leadership development.** Third, you need to get your people ready to take advantage of the opportunities you see. Otherwise you'll never achieve your strategic goals. **That's a general rule, by the way. Once you get beyond the survival stage, a shortage of people is the only obstacle to growth.** There's never a shortage of opportunities, and capital isn't a problem, either. In most cases, you're generating enough cash internally to finance your growth. If not, there are numerous sources of outside capital available to fill in the gaps.

Having a culture of ownership gives you an enormous advantage in this regard. What builds and sustains the culture are the mechanisms you use to educate and train your people and to create leaders at every level of the organization. As a result, the company becomes an incubator of potential entrepreneurs.

We saw that effect clearly in SRC. We had a whole generation of middle managers who'd come up through the ranks, starting as hourly employees, becoming group leaders and supervisors, then advancing from one position to the next until we'd run out of places to put them. They'd been practicing the disciplines of the Great Game of Business for years. They had a solid grasp of the numbers. They knew how to put together an annual plan, how to forecast, how to develop contingencies, how to communicate and motivate, how to make the big play. They understood our system and our culture. They'd been through the whole informal learning process, and they were ready for the next course. We saw the start-ups as a way to provide them with new challenges and opportunities, while simultaneously giving other people a chance to move up.

We'd need replacements, after all, for the managers who were going to the new businesses. Fortunately, we had an abundance of talent in our hourly, professional, and supervisory ranks. There, too, were people who'd been stuck in their jobs too long, who'd learned a tremendous amount about business through the Game, and who needed new challenges and opportunities. They understood the language of numbers. They had experience in working as members of a team, in setting and meeting goals. Now they were ready for another level of responsibility. By moving the middle managers to the new subsidiaries, we'd create a range of job openings for people down the ladder . . .

. . . which would mean we'd have more entry-level positions available. We'd be able to bring in a whole new group of young people, who would play the Great Game of Business, learn our system and our culture, and get ready to move up when their turn came.

In other words, the decentralization strategy would serve as a mechanism for rejuvenating the company and reinvigorating the community while allowing us to address our weaknesses as a business and develop an exit strategy at the same time. We'd be creating new career paths for people, providing them with experience and skills that would help them no matter where they wound up.

4. **Financial discipline.** The fourth imperative involves improving your ability to make wise decisions about spending your cash. Specifically, you need to make sure you're using your cash to build the future rather than simply to maintain the past. That means, among other things, fighting against the natural tendency of many costs—especially labor costs—to rise over time.

Here, too, we saw our strategy helping us strengthen the company by reducing costs in our established businesses as we moved managers into the start-ups. In effect, we'd be replacing high salaries with low salaries, since someone who's starting out in a job almost always earns less than someone who's been doing it for years. The lower our fixed costs, the better our margins—and the more cash we'd have available for other purposes.

I suppose you might say we were downsizing. We were, in fact, using the new strategy to help us cope with the same economic forces most companies were contending with in the late 1980s. We, too, were getting squeezed by our customers. We, too, were being forced by competition to reduce prices. We, too, were under unremitting pressure to cut costs. We, too, wanted to build shareholder value.

On the other hand, we couldn't justify using layoffs as a management tool, and the new strategy offered us an alternative. Instead of getting rid of our middle managers, we'd ask them to help us grow. By moving them into the new businesses, we'd reduce our payroll in Heavy-Duty, where most of them came from, but without losing all the talent those people represented—and without sending a terrible message about loyalty that came back to haunt other downsized companies in the 1990s, when they suddenly found themselves dealing with the worst labor shortage in memory.

Moreover, we had the additional lever of equity to use in maintaining financial discipline, and a powerful lever it can be, especially in a tight labor market. There's no better way to keep your operating costs down while providing people with the rewards they deserve for helping to make the business successful. (See "The Equity Advantage," page 193.)

5. **Experimentation.** There is at least one other thing that you must do to remain competitive over the long haul. You need to keep trying out new ideas, taking chances, running into obstacles, making mistakes, and doing all of the other things that allow you to learn and move forward. The question is, How do you avoid endangering the company at the same time?

Therein lay a major benefit of our new strategy. We could use the start-ups to experiment without putting the rest of the company at risk. If one of the huts blew up, the village would still be safe.

We couldn't be sure, for example, how our people would respond if we brought them in as equity partners in a new business, or what ramifications the practice might have in other parts of SRC. Nor did we

THE EQUITY ADVANTAGE

There's a great benefit you get from sharing equity in a business. You can, in effect, pay people more money without putting the additional cost into the product—which gives you a huge competitive advantage.

It's a particularly big advantage when you're competing with other companies, not only for customers, but also for employees, as every business is these days. Why? Because we all have limits on what we can afford to pay people for most jobs. You may desperately need the people to take advantage of market opportunities, but you're playing a dangerous game if you try to attract or keep employees with higher salaries. You could easily upset your compensation structure and wind up paying too much for labor. Then you'll be forced to make up the difference somewhere else. Maybe you'll take it out of profits; maybe you'll skimp on investments in other areas of the business; maybe you'll raise your prices. One way or another, you're going to make your company vulnerable. You'll hurt your cash flow and become less competitive. Instead of adding jobs, you may eventually be forced to cut them.

Equity allows you to sidestep the problem because it doesn't add to your operating costs. A guy might be earning $10 an hour in base compensation, but he could be making two, three times that amount in the form of equity appreciation, and the company doesn't have to pay for it—at least not right away.

So who *does* pay for it? Most people would say that the other shareholders do, by diluting the value of their stock, which is technically true. When you divide the pie among more people, each person gets a smaller slice. But that doesn't take into account the increase in stock value you can have as a result of equity-sharing.

I'm not saying it happens automatically. You have to take advantage of the leverage that equity gives you with the people who receive it. But if you can show them what it means, how it works, and what they can do to drive its value, you can overcome the effects of dilution. The whole pie will grow, and so will the individual slices. In that case, equity-sharing becomes a benefit that pays for itself.

That's possible because equity has the potential to change the fundamental relationships in a company. It puts everybody in the same boat, and it allows you to talk sense to people about business. You can explain the logic behind your compensation system, and they'll listen because you've given them a reason to care about it.

So they can see, for example, why you need to set base pay at a competitive level. We try to keep ours low enough to minimize the danger of ever having to lay people off—even in downtimes, even when the market is weak. On the other hand, we also want people to know that we'd prefer to pay people above-market rates, but we can afford to only if we have above-market performance. When we do outperform the market, we pay everybody a reward through our bonus program.

At the same time, of course, we're increasing the value of the company, and everybody is helping to one degree or another. Equity is the means by which we compensate people for their contributions, and it has the potential to provide the greatest rewards of all. The better people understand that, and the more they're motivated by it, the bigger the payoff will be for everyone—including the original shareholders who diluted their stock by sharing equity with the other employees. Not only will they suffer no loss due to the dilution, but they could see a substantial increase in the value of their holdings.

That's the beauty of capitalism, or at least of this particular approach to capitalism. When you bring everybody into the game, everybody can come out a winner.

know how it would work out to form joint ventures with some of our customers, as we were thinking of doing. And what about the service and retail businesses we had in mind? We were dyed-in-the-wool manufacturers. There was no question that we had a lot to learn about operating outside of our normal habitat. How long would it take to get acclimated? How many failures would we need—and at what cost?

One way or another, we knew we'd have problems in the start-ups. In fact, we *hoped* we'd have problems. We wouldn't get anywhere unless we did.

That was one of the big lessons of our journey: You move ahead in business by running into obstacles and overcoming them. Every important discovery we'd made, every major step we'd taken forward, had come by working our way out of some predicament. The collapse of International Harvester, the 89-to-1 debt-to-equity ratio, the trouble with Dresser, the problems with RSC, the confrontation with McCoy, the loss of the GM contract, the search for a way out—those had been the business courses we'd taken, and we'd learned a tremendous amount from each one.

With the new strategy, we thought we had a way to harness the process. We could set up a business knowing that we were going to run into obstacles and welcoming them. Why? Because we wanted to see what would happen, what we could learn, what unexpected discoveries we could make. In effect, the strategy offered us a methodology for conducting the type of ongoing experimentation that every company must do to move forward, and at minimal risk.

Focusing on the Future

The experiments couldn't help but make SRC a stronger, better company. Then again, I could say the same thing about the other benefits of the new strategy. Together, they had the potential to take SRC to another level. By that, I mean they would turn us from a company that was good at operating in the present into one that was constantly preparing for the future.

That's a major transition for any business. When you pass that threshold, you come of age. In the early days, every company lives day to day, week to week, and month to month. Later, as your cash flow stabilizes, you get the knack for operating from year to year. But you don't reach true maturity until you learn how to think and plan three, four, five years into the future—until you're always looking ahead, always doing today what will make your business stronger tomorrow. At that point, your company acquires staying power. You begin to build dependable, long-term value, for which any investor would be willing to pay a premium.

Not that the transition is easy. When you fundamentally transform the way a company operates—particularly when you decentralize the business as much as we were doing—many people have to change their roles, especially the people at the top.

For one thing, you have to let go of a lot of functions you've grown used to handling, including some you're probably quite good at. You may have been a whiz at operations, but now you have to play a strategic role. You need to be spending time on different kinds of activities, and it may take a while to figure out what they are. It will take even longer to figure out whether or not you have any talent for them. Until then, you can't really be sure. So there's an element of uncertainty, maybe even doubt.

Meanwhile, you've turned over operational responsibilities to other people, some of whom will undoubtedly have management styles very different from yours. No matter how good they may be as managers, you'll see them doing things you don't like, wouldn't have done, and think may lead to trouble someday, but you'll have to bite your tongue. You could be wrong, after all, and even if you're right, you'll make yourself wrong by butting in. You'll succeed only in undermining them, which will make it impossible for them to do their jobs and torpedo the whole transition process.

I can't tell you how to avoid all these challenges, but I can offer some suggestions on coping with them:

- **Move your office.** You can reduce the temptation to meddle by physically removing yourself from the premises. That may be hard, and you may not like the change at first, but over the long term it will be good for both you and the company.

I have to admit that I hated the idea of moving my office out of the Heavy-Duty building, where I'd been stationed ever since I'd arrived in Springfield in 1979. I recognized, however, that I had to make room for Heavy-Duty's new general manager, Dan Rorke, my old boss from International Harvester, who'd joined SRC in 1988. So we bought a building on the other side of town and reserved a portion of it for "corporate offices."

I was miserable. I felt like a duck on a bicycle. I'd spent my entire career working in factories. Never before had my office been more than a few steps from the shop floor. It took a long time for me to get used to my new digs. But moving was the right thing to do.

- **Get outside the company.** A great opportunity awaits you when your company finally reaches the point at which operational responsibilities can be delegated. Suddenly you're free to spend a lot more time learning from other companies. You can join their boards. You can play a more active role in industry associations. You can become a member of a networking group, go to business conferences, become a mentor to young entrepreneurs, and so on. In the process you'll be broadening your horizons, and both you and your company will benefit—often in ways you won't realize until much later.

Through such activities, you can acquire an incredible education. I certainly did. In particular, I became much more adept at viewing SRC from the outside in, at diagnosing our strengths and weaknesses, a critical skill in the transition process. I also kept myself out of the hair of the general managers as they were establishing themselves in their respective businesses.

- **Use the variances to avoid micromanaging.** Of course, even in the most decentralized companies, the company's leaders need to keep informed about what's going on in the different parts of the business. There are times, moreover, when you have to step in. But how do you know the appropriate response in any given situation? When should you panic? For that matter, when should you cheer? Or get angry? Or offer help? Or shut up?

It helps to have some sort of system like the Great Game of Business. Twice a year, we'd hold a three-day sales meeting, in which people from each business would give the rest of the company a detailed report on what had happened in the previous six months, what they expected to happen in the next twelve to eighteen months, and why. And, every January, I'd take to the board of directors an annual plan that we'd worked out together, signed off on, and were committed to achieving. It was, as I liked to say, an agreement among consenting adults. As long as the different businesses were living up to their end of it, I generally didn't interfere.

I relied mainly on the huddle process to monitor how they were doing. Each of the individual businesses continued to hold weekly huddles, and I'd get the numbers afterward. Then, every other week, I'd have an hourlong huddle with managers from all over SRC and see exactly how each business was doing in relation to the annual plan and where the variances were coming from. In general, I didn't get worried about variances of less than 5 percent in either direction. If a variance was greater than 5 percent, I'd ask why—and insist on getting an answer that made sense.

By watching the variances over time, I could see where the problems were and how they were being handled, and I could figure out how worried I should be. Unless someone was in serious trouble and needed help right away, I didn't get involved. It often takes months for a team of people to figure out how to work a plan. You can do a lot of harm by stepping in too soon. I'd generally wait two or three quarters before doing anything drastic. Even then, I preferred to deal with a situation through the annual planning process, when we'd take whatever steps we thought were necessary to fix the problems in the coming year.

The New Priorities

Once you've turned most operational decision making over to other people, you're still faced with the biggest question of all—namely, Where exactly should you be focusing your attention anyway? From a practical standpoint, what should you be doing?

I don't know how other people approach that challenge, but I was guided mainly by my obligations to the shareholder-employees of SRC. I think that's an advantage you have when you distribute equity widely in a business. You have a kind of freedom that comes from knowing you're acting as the steward of the community. You're not just promoting your own interests, or those of a small group of owners. Rather, you're helping to create the conditions that will allow people throughout the company to make their own choices when the time comes.

I wound up focusing on five areas of the business that I sensed would ultimately determine the amount of control we'd have over our destiny.

Not that I formally designated them as priorities. They were simply the things that I decided, more or less intuitively, it was important to spend my time on. You can think of them as a series of questions:

1. *What new ventures should we be starting, and why?* There is never a shortage of opportunities. Once you become aware of them, you can walk through your company and, at every turn, come across an operation that seems as though it's just waiting to be spun off as a separate business. We had one hourly guy, for example, who'd developed a process that was saving us thousands of dollars in turbocharger costs. Couldn't we set him up in his own company? What about having someone produce brake shoes? Or transmissions?

Then again, you can also ask your people for their ideas. We did that, and the suggestions poured in. Unfortunately, they were all over the lot—a liquor store, a Laundromat, a bar, a beauty salon, an Amway distributorship in Mexico. I had to explain that there were some limits. We needed to focus on starting businesses that made sense in the context of SRC. Nevertheless, it was great to see other people as excited about the possibilities as I was.

We wound up starting four new businesses in the first year. We've started another 35 since then. In general, we've tended to choose the ones that meet the following criteria:

- we have people who are ready to run them
- they serve an important strategic purpose (diversification, for example)
- they can help us meet our business goals, specifically our target of fifteen percent sales growth per year
- they will allow us to experiment in areas we consider it important to explore (e.g., joint ventures with customers)

To be sure, all of the new businesses didn't work out as we'd hoped, but we learned as much from the failures as from the successes.

2. *What other trapdoors and contingency plans can we build into the company?* Each new business is a trapdoor in its own right, since you can presumably sell it someday to raise cash if you have to. On the other hand,

you don't need to limit your contingency planning to starting businesses. If you think you're going to need cash in the future, there are plenty of ways to generate it.

As far back as 1987, for example, we invested $250,000 in an office building for doctors that was being developed next to one of the major hospitals in town. One year later, we sold our stake for $560,000—an annual return on investment (ROI) of 125 percent.

And that was just the beginning. In 1996, we bought a stake in a company in Tulsa, Oklahoma, that made oil-drilling equipment. In part, we wanted to see whether we could successfully integrate another company into our culture, but we also saw the acquisition as a good investment, since the market for oil-drilling equipment was just beginning to rebound at the time. As a business, the company turned out to be one headache after another. We could never overcome the legacy of mistrust left by the previous owners. As an investment, however, the acquisition was an unqualified success.

Meanwhile, we've continued to make investments with an eye toward generating cash in the future. We own 5 percent of an extremely successful bank we helped start in 1998, and we could sell our stake at a substantial profit if we wanted to. We also own seventy acres of prime, undeveloped, commercial land that we bought at a very good price in 1998. We can use it ourselves or sell it in the future, depending on our needs.

The point is that there are numerous contingency plans you can create outside the business if you bother to look for them. It was our need to protect the community that got us looking in the first place and that keeps us looking now.

3. *What new things can we learn about the art of doing deals?* Every business you start, acquire, or invest in involves a deal of some sort. The more you experiment, the better you'll get at doing deals as you go along.

One of our first spin-off businesses, for example, was a joint venture called Newstream Enterprises. We actually stole the business concept from some clever entrepreneurs who were selling kits to overhaul Navistar engines. The entrepreneurs would buy the parts from Navistar, put them together in sets, shrink-wrap them, and sell them through Navistar dealers.

We decided to set up our own kitting company with Navistar. SRC would run it and own 51 percent of the equity. Navistar, which had the other 49 percent, would provide parts and distribution. Not only did Newstream turn out to be a phenomenal cash-flow generator for both companies, but it taught us important lessons about joint ventures that we were able to apply in later deals.

Among other things, we learned that it's smart to put a buyout clause into a joint-venture agreement with a major manufacturer. Otherwise you may never be able to take out the equity value you've helped create. What a small company brings to the party is its ability to get a new business up and running. The large manufacturer, on the other hand, brings an ongoing supply of parts and a distribution network. It's an unequal partnership. You'll contribute all you have to offer in the first few years, after which you'll lose your leverage. If you don't have a buyout clause, you'll have no way to cash out.

We applied that lesson to one of the biggest deals we've undertaken, a joint venture with John Deere to remanufacture engines for its agricultural and construction equipment. The company, called Regen Technologies, was launched in 1998, and we had high hopes for it. We expected that, in five years, Regen could be as big as Heavy-Duty, with sales of $56 million and 300 employees. Drawing on our experience with Newstream, we put a formula in the contract under which we'll be able to sell our interest to Deere after a certain period of time. Not that we'll necessarily exercise the option to sell, or "put," as it's called. Our intention is to grow the business and the people in it. But if we did decide to liquidate our stake in Regen, that deal alone could someday raise enough cash for us to buy out 20 percent of our shareholders.

The point is that, as you go along, you need to learn as much as you can about the art of doing deals. Each new subsidiary, acquisition, or sale can be a school.

4. *Is our management system working, and how can we improve it?* I knew we needed a strong management system to be successful over the long haul. You can't count on individuals to carry you indefinitely. Individuals don't last. They die, or they retire, or they simply move on. Then they're succeeded by other individuals with different strengths and weaknesses.

The system provides the continuity and the structure that allows the culture to endure. Not that individuals aren't important, but they can't be too important. You can't depend too much on their individual qualities. And that goes for everyone, right up to the CEO.

We, of course, already had a management system, but it was a work in progress, as all management systems are to some degree. There were times when the system broke down. Some of the new companies we set up didn't practice the Great Game of Business, or they just went through the motions. I tended to let them go their way and see what happened. Invariably they got into trouble. Morale went down, and performance plummeted. Sooner or later, I'd have to step in.

On the other hand, I was also wary of becoming complacent about the Game. You have to keep working on a management system, or it will atrophy. People will start taking it for granted. They'll forget why you developed it in the first place and what it's supposed to be doing. They may even question whether the routines are worth the effort.

I didn't want people playing the Game for my sake. You gotta wanna, as we say at SRC. So, at one point, I brought sixty managers together from all over the company for a two-day conference to find out whether they really wanted to keep it. (They did.) At another point, we suspended the companywide huddles and sales meetings, and I let everybody know that we were open to trying something else if people came up with another way of communicating. (They didn't.)

Meanwhile, we continued to look for ways to improve the system. For example, we developed the morale survey I mentioned in Chapter 7. We also began doing what we call employee annual reports, designed to update our employee-shareholders on the state of their careers. (More about them in Chapter 14.)

You're never through making those kinds of improvements. The system is never finished. That's where leadership comes in. Leaders look for the parts of the system that need fixing, or improving, or that haven't been developed yet—so that people have the tools they need to keep the culture alive.

5. *Are we doing all that we should to develop our people?* In the end, of course, everything depends on the growth of your people. That's another rule, and one of the most important.

OWNERSHIP RULE #12

A company is only as good as its people.

To build an ownership culture, you need to get the cycle of leadership development going—with people coming in, learning skills, moving up and making room for others, learning more skills, moving up again, and so on. Setting up such a process is a long-term, arduous, often frustrating undertaking, and it will absorb a huge amount of time and energy, but it's where all the big rewards come from.

I saw people development as my primary responsibility, but I had a hard time getting other people to understand how I saw the process working, or to share my sense of urgency about getting it started. We'd talk at length, for example, about the need to have succession plans in all the companies. I wanted everybody in a supervisory or professional position to give me the names of two people who could be replacements for the person if he or she moved into a new role.

Those replacement lists were critical. They'd tell us what training programs we needed. They'd show us who the up-and-comers were—which people were seen internally as the future leaders of the company. The lists would help us develop a new stock option plan we were intending to introduce. They would tell us how fast we could start businesses, who was ready to lead them, what it would take to achieve our strategic goals, and on and on.

But try as I might, I couldn't get people to give me the lists. I begged. I pleaded. I cajoled. Finally, I just threatened. Any subsidiary that didn't submit a list would have to pay a fine to the corporate office. The fine would amount to 1 percent of sales—and would come straight out of bonuses.

Thereafter we got the lists, and they were as informative as we'd expected.

Looking back, I'd have to say that our experience with the lists wasn't all that unusual. Most of the challenges you face in this journey are people challenges, and there's none bigger than the challenge of getting people to the point of getting it. By that, I mean getting people to really understand ownership—to have a total understanding of what's involved in running a business and what it takes to enjoy the rewards.

You can do a lot of it with incentives, training programs, games, and informal learning mechanisms, as well as the occasional threat. When they don't work, however, you may have to try what is probably the most effective teaching process of all—but also one of the least predictable. It's what I call reality testing.

OWNERSHIP RULE #13

Ownership is all about the future.

The value of a business depends not on how much money you made yesterday or are making today but on what you're going to be making down the road. That's why buyers are willing to pay a multiple for your stock. They believe the returns they'll get in the future will pay back their investment many times over. It's all about future earnings, future growth, future ideas, future cash flow.

Now, that's a big concept, and getting people to understand it is the key to developing an ownership mentality in a company. They need to realize that they can directly affect the value of their stock—and their own economic situation—by learning how to operate in the present with an eye toward the future.

FIELD NOTES

Lessons from Companies with an Ownership Culture

Commercial Casework, Fremont, California

A culture of ownership changes the role of managers, especially CEOs, by allowing them to let go. Instead of managing people, they can manage the system, which gives them a new level of freedom as well as a tremendous amount of satisfaction.

Bill Palmer, for example, is the CEO of Commercial Casework, a $16-million, unionized architectural woodworking company in Fremont, California, that began playing the Game in 1992. In the next seven years, annual revenues grew an average of 19 percent, and annual profits an average of 52 percent. By 1998, Palmer felt confident enough about the employees' business knowledge to set up a special committee, made up largely of union members, to review ideas for capital investments.

The committee began to meet weekly. One day early on, Palmer went into the meeting room—and almost had a heart attack. On a flip chart was a list of various possible equipment purchases and the price of each one. The total came to about $1 million.

Palmer was tempted to say something but managed to hold his tongue. In the following weeks, he noticed that items were being crossed off the flip chart. When the committee submitted its final list, there were only two recommendations on it, one fairly expensive piece and another relatively cheap one. The committee members explained the benefits of each in terms of safety, quality, and—most important—the labor cost savings and payback time. "They'd done a great job," Palmer said, "but I couldn't help asking them what had happened to all the other pieces of equipment on their chart. They said, 'Well, there were a lot of things we'd love to have, but they just didn't make economic sense. The payback wasn't good enough.'"

The capital committee has since become an integral component of Commercial Casework. Membership changes annually. In 2001, as the recession was hitting, the committee recommended the purchase of something called a wide-belt sander. When Palmer asked why, the committee representatives brought out their numbers. "They made a great argument," Palmer said. "They showed it would substantially cut our labor costs. So when we're slow, we can save on labor, and when business picks up, we can produce more with fewer people. They also showed it would have a big impact on quality, which is critical in a tough market when customers are paying more attention to quality than ever before." The committee had rejected other ideas because they weren't cost-effective, but the numbers indicated that the sander would pay for itself in thirty-six months. The company made the purchase.

13

Reality Testing

There's a critical discovery you make somewhere along the road to becoming an owner.

When people do make the connection, a transformation occurs. They think about the concept for a while, and pretty soon a bright light goes off in their head. They realize, "Gee, if we can grow our sales at 15 percent per year, we can probably grow our earnings and cash flow at the same rate, and if we can keep doing it, we'll be on our way. If we can figure out a formula for growing 15 percent year after year, if we can establish a long-term track record, if we can build in mechanisms to maintain our growth rate even in a bad economy, my God, we'll be in control of our destiny."

To one degree or another, the whole process of building an ownership culture is geared toward leading people to that epiphany. It isn't easy. In effect, you're asking people to make a fundamental change in perspective, a leap of consciousness, and all kinds of things come along to block the message, as we discovered over and over again in the course of our journey. There are old habits of mind that people have grown up with. There's the training of the industrial economy, the narrow focus on just doing the job. There are the pressures of performing day to day. There are the usual misunderstandings and suspicions. There's the natural inclination of people to view themselves differently from the way the market views them. And on and on.

Overcoming those obstacles is essential if you want to create a company of owners, but you need tools to get through to people. I've always found that the most effective tool is reality itself. The better people understand how business really works, the easier it is to make the necessary connections. That is, in fact, the basic idea behind the Great Game of Business. It's a set of mechanisms designed to teach everybody the realities of business, while keeping us all informed about what's going on in the company and focused on what we have to do to achieve our goals.

There are times, however, when even a system like the Great Game of Business isn't enough. Try as you might, you find that you can't get through to people with facts, reason, and logic. The emotions are too intense. Communication breaks down.

At that point, your only recourse is to create a situation in which people are forced to confront real choices in the real world and make real decisions for themselves. You put them through an experience, which is the key to accelerated learning. People learn more from experiences in real life than from any other form of teaching. It's the fastest way of getting people to change.

To be sure, there are risks in taking such a course. For one thing, you lose some control of the situation, since you're putting other people in the position of making their own decisions. That's unavoidable. You can't fake a challenge of this type. People really have to be free to make whatever decision they think is right for them, and you have to be ready to accept the consequences.

On the other hand, you have a lot to gain when they do make their decision. To begin with, you get a clear resolution of the issue. Second, you get a kind of commitment and buy-in that's impossible to obtain any other way. Third, and most important, you get critical information about what people really want—information that you need to be an effective leader. What's more, the information may surprise you.

We had a good example of this technique in action midway through the implementation of our strategy to grow the company by decentralizing it and spinning off new businesses. About four years into the process, we reached an impasse so serious that I realized we could no longer continue to exist as one company without resolving it.

And so it was time for a reality test.

What Is a Successful Business?

The problem was a huge gulf that had developed between Heavy-Duty and the rest of the company. Heavy-Duty was our largest and most profitable subsidiary, the heart and soul of SRC, where we'd invented the Great Game of Business and survived all the trials and tribulations of our early years, and it was vital to the success of our strategy.

By all the standard measures, moreover, Heavy-Duty was doing extremely well. Month after month, it turned in great numbers, regularly beating its plan. Its performance was, of course, a direct reflection of the quality of its workforce, which was extraordinary. A lot of the people had been working at the factory since it was owned by International Harvester; some of them had been there longer than I had. They'd gone through the best of times and the worst of times together, and they'd played a major role in bringing us as far as we'd come.

In the process, they'd learned a great deal about making money and generating cash. They practiced open-book management as well as any group of people in the world, which wasn't surprising. By the time Dan Rorke took over as general manager of Heavy-Duty in 1991, most people there had been playing the Great Game of Business for seven years. They had the routines and disciplines down cold.

And people continued to do great things on Rorke's watch. One of Heavy-Duty's salespeople, for example, took an idea for a bass fishing contest and turned it into an important mechanism for building stronger ties with the Navistar dealers who carried our products. (See "How to Turn an Ownership Culture into a Marketing Tool," page 210.) The contest proved so popular that we soon had other customers banging down our doors to stage similar events for them.

HOW TO TURN AN OWNERSHIP CULTURE INTO A MARKETING TOOL

Many benefits flow from having a strong ownership culture, but there was one we didn't expect and would never have predicted. It turns out that the culture can be a powerful marketing tool.

We made the discovery several years ago, as a result of our efforts to develop closer ties with the dealers who sell the engines we remanufacture for Navistar. To win the dealers' loyalty, we realized that we first had to differentiate ourselves from the 9,000 other engine rebuilders in the continental United States.

But how? Like most companies, we operate in an intensely competitive marketplace and have increasingly found that we can't rely on factors such as price and quality to set us apart. So what advantages do we have? We were sitting around one day, racking our brains for an answer, when an odd thought occurred to me: We lived in Springfield, Missouri, and our competitors in the truck market didn't. Everybody else thought I was nuts. "Fishing," I said. "The best bass lakes in America." They got it. Before long, we'd mapped out a five-year marketing plan—built around fishing.

The idea was to hold a bass-fishing tournament every year for the dealers who sold the largest number of our products in that particular line. Dealers who qualified could automatically return each succeeding year provided they increased their sales of our products by 15 percent annually. Meanwhile, we'd keep bringing in twenty new dealers per year until we had a hundred participants in the fifth year.

To whet the dealers' appetites, we promised not only to cover their expenses but to give them a chance to win serious prize money—up to $5,000 in each of the first four tournaments, and a grand prize of $50,000 in the fifth year. We'd also provide each participant with a guide. Fortunately, SRC is loaded with experienced fishermen, and so we had no trouble recruiting the people we needed: fuel-pump assemblers, welders, machinists, an engine tester, a production manager, a bookkeeper, the company president, you name it.

On paper, at least, it looked like a good investment. While we'd have to spend about $280,000 on the tournaments, we figured that the profit from the additional sales would give us a nice return—assuming the plan worked, that is.

In the end, the plan worked better than we could ever have imagined, and for reasons we didn't anticipate. It turned out that the dealers just *loved* coming to Springfield and spending time with us. Many of them became fast friends with their guides and stayed in touch throughout the year. The tournaments themselves began to resemble family reunions, where the people who made the products and the people who sold the products would get together, not to fight about warranty claims or haggle over prices, but to tell stories, play games, and reminisce about old times.

Slowly it began to dawn on us what was going on here. In effect, we were using the tournaments to introduce our customers to our culture. We were inviting them into our community, building the same bonds with them that we have with one another. We were showing them how we manage to work and have fun and make money at the same time, and we were giving them the chance to do it with us. Most of them seemed to find the offer irresistible.

Our culture, we discovered, could be one of our most powerful marketing tools.

Then there was the production manager who began putting out a weekly report showing each department exactly what it had to do to hit the maximum bonus level for the quarter. The result was that Heavy-Duty began to max out its bonus with astonishing regularity.

And when Rorke challenged people to set a new safety record, they got so carried away that they went more than 1 million consecutive man-hours without having any time lost due to injuries on the job. The federal Occupation Health and Safety Administration (OSHA) recognized Heavy-Duty for having gone longer without a lost-time accident than any other factory in southwestern Missouri.

So I'm talking here about a business that, from one perspective, was doing spectacularly well. From another, however, Heavy-Duty represented the biggest obstacle to our long-term success and a danger to everyone else in the company.

The problem, as I saw it, was that Rorke and his team weren't preparing for the future. They were churning out profits, all right, but how? By taking the business we'd built during the first seven years and milking it for all it was worth. Meanwhile, they weren't helping us lay the groundwork for the business we had to become—a business that would allow us to take care of our future obligations and remain in control of our destiny.

To succeed long term, we had to diversify, innovate, develop leaders, experiment, and do all of the other things we'd contemplated when we'd put our growth strategy together. I didn't think Heavy-Duty was doing any of them—or at least not very much of them. But there were two specific areas in which it was falling short. First, it wasn't doing enough to diversify its customer base. Second, we weren't getting the people from Heavy-Duty that we needed to run the new businesses.

On the first issue, Rorke and I simply disagreed about the danger. He wasn't particularly worried that Heavy-Duty did 50 percent of its business with one customer, Navistar. I was scared to death that we could have a repeat of the GM episode. Navistar was facing the same competitive pressures as all the rest of us. What if someone else came along with a better offer and took away the account?

Rorke told me I was getting upset over nothing. The Navistar dealers loved us. If Navistar itself decided to go with another supplier, we could always sell directly through the dealerships. Of course, I remembered our last experience of competing with an OEM to sell through its dealer network. Dresser had clobbered us.

In my mind, the issue was very clear. If we ever lost the Navistar account, we'd face a choice: either lay off a large percentage of our workforce or find the new business we needed to keep them employed. So what excuse was there for not trying to get the new business now? If we didn't, we'd be putting jobs at risk, and we'd be doing it *knowingly*. As managers, we'd be gambling with the livelihoods of people who'd put their trust in us.

I couldn't justify taking that kind of a risk—not if we had an alternative, and we did. We could reduce our dependence on Navistar. We could bring in the new customers sooner rather than later and get its percentage of Heavy-Duty's business down to a safer level.

To be fair, Rorke insisted he was diversifying, and he was, in his own way. But the programs he had in mind would take years to develop, and it was by no means certain that the business we got from them would ever amount to much. In my mind, we had to be figuring out how to diversify the customer base *now*. Rorke didn't agree, or at least he didn't share my sense of urgency. As a result, neither did anyone else at Heavy-Duty.

So that was one major problem.

The other one had to do with our ability to carry out our strategy for growing the company. We needed people to build the new businesses, and our best source of recruits was Heavy-Duty—or it should have been. In fact, after taking out the first group of people, we couldn't pry anybody loose. Rorke insisted he needed all of the people he had, and he'd get furious if one of the other general managers tried to recruit someone away without first asking his permission. When they did ask, however, the answer was almost always "no."

As a result, we couldn't take advantage of our greatest strength as a company. Some of our best people were bottled up in Heavy-Duty, and we couldn't get them out. What's more, we weren't doing anything to make them available in the future. There were no succession plans in Heavy-Duty. People weren't being asked to identify their replacements. We weren't developing career paths, or implementing training programs to give people the skills they'd need to get ahead. For that matter, we weren't even asking them what they might want to do in the future.

From the standpoint of leadership development, the place was stagnant. A lot of people had been in the same jobs for five, six, seven years, or more. They'd stopped learning, stopped growing, and they were clogging up the pipelines. For every person stuck in a professional or supervisory position, there was somebody else down the ladder who couldn't move up. Meanwhile, the rest of the company couldn't get the talent it needed to grow.

So those were the two business issues that concerned me: no succession planning and not enough diversification. Behind them, however, was another issue that had more to do with our corporate culture.

Two Managers, Two Cultures

Rorke and I had very different ways of managing, which in itself was no big deal. The difference was largely a matter of style and personality, not performance. We were both pretty good at getting the results we wanted, hitting our targets, meeting the plan.

As time went along, however, I began to realize that something else was happening as a result of our different management styles. They were producing different types of communities, and that did matter. Why? Because it was producing a split in the company that threatened our ability to function as one business.

Rorke's style was to protect people. As a leader, he functioned more or less as the guardian of his employees, creating an environment in which they felt safe and comfortable and were thus free to focus on doing their jobs. His people referred to him as "Big Daddy." He wasn't a pushover by any means, but neither did he challenge people much. As long as you did your part, he left you alone and made sure you didn't have a lot of negative distractions—like fear, for example. He didn't like to worry, and he didn't want you to worry, either. What's more, he gave you the sense that you didn't have to worry. He always seemed to have the situation under control.

I had a different idea of my role as a leader. My job, I thought, was to help people understand reality, and in business the reality is that you are constantly facing threats, some of which you can identify, some of which you can't. So you need an element of fear. You need to be aware of the real dangers that are lurking out there in the market and that could cost you your job if you're not careful. Otherwise you won't do what's necessary to protect yourself and the people you work with. You'll get complacent. You may even get arrogant. You'll think you're doing great because you're generating a lot of profit. You won't realize how quickly the situation could turn around.

Now, it's possible to make a case for both ways of managing, but there's no question that they produce very different corporate cultures. I wanted a culture in which people were always a little uncomfortable. Not that they should live in constant fear, but they needed to realize that their only real security would come from working together to protect themselves against the dangers they faced. So they had to be aware of the dangers and the role that each person, each department, each part of the business played in overcoming them. That way, people would understand why it was important for them to do their part and to support others in doing theirs.

As long as they did, moreover, they could create good lives for themselves. They could make money and have fun and take advantage of the opportunities that business offers, including the opportunity to get ahead, to move up in the world, to have not just a job but a career. Granted, some people might not want that opportunity. Changing jobs can be scary. You always face the possibility of failure, not to mention rejection by your peers. But I thought we should be challenging people to think about the possibility, to dream a little, and then we should be doing all we could to help them achieve their dreams—for their sake and everybody else's. As a community, we needed people to be learning, growing, and moving up in order to protect ourselves.

I don't know what Rorke thought about the kind of culture I had in mind, but he was obviously creating a very different one at Heavy-Duty. Mine was full of change; his wasn't. I wanted to move people around; he wanted to leave them alone. I wanted people to be aware of the dangers in the market; he wanted them to feel safe and protected.

For all I knew, the people at Heavy-Duty might have preferred his culture to mine. Change is always uncomfortable, after all, and who doesn't like to feel safe and protected? If you're also making money and having fun—as they were—so much the better.

There was another problem, however. Rorke needed an enemy. Many good managers like to have an enemy. By that, I mean someone or something you can use to bind people together in a common cause. I wanted the enemy to be the external threats—the marketplace forces that could take away our jobs. But Rorke didn't want to manage that way, and so he had to look elsewhere for an enemy. He found it in the rest of the company.

I don't mean that he actively worked against us or wished us any harm, but he subtly promoted a sense of "us versus them." It's a common trick. I sometimes used it myself in my days as a manager at International Harvester. You create a little bubble around your organization, and then you manage within the bubble, building a sense of loyalty to the team by suggesting that you're competing against everyone else in the company.

I have no doubt that Rorke knew exactly what he was doing. After becoming general manager of Heavy-Duty, one of his first acts had been to move his salespeople out of the offices across town where they'd been working and back into the factory. When people work in the same location, he said, they think of one another as individuals. When people work in different locations, they think of the other group as "those assholes."

I could see that, little by little, the rest of us were becoming "those assholes" to the people at Heavy-Duty. They all but said so in the mission statement that Rorke had them draw up at one point. Their mission, they decided, was "to improve the quality of life of the people associated with the Heavy-Duty division of SRC, particularly its employees." There was no mention of the other people who worked for SRC.

Rorke himself acted as if Heavy-Duty were in competition with the other SRC companies. He'd always object, for example, whenever we'd let a new piece of business go to one of the subsidiaries rather than to Heavy-Duty. On the shop floor, meanwhile, there was a widespread belief that we were using the profits being generated by Heavy-Duty to finance somebody else's business, and people resented it. They thought we were taking the money away from them and giving it to strangers.

Over time, the gulf seemed to grow wider. What should have been routine matters were blown way out of proportion. At one point, we changed an ESOP rule, reserving the option of cashing people out over ten years instead of paying them in one lump sum. The change was necessary to protect the company, but people at Heavy-Duty reacted as if I and the other members of the corporate staff had double-crossed them, and nobody stepped in to tell them otherwise.

We got a similar response when we instituted a rule against smoking indoors. The next thing I knew, a petition was being circulated at Heavy-Duty denouncing "corporate" for infringing on the freedom of smokers.

Obviously, something was wrong. Our system wasn't working, at least not inside Heavy-Duty. We were trying to promote trust, but we were getting suspicion. People didn't understand what we were doing and why, and they assumed the worst. We'd developed a whole strategy for their benefit, but they didn't get it, and nothing was being done to explain it to them.

What bothered me most, however, were signs that the leaders of Heavy-Duty were losing touch with the realities of the marketplace. That's one of the hazards of managing in a bubble. For you and your people, the company becomes your whole world. All you see are the other teams, or departments, or divisions. If you're not careful, you may forget that your *real* competition lies outside the walls of the company.

I realized that Heavy-Duty had reached that point in the fall of 1994. I was in a restaurant, talking to one of Rorke's top people. I asked her how she and her colleagues were benchmarking their performance. I wanted to know which companies outside SRC they looked to as role models.

There weren't any, she said. "We benchmark against ourselves."

I knew right then something had to happen. The gulf between Heavy-Duty and the rest of us had grown so wide that we were operating on totally different premises. I thought Heavy-Duty had significant problems that we'd pay a heavy price for in the future if we didn't fix them now. Rorke's people thought Heavy-Duty was so strong they had nothing to learn from anyone else.

Clearly we had to resolve this difference of opinion one way or the other. The question was, How? The answer, I decided, was to give Rorke and his managers a chance to do their own buyout.

The Logic of Giving People Choices

You might wonder why. There were other options, I suppose. Another CEO might have tried, say, reading the riot act to Heavy-Duty's managers, or breaking up the team, or maybe even replacing Rorke with another general manager. But I don't operate that way.

For one thing, it doesn't work. I believe in that higher law of business, "You gotta wanna." There were legitimate differences of opinion involved here. I couldn't resolve them by forcing Heavy-Duty to accept my point of view. If the people there didn't want to do things my way, they wouldn't, and I couldn't make them change against their will. I'd be foolish to try. Besides, what if I was wrong, or overreacting?

Then again, I strongly believed I was right, in which case there was only one conclusion to draw: Heavy-Duty was at the peak of its value. Remember, I thought Rorke was living off the past and not preparing for the future. Granted, his numbers looked great, but—in two, three, five years—I expected them to look a lot worse, assuming he stayed on his present course. So now was the time to sell, at least from the shareholders' standpoint, and I had a responsibility to do what I thought was best for the shareholders.

To be honest, however, I had an additional motive for giving Rorke and his managers a chance to buy Heavy-Duty. It was my only hope for getting them to see things my way. I'd run out of arguments. They weren't getting through, and I didn't think they'd ever get through as long as Heavy-Duty continued to perform so well.

Even under the best circumstances, it's extremely difficult to change the mind-set of a company that's going gangbusters. When you tell people there's a problem with what they're doing, they don't believe you. They don't want to hear you. They're used to thinking a certain way, and they've been successful with it. Why should they do anything different?

And I was asking a lot of Rorke and his team. I was telling them, in effect, to stop focusing on making money in their core business and to start spending money on new product lines and businesses—some of which were bound to fail. That's a tough case to make when, month after month, a company is turning in great numbers. People accuse you of being ungrateful. They wonder how you can have the nerve to criticize them when they're carrying the rest of the business.

In any event, I wasn't making any progress, and I figured I had one last shot at bringing them around. I'd give them a reality test. I'd create a real-life experience for Rorke and his managers—a compressed version of the same experience my own team had gone through almost twelve years earlier. How they'd respond, I couldn't predict. But I knew they'd learn something, and so would I.

That doesn't mean we weren't serious about selling Heavy-Duty. You don't go into this kind of deal simply as an educational exercise. There's too much at stake for too many people. I myself was dead serious. Given the right price and the right terms, I was ready to let Heavy-Duty go. I'd been assuming for a while that we were going to sell parts of the company to raise cash at some point. I hadn't expected it to happen quite this way, or quite so soon, but that didn't bother me. As long as we could get $13 million to $15 million out of the deal free and clear, after taxes, we could take care of all our financial obligations and go our separate ways.

And maybe parting company was the best result for everybody involved. Maybe it was time for Heavy-Duty to leave the nest. I felt a little like a parent with a kid who's been living at home too long. Rorke and his crew at Heavy-Duty were ready to have their own experiences out in the real world. They just needed a push. So I sent them out to meet some new people they could do business with. I said, "We ain't getting anywhere here. Go see what you think of these guys."

Step One: Set the Stage

Over the years, we'd been approached from time to time by investors and investment bankers who'd heard about SRC and were interested in acquiring all or part of the company. I would always talk to them, listen to what they had to say, and in the process gain valuable insights into their way of thinking. But we'd never gone beyond preliminary discussions. I didn't want to waste their time, and we hadn't been ready to sell anything. Yet. I'd told them so and promised a couple of them I'd get back in touch if our position changed.

In the spring of 1994, a letter arrived from another suitor, a mergers-and-acquisitions group headed by a man named Jim Carlisle. Based in La Jolla, California, Carlisle Enterprises specialized in industrial and aerospace manufacturing deals. The letter inquired about our interest in selling assets and was signed by Dennis Dunn, a managing partner. I called Dunn back and invited him to come visit us. I also called one of the investment bankers I'd met previously and told him we were ready to entertain offers if he wanted to make one.

From then on, we were officially "in play."

On June 8, Jim Carlisle and Dennis Dunn flew in to Springfield, and we spent the day together. I gave them the grand tour. They wanted to know what we had in mind. I said we were thinking about selling Heavy-Duty, probably in conjunction with Engines Plus and one of our newest start-ups, Loadmaster, which was developing an engine powered by natural gas. Together, they made an attractive package, with strong current earnings and great growth possibilities. I also made it clear that neither I nor the other corporate officers would be part of the deal. On the other hand, I said, we had some managers who might be available if Carlisle were willing to give them a piece of the action.

Carlisle and Dunn were very interested. What's more, they struck me as people we could do business with. They were intelligent, professional, and experienced, and they appeared to share our values, or at least some of the most important ones. They made it clear that they wanted our people more than our assets. They wouldn't even consider doing a deal without the support and participation of the Heavy-Duty management team. They were all in favor of equity-sharing, and they loved the Great Game of Business, which they were familiar with before they came.

All in all, I thought they'd be reasonable people to work for, with reasonable investment goals. As long as the goals were being met, Rorke would probably have a free hand to run the business as he saw fit. In any case, I felt Carlisle could be counted on to deal fairly with the people at Heavy-Duty. And one other thing: They had deep pockets. They could come up with the amount of cash that we'd need to do a deal, and that Rorke would need if he ever did lose the Navistar account and had to try selling directly to the dealers.

So we had at least one group of potential investors. Now we needed to get our own people lined up. I'd already told Rorke that I was meeting with some people who might be interested in buying Heavy-Duty. He was obviously the key player. There couldn't be a deal without him. I figured he'd be interested in at least exploring a buyout, given the opportunity to acquire an equity stake larger and more lucrative, potentially, than anything we could put together for him at SRC.

But I also knew that he'd need a strong financial person to put the deal together, just as I'd needed McCoy. So I'd also spoken with Marty Callison, our former CFO, who'd left the corporate staff a couple years earlier and moved into operations. He was now general manager of Newstream, our joint venture with Navistar. Callison was one of the people who'd narrowly missed the cut for the original SRC buyout group, and who'd made enormous contributions to the company thereafter. I knew he wanted—and deserved—a shot at the brass ring.

As for the rest of the buyout group, I'd let Rorke figure that one out. In fact, I'd insist on it. I wanted him to face the same hard choices that I'd made, for better or worse, back in 1982.

Before we could move forward, however, we needed to bring the directors and major shareholders into the loop, since they'd eventually have to approve any such deal. As it happened, we had a board meeting scheduled for June 10, at which they'd all be present. I thought I could use it to raise the possibility of selling Heavy-Duty, Engines Plus, and Loadmaster and to take a reading of the response. Not that I wanted a yes or a no. We'd all need to see a firm offer before we came to that crossroad. The question was, Did we have a consensus in favor of trying to get a firm offer?

I wanted people to consider the idea in a specific context. I wanted them to think about how we were going to grow the business, bearing in mind that sooner or later we'd have to be in a position to cash our shareholders out. So when we sat down together on June 10, I laid out the five strategic options that I thought we had:

1. Continue to grow our existing businesses 15 percent a year
2. Develop new businesses and product contingencies, especially those with good gross margins
3. Acquire businesses, particularly those that would allow us eventually to develop our own distribution system
4. Work toward an initial public offering of stock
5. Sell Heavy-Duty, probably in conjunction with Engines Plus and Loadmaster

You could almost hear the gasps in the room when I got to the last option. For most of the people, the idea came as a complete surprise and a shock. We had a discussion of the different options, with particular emphasis on the possible sale. I asked people to think everything over and let me know in writing what they thought we should do. Rorke, meanwhile, got the green light to give the Carlisle people the information they needed to determine whether they really wanted to make an offer and, if so, for how much.

Step Two: Be Clear About the Choice People Have

The opinions, when they came in, were all over the lot, but there was a general consensus that we should at least explore any offers we could get and give the employees of Heavy-Duty a chance to buy the company if they wanted to. Oddly enough, Rorke was among those with the most reservations, although by then he was already working on a deal.

For one thing, he'd decided on the people he wanted to include in the buyout group—ten managers, including himself and Callison. Carlisle, meanwhile, had retained the services of a couple of former manufacturing executives who would oversee the operation if the deal went through. On July 20, they came to town and spent a couple of days with Rorke's team.

After they left, I met with Rorke's group of ten. I wanted them to understand how the deal got started. I explained my concerns about the lack of succession planning in Heavy-Duty, the failure to diversify, the continued dependence on one customer, the fact that we weren't moving people up. I said I thought that they'd been focusing too much on maximizing profit and not enough on using the profit to address our weaknesses, and I was worried about the three hundred families who could be hurt if something bad happened. Besides, I added, they were obviously unhappy with our corporate leadership. Maybe it was time for them to be on their own. We had philosophical differences about strategy. By selling Heavy-Duty, we could each go in the direction we thought best, and everyone would win.

I was very candid in my criticisms of Heavy-Duty. I can't say people were thrilled with what I had to say. It was a stormy session. But at least, when I left, they were clear about the choices they had. They could stay at SRC and do things my way, or they go out and seek their fortune with Carlisle. The decision was theirs.

Step Three: Stand Back and Let Events Take Their Course

Over the next eight weeks, the Heavy-Duty managers had what they all later described as one of the most intense educational experiences of their lives. There were constant discussions and meetings, debates over strategy, negotiations with Carlisle, negotiations with SRC, bull sessions about values and opportunities, speculation about alternatives.

The Carlisle people had offered up front to include seven of Heavy-Duty's managers in the deal and give them 15 percent of the equity, but Rorke had sensed some flexibility. What Carlisle really wanted, he thought, was a 35 percent return on investment, compounded annually, with an intention of cashing out after five years.

Throughout July and August, Rorke and Callison kept working over the numbers, trying to come up with a scenario that would allow Carlisle to achieve its goals, while giving the management group a bigger piece of the pie. Specifically, Rorke wanted to expand the core group from seven to ten people and make it possible for them to increase their combined equity stake from an initial 15 percent to 35 percent at the end of the period, provided they hit their targets. He also wanted to give supervisors a shot at earning an additional 10 percent of the equity over five years, and he wanted to continue to have a generous bonus program for hourly and salaried people.

The Carlisle people didn't seem to have a problem with any of that, as long as they got their compounded 35 percent annual return on investment. They did ask Rorke about the situation with Navistar. He gave them the same answer he'd been giving me, and they accepted it. Then again, Rorke was well aware that Carlisle would insist on meeting the targets no matter what happened with Navistar—even if it meant laying off a substantial portion of the workforce at some point.

Within Rorke's group, there was a range of opinions about the deal. One member of his team was adamantly opposed to it and refused to meet with the others. A couple of the others were skeptical, but they said they'd go along with whatever the group decided. Rorke himself appeared to be on the fence. The rest, however, tended to view the deal as the opportunity of a lifetime, which—for several of them—it might well have been.

In early August, Rorke sent Jim Carlisle a proposal for a deal between Carlisle Enterprises and his own management team that would allow negotiations to begin with SRC for the purchase of Heavy-Duty, Engines Plus, and Loadmaster. Soon thereafter, Carlisle put in a bid of more than $20 million for the three companies.

It was a good offer, no question, especially when you consider that SRC as a whole had just been valued at $23 million. We figured we'd probably have to pay about $10 million in taxes on the sale, but that would still leave us with $11 million to $12 million in cash, which was getting close to my magic number. I called Jim Carlisle, thanked him for the offer, and told him I'd be back in touch shortly.

Step Four: Let the Numbers Be Your Guide

The Carlisle people were clearly eager to do a deal. Meanwhile, the other investment banker I'd called had also made an offer. One way or another, I thought we could eventually get the amount of after-tax cash we were looking for. So I and the other major shareholders had some choices to make. I could easily imagine a future in which we'd continue our journey without Heavy-Duty, and we might all wind up happier and more successful in the end. The secret, as always, was in the numbers.

Without Heavy-Duty, Engines Plus, and Loadmaster, the company would consist of Sequel, our automotive subsidiary, which was struggling, and a bunch of shaky start-ups. Between them, they were earning a pathetic $250,000 on sales of $48 million. Their combined book value—assets minus liabilities—was about $4 million.

But let's say we got our $15 million after taxes, and suppose we kept the $15 million and invested it in a venture capital or private equity fund of some sort. If we could earn 10 percent per year ($1.5 million), our balance sheet would suddenly look great. Book value would jump to $19 million. Our profit before tax would rise to a modest but respectable $1.75 million ($1.5 million plus $250,000), still on sales of $48 million.

So what would we do next? We'd go to work on the remaining companies, make them profitable, grow them 15 percent a year, and double our annual sales to $100 million in five years. Then we'd sell off another $50-million piece of the company and keep going.

There was one difficult problem I'd have to deal with. Several of the original SRC shareholders were now working in the corporate offices. The new company, with its thin operating margins, simply couldn't support all those salaries, and so some of my old friends would have to leave. Not that they would suffer. Each of them had plenty of stock, which would be worth a considerable amount of money after the sale. But how could we pay them and still keep the $15 million, which we'd need to build the new company?

In this case, I could see how the ESOP laws might come to our rescue. We could use a "leveraged ESOP" (see "How a Leveraged ESOP Works," page 226) to cash out those shareholders and simultaneously solve another problem that was bugging me—namely, the fact that most of the subsidiaries' employees had no equity stake. We'd been scared to bring them into the old ESOP while we were still struggling to figure out how to cash out the people who were in it already. After the sale, we'd set up a brand-new ESOP, which would then borrow from a bank enough money to buy 30 percent of the new company's stock. Let's say that the new company, with its $15 million in cash, was worth $22 million altogether. The ESOP would borrow 30 percent of $22 million, or $6.6 million, and we'd use the money to cash out the shareholders who had to leave.

Understand, I hadn't worked out all the details. I assumed, for example, that we'd find something better to do with the $15 million than leave it in a venture capital fund. My point is just that, with a couple of

HOW A LEVERAGED ESOP WORKS

Typically an ESOP is used to cash out an owner. Let's say the owner is a guy who wants some liquidity for whatever reason. He sets up an ESOP and sells 20 percent of the company's stock to it for, say, $1 million. In other words, the company as a whole is worth $5 million. The ESOP doesn't have any cash, so it borrows the money from a bank, using the stock as collateral. The owner gets his $1 million, the bank gets the interest plus various tax benefits, and the ESOP gets the stock and the debt.

Now let's say that, in year one, the company makes a cash contribution of $500,000 plus some interest expense to the ESOP. The money, which is deducted from pretax earnings, is used to pay down the debt, thereby releasing 10 percent of the company's stock to the employees. Maybe the company also decides to pay a dividend. Suppose the ESOP's share of the dividend comes to $50,000. That's tax deferred. So the money used to pay the debt and the interest expense all get paid out of pretax profits, and the taxes on the dividend get paid sometime in the future. Meanwhile, the owner has his $1 million.

When most people decide to start an ESOP, that's what they look at. They see it as a way to cash out an owner tax-free, in one fell swoop. He puts stock in the ESOP and walks away with his money, which he can then put in a self-directed IRA, thereby avoiding taxes until he's ready to spend it. There are very few restrictions. You can put as much stock into the ESOP as you want and take out whatever it's worth. It's a great deal.

serious offers in hand, there were suddenly all kinds of options and choices open to us that we'd never had before. I could imagine us churning out companies indefinitely—starting or buying them, building them, spreading ownership, teaching people the Great Game of Business, sending them off to play it on their own. We'd still have our dream, and we'd still have our village, but we wouldn't expect people to stay in it forever. Our hope would be that they'd eventually leave and start another village somewhere else.

So we'd come to an interesting crossroads. We could take one direction and stay together, understanding that we were all going to get behind the new strategy and grow the company to $200 million in the next few years. Or we could go in another direction, split the business in half, each take our $50-million pieces, and pursue our dreams separately. I'd be happy with either course. The question was, What did Rorke and his people want to do?

Step Five: Insist That People Make Their Choice

I knew they were thinking about it, and they weren't alone. Word had reached the shop floor that Heavy-Duty might be sold, and I began to hear rumblings of discontent. Several hourly guys came to me and said there was considerable anxiety about the prospect of a sale. People couldn't see what was in it for them. I reassured the guys that, so far, we were just talking.

Meanwhile, an important change was occurring in the thinking of the Heavy-Duty managers. The harder they looked at the numbers, the more they wondered why they needed Carlisle. They could see that there was a real possibility of creating a significant amount of wealth in the next five years—and that under the terms of the deal, most of it would go to Carlisle, which was contributing nothing but money. If Carlisle were cut out of the loop, they realized, all of that wealth could go instead to the people who'd worked to create it.

In retrospect, that realization was the turning point in the Carlisle episode, although I wasn't aware of it at the time. I did know something was going on, however. At one point, Rorke and Callison had asked me if we'd let the group buy Heavy-Duty with a bank loan and a note from SRC, but I couldn't do that. For one thing, the note would have to be too large, $13 million or $14 million. For another, I wasn't confident they could hit their targets unless they changed the way they ran the business. If they got in trouble, we'd have to take back the company, which would be extremely messy. Nevertheless, I found it interesting that they'd asked the question.

I guess they were asking themselves a lot of questions. As time went by, more members of the group began to have misgivings, even some of the managers who had the most to gain from the deal. They started to wonder whether they really wanted to work for people they didn't know and probably would never get to know. It also began to sink in that the hourly employees had no reason to support the sale and might resent it.

But mainly, a couple of the managers said later, they started to feel uncomfortable about the change in priorities. They'd grown up in a company that had always put protecting people at the top of the list. If the deal went through, they'd have one overriding goal for the next five years: return on investment. Did they really want to make that switch?

For me, the key moment came at the end of August, when Rorke and I sat down alone over breakfast one morning and had a long talk. He told me he had no personal desire to do the deal. He had nothing against me or the other corporate people. He thought we needed to level the playing field, as he put it, by giving more equity opportunities to the people who were contributing the most to the company's success, but he thought we could do that without breaking up SRC.

If there were strategic reasons for selling Heavy-Duty, he said, that was another story. He and his people were grown-ups. They could deal with whatever came along. If we thought now was the time to sell, they'd go. As for the Carlisle people, he said he didn't know them that well. They seemed okay, but you couldn't tell much from a few meetings.

I raised the question of strategy. He said he had no problem with our strategy. He thought it was good, but he wasn't sure everybody understood it. He said he thought that I sometimes got too far ahead of people. "You've spent a lot of time outside the business over the past three, four years," he said. "You've been serving on other company boards, giving speeches, talking to bankers, investors, CEOs. I think you sometimes assume everybody's learned the same things you have." He said I needed to take a little more time to explain what I had in mind. I admitted he was probably right about that.

We talked for about three hours altogether. It was the best talk we'd had in six years. When it was over, I knew in my gut that the sale probably wasn't going to happen.

Step Six: Deal with the Consequences

Ironically, we had more reasons than ever to go forward with the deal at that point, thanks to an unexpected event. In the midst of our discussions with Carlisle, the hot business trend of the moment suddenly hit our industry and our town. One of our major competitors in the automotive market, who happened to be based in Springfield, was acquired for $100 million in a "roll-up" of remanufacturers in the automotive parts industry.

The price tag took my breath away. The competitor wasn't much bigger than SRC. Its owner was selling the business for the amount of its annual sales, which was extraordinary. I understood that the roll-up people had specific strategic reasons for acquiring that particular company, but even so, the deal bolstered the argument that now was the time to sell. Remanufacturing was hot. We might never again be able to get such a good price for Heavy-Duty. So, no matter what Rorke and his people were feeling, we had to take Carlisle's offer very seriously, and we did.

In the end, the deal came apart over a couple of problems that dramatically reduced the amount of cash we'd have after the sale. First, it turned out that we were going to owe $2 million more in taxes than we expected. Beyond that, we'd have to spend another $8 million to satisfy our obligations under the ESOP. By late September, Carlisle had increased its offer to $25 million, but after paying taxes and buying out the ESOP members, we'd have wound up with just $9 million in cash from the sale.

So we had a big problem. When I sat down with the Carlisle people, I explained it to them. They were surprised. We'd never discussed the ESOP angle before. Then again, they really wanted to do the deal. They offered to bring in experts to help us come up with a solution. We did, in fact, keep talking for a while, but Carlisle never came back with the one thing that would have forced us to reconsider: a significantly larger offer.

Step Seven: Make Sure You Get the Message

With the Carlisle deal effectively dead, it was now my turn to do a lot of thinking. I'd given Rorke and his people a choice, and they'd made it.

We were going to stay together. Everybody was going to get behind the strategy. We'd diversify. We'd do succession planning. We'd move people around, shake things up, support the subsidiaries, start other companies, and so on.

But, as I noted earlier, reality testing does more than resolve issues and create conditions under which people can buy in to decisions. The process also gives you information about what they want, and it's not necessarily what you expect to hear.

In the wake of the Carlisle episode, I realized I'd been given a message, and it had come from all parts of Heavy-Duty. People wanted to keep the company together. They liked what we'd built. I'd tried to push them out of the nest, and they'd come back saying they really didn't want to leave after all. That was a shock to me. I thought, "Man, the kid's going to stay in the house forever!"

So there I was, staring at my old problem again: How do I get out with a clean conscience? I'd thought I had it solved. We were going to start all these businesses and—when the time came—break up the company and sell everything off. Nobody would be left holding the bag or denied a fair share of the rewards. We'd all be able to move on.

Now people were telling me, in effect, that they didn't like my plan. They weren't thinking, first and foremost, about the wealth they were creating and the financial rewards they were going to get. They were thinking about the community they were going to lose. They wanted to stay in it until they retired.

But then, of course, they *would* expect to get their financial rewards—which meant we had to go back to the drawing board. Should we reconsider the possibility of going public? Should we think about doing our own industry roll-up? We had to come up with a new set of answers, since we all were going to leave at some point, and the company would then be obligated to buy back our stock. Where would the cash come from to pay for it if we couldn't raise it by selling our most valuable businesses, such as Heavy-Duty?

Moreover, there was another, trickier question we had to answer—one we'd neatly avoided with our plan to break the company up. Who was going to run SRC when I and the other senior managers left or retired? That wouldn't have been a concern if we'd sold all the businesses, but it was a huge issue now.

So we finally crossed the threshold we'd been working up to for so many years. In the months following the Carlisle episode, I began to focus directly and explicitly on the challenge of building a company that could endure. What could we do to improve its chances of surviving and being passed on from one generation to the next? It wasn't just a matter of keeping the company together, which we might be able to do just by selling it. What people valued was the culture. Our challenge was to preserve that culture and still live up to the commitments we'd made.

Fortunately, I realized, we were already on the right track. Whatever the future held, we needed to accelerate the process we'd begun when we set out to turn SRC into a community of businesses. We needed to start or acquire more companies. We needed to continue diversifying, innovating, and experimenting. We needed to keep on expanding the range of options and choices we'd have for raising cash if we needed it. The more options we had, the less likely it was that we'd ever be forced to choose an unpalatable one.

Above all, we needed to get our people ready for the challenges that lay ahead. We needed to focus more than ever on succession planning, career development, education, and all the other things we'd been talking about ever since we rolled out our new strategy.

Now, however, we had to take those efforts to another level, which raised a whole new set of issues. How, for example, should we identify the specific individuals who would eventually be running the company? What sort of training should we give them? How should they be compensated for the additional responsibilities we'd be expecting them to assume? What kind of an equity stake should they have?

And what would happen when I and the major shareholders actually left? Would the new leaders acquire our stock? Could they afford to, or would we be forced to bring in outside equity?

We'd come to the next big obstacle in our journey. Somehow we had to figure out a way to fulfill our promises, cash everyone out, keep the community together, turn it over to the next generation of leaders, and still leave enough on the table for them to get their just rewards when their time came. It was a taller order than I'd bargained for.

14

Passing the Baton

For most of my life, I assumed that the whole idea of business was to build a successful company. Once you'd accomplished that, I figured, you could declare victory and move on. It was sort of like one of those carnival games in which you keep whacking on the platform until the puck goes up and rings the bell. It turns out, however, that in a company with a strong ownership culture the sound of the bell doesn't necessarily mean you've won. It may just mean you have an even bigger set of problems to deal with.

That's more or less the situation I faced in the wake of the Carlisle episode. Believe me, there is no more difficult challenge in business than orchestrating the clean transfer of ownership from one generation to the next in a successful employee-owned company. By "clean transfer," I mean that both sides come out winners. The departing shareholders get the financial rewards they've earned, and their successors get a fair opportunity to do the same thing for themselves.

There are actually three parts to the challenge. The first one is financial, and it centers around the value of the older generation's stock, which represents a claim on the company's assets. The more successful the company, the more valuable the stock and the larger the claim. If the company happens to be both well established and publicly traded, that claim won't necessarily be a burden because the stock can be sold in the public equity market. But most businesses aren't publicly traded, and it's seldom possible to go public just to raise money for cashing out shareholders.

So, in the vast majority of cases, the stock of the older generation becomes a huge burden, because the departing shareholders must be paid.

One solution, of course, is to sell their stock to private investors from outside the company, but then you change the business in a fundamental way. After all, the investors have their own agenda, and it may or may not include maintaining an ownership culture in your business.

I suppose another solution, at least in theory, would be to have the younger generation purchase the stock directly from the older generation, but that's seldom practical. Working people don't have access to that kind of money except in bizarre situations like the one we faced back in 1983.

If you want to keep ownership—and control—inside the business, you generally have little alternative but to figure out how the company can pay off the debt, and there are only two options. One is to raise the necessary cash by selling assets. The other is to take it out of the company's cash flow. Either way, you'll be using your resources to do something other than build the business.

Which brings us to the second part of the challenge of transferring ownership: getting people ready for it. Leadership succession is a tricky issue in every business, but you face some special challenges when you're preparing to turn over the reins in a private company with employee-owners. How, for example, do you make sure that everyone gets paid—including yourself?

After all, you'll probably be leaving with an IOU from the next generation in the form of an interest-bearing note. That IOU won't be worth much unless the company is viable and generating enough cash to pay the note off. So whatever altruistic motives you may have for caring about the company's future, you also have some pretty compelling personal reasons to make sure there's a crackerjack team in place that's ready to run the business after you're gone.

But how do you identify the members of that team? Do they work for you already, or do you have to recruit them from outside? How do you train them? How do you compensate them? How do you make them understand and accept the responsibility they're taking on? How do you provide them with an opportunity that they're going to get excited about and that will make all their sacrifices worthwhile?

Above all, how do you prepare them for the challenges they're going to face in the future—including the challenge of orchestrating their own transfer of ownership and getting paid for their stock when the time comes?

The task of preparing the next generation is complicated, moreover, by the third aspect of the challenge—the psychological one. Change is always difficult, and a transfer of ownership is one of the biggest changes a company can go through. No matter how skillfully you manage it, there will be powerful emotions floating around, notably fear, and they'll be especially potent in a company with a strong ownership culture. The more comfortable people are with the culture, the more anxious they'll be that they might lose it.

On top of that, you may have another psychological issue to contend with. It may also be necessary to change the way people think about the business. Otherwise, you're liable to have a very difficult time generating the cash you need to pay off the debt and continue growing the company at the same time.

Optimization and Innovation

That problem has to do with what I think of as optimization versus innovation. By optimization, I mean getting as much profit as possible out of your products and services. When you're geared toward optimization, you tend to focus on selling things you already know about and on figuring out how to make more money from them. You look for ways to squeeze nickels out of the production process by cutting costs and improving efficiency. You grow by taking market share away from your competitors.

Optimization is one path to success in business and something that every company needs to strive for. But the best opportunities to create wealth often lie elsewhere—not in optimization, but in innovation.

Let's say, for example, that the most profitable company in your industry has 7 percent net income, and your company is doing 5 percent. You can create some additional wealth by continuing to optimize and improving your net income to 7 percent. But you can create much more if, at the same time, you spin off another business with significantly higher margins.

We'd tried that in 1994, when we spun a logistics company out of Heavy-Duty. The idea had grown out of our frustration with being in such a capital-intensive business that absorbed so much cash. We figured we could make more money, and generate more cash, if we started some service businesses. But what did we know how to do?

Well, for one thing, we knew how to process cores—the worn-out engines and engine components that we turn into remanufactured products. As it happens, processing cores is a huge pain in the neck for most people, especially truck, automotive, and heavy-equipment dealers, mainly because of the accounting involved. Each core comes in with a credit that has to be refunded to the customer. The manufacturer will reimburse the dealer for the credit, but only when the core is returned. What's more, a single dealer may be handling cores for ten or fifteen different manufacturers, and so all of those cores have to be sorted, packed up, and shipped. The paperwork has to be completed. Freight and handling charges have to be taken into account. It can be a nightmare.

We thought, What if we set up a company that did all that for dealers? We'd tell them, "Put all your cores in a trailer and send them to us. We'll take care of everything from there." Not only could we make money on the processing, but we could also get into core distribution. Since we'd have all these cores coming through, we could set up distribution points around the country. When salvage yards needed a particular type of core, they could come to us, and we'd earn an additional profit on the sale.

So we started the logistics company, Encore, using the expertise we'd developed doing our own core processing in Heavy-Duty. When we remanufacture the cores, we have a typical manufacturing margin. When we sell our ability to process them, we have a much higher service-company margin. That's what I mean by innovation.

In most businesses, there's a natural tension between optimization and innovation, and it parallels the tension between operational thinking and strategic thinking. People with an operational perspective tend to focus on optimizing. If you think strategically, however, you can't help but realize the importance of innovating.

Not that one is inherently better than the other. You can't be successful in any business unless your people can do a good job of optimizing. But there comes a point when optimization isn't enough anymore. You've squeezed just about all the profit you can out of your current lineup of products, services, and businesses. The future growth you need has to come from innovating—from doing new things, selling new things, starting new things.

If a company hasn't reached that point already, it surely does when a generation of shareholders has to be cashed out. By then, moreover, you're likely to have another issue to think about as well. Not only do you have to promote innovation to cover the debt you're assuming, but you also have to get the next generation of leaders involved in the strategic thinking that lies behind the innovation process. Otherwise, they won't be ready to take over when the time comes.

We found ourselves wrestling with all of those issues as we tried to figure out what it would take for SRC to survive beyond the first generation of shareholders.

Finding the Next Generation of Leaders

If I had to say when the process of transferring ownership actually began at SRC, I'd point to October 6, 1999. On that day, following one of our semiannual sales-and-marketing meetings, we brought together sixty of our people in a conference room at a resort in Branson, Missouri, about thirty miles outside of Springfield. Most of them were managers or supervisors, although there were a few professionals mixed in. All had been identified as candidates to become the future leaders of the company—or perhaps I should say they'd identified themselves.

Companies tie themselves in knots trying to determine the right criteria for leadership and to pick out the individuals with leadership potential. I believe you can save yourself a lot of trouble by letting your people tell you who the leadership candidates are.

We did that using three simple mechanisms. First, we looked at the lists we'd received from our managers, supervisors, and professionals when we'd asked them to name their replacements. Lo and behold, many of the same names were on different lists. Those were obviously the people seen by their peers as the company's rising stars.

In addition, we give out "Top Gun" awards every year to people singled out for special recognition by the company's managers. The rule is that managers have to choose people who've made significant contributions beyond their departments, doing things that have an impact on the company as a whole. I looked at the employees who were repeatedly nominated and added them to our pool of potential leaders.

Then there were the people who'd identified themselves as future leaders by the career paths they'd chosen. The mechanism in this case is what we call an employee annual report. It's built around a four-page form that people fill out with their supervisors during personal development interviews held at least once a year. We ask employees to write down the next job they'd like to have and tell them exactly what they must do to qualify for it. Just to make sure they get the point, we give them a list of all the jobs the company has to offer—from receptionist to president—prior to the meeting.

So, through the employee annual reports, people actually tell us whether or not they want to be leaders in the company. We can then see how serious they are by watching what they do with the opportunities they're given.

With those three mechanisms, it was easy to identify our most promising candidates for leadership, or at least the homegrown ones. In addition, we'd hired three or four people from outside SRC to high-level positions. They were also members of the group that assembled in Branson.

The purpose of the meeting was to launch a program for training leaders, which I know some people think can't be done. They believe leaders are born, not made, implying that leadership can't be taught. I don't buy it. God-given gifts no doubt count for something, but more people have those gifts than we generally recognize. What counts most is experience. To become an effective leader, you need to walk both sides of the street and get run over a few times. You need to pay your dues by wrestling with real problems in the real world.

The question is, How do you give people that kind of experience while they're still working in the business?

We'd always hoped we could do it through the mechanisms of the Great Game of Business, but as our outside directors often pointed out to me, we hadn't yet succeeded in putting together a team of people to whom we could turn over the company should anything happen to me and the other top executives, especially our vice president of operations, Mike Carrigan, and our general counsel and CFO, Dennis Sheppard. (Dennis had left his law practice in 1990 to come work for SRC full-time.) There was, I realized, something missing from our education program. We were teaching many important business skills, but not leadership—or at least not the type of leadership required to run a company like ours.

Frankly, I wasn't sure that people understood what that kind of leadership entailed. Almost all of the long-term thinking was being done by the senior executives, and everybody else pretty much deferred to us. We were the ones who focused on strategy and innovation. The managers of the subsidiaries focused on operations and optimization. As much as we'd tried to force them to broaden their horizons, most of them still didn't get the strategic part of the equation. In fact, some people suggested that our system encouraged them to think operationally by putting so much emphasis on the annual plan. I wasn't sure that I agreed, but I could see we needed a new mechanism. So we came up with one: *leadership groups*.

The Branson meeting marked the start of the process. Over two days, the attendees had to decide on the most critical long-term issues facing SRC. Carrigan, Sheppard, and I did not participate in the session for fear of skewing the discussion. Instead we brought in an outside facilitator, who worked with the group and reported back to me. In the end, they came up with six key problems:

1. What should be the succession process in the company?
2. How can we take better care of our people?
3. How can we use twenty-first-century manufacturing methods to make ourselves more competitive?
4. How can we broaden our customer base and get closer to our end users?
5. How can we raise the capital we'll need in the future to buy out shareholders and build the company?
6. What should be our strategy with regard to information technology?

Once we had the issues, we divided the future leaders into six groups and gave each group one problem to work on for the next year. Again, the three top executives kept their distance. We made it clear that we wouldn't play any role in the groups' deliberations, but we'd expect to receive an interim report from each group after six months and a final report at the end of the year. That was the rule: The groups had to come up with an answer.

Leadership Lessons

Like so many things we do, the leadership groups were an experiment. We couldn't say in advance exactly what would happen, but we knew it would be interesting to watch and see. In addition, there were at least five specific benefits we saw coming out of the program:

- We'd teach people the importance—and difficulty—of reaching closure on an issue, which is one of the critical disciplines of leadership.
- We'd show people what it means to look at a company from a strategic perspective.
- We'd give them an introductory course in the challenges of cashing out shareholders.

- We'd see how people interacted with one another and in the process gain valuable insights into the leadership qualities of our various candidates.
- We'd learn something new about our company and our culture.

It was, in fact, a fascinating exercise. In the beginning, people walked around feeling confused and disoriented. They didn't know where to begin. The meetings were chaotic. The participants would get sidetracked onto tangential issues, then go off in half a million cockamamie directions. Managers from the different subsidiaries would push their own priorities. Several of the groups wound up working on the same issues.

When people asked my advice, I steered them back to the original topic, urging them to keep it as narrow as possible and to focus on coming to a definitive resolution of the issues involved. Mainly, however, I sat back and observed. I wanted to see which people would take charge, how they'd do it, what the internal dynamics of the different groups would be. How would they divide up the workload? What kind of a decision-making process would they set up? How would they deal with the different levels of sophistication that existed in each of the groups?

As time went along, the chaos subsided. The groups began to organize themselves, choose their leaders, and assign responsibilities. By the midyear review, four of the groups had made substantial progress. They came in well prepared and put on excellent presentations. As for the others, they more or less gave us the time of day.

Of course, a bad presentation can be a good opportunity to deliver a message, and I didn't waste it. "Don't bullshit us," I said. "Coming in here with a canned response you got off the Internet isn't leadership. You're only trying to appease your bosses. If you're going to be a leader, you can't just be thinking about getting through the day, finishing the project, checking the assignment off a list. This thing is about the long-term success of the company. What leaders do is think about the long term."

In the end, the groups had even more trouble reaching closure than I'd expected. They would talk all the way around an issue, look at it from every conceivable angle, but they couldn't bring themselves to make the tough call. Instead of facing up to the need for employees to start sharing health-care costs, people would recommend that we put more emphasis on wellness programs. That was typical.

Nevertheless, we all took away important lessons from the experience. The participants got to look at the company through a different prism. For a whole year, they struggled with issues they'd never spent much time thinking about before, and they became aware of some of the complexities a leader has to deal with.

The information technology group, for example, began by focusing on the efficiencies we could achieve if we centralized our computer systems, rather than letting each subsidiary develop its own. Then someone pointed out the problems too much centralization could create if we decided to sell one of the subsidiaries, or take it public, as we might have to at some point in the future. The group had to go back and reexamine everything it had done.

Similarly, the taking-care-of-people group ran into the difficulty of choosing between funding the ESOP, putting more money into 401(k)s, dealing with skyrocketing health-care costs, and developing a cash reserve in case the economy turned bad. The succession-planning group suddenly realized why we needed a much better process for continually replacing people at all levels of the company. As for the group on future capital needs, it wound up going down all the same roads that I and the other senior executives have been exploring for more than a decade.

The Downside of a Great Culture

I suspect I learned more from the leadership groups than anyone else, however. For one thing, I found out a tremendous amount about the leaders themselves—who implemented, who procrastinated, who took control, who lay low. I also saw more clearly than ever the challenge of getting people to accept the kinds of changes you have to make if you want to remain in control of your destiny and deliver on the promise of ownership.

There's a downside of having a great culture. When people like working in a company, they tend to stick around for a long time. That's good, except that after ten or fifteen years, they start losing touch with the outside world. They know only what they've learned in your business, which poses two great risks.

One risk is that people will become arrogant and start benchmarking against themselves instead of their competitors, which leaves the company vulnerable to all kinds of unpleasant market surprises. The other risk is that people will grow complacent. They'll feel so comfortable with what they have that they'll resist attempts to change it—even if the changes are essential to the long-term success of the business.

So, ironically, the same thing that makes you strong today can become an obstacle to creating the organizational changes that will allow you to grow and prosper in the future.

You can begin to address the problem by forcing people to go out and see what other companies are doing, especially your competitors. To some extent, we use our sales-and-marketing meetings for that purpose, and I'd hoped the leadership groups would take the process to the next level. I wanted people to come back with a clearer sense of the changes happening in the world and the long-term challenges we face in meeting them.

Maybe the groups would suggest radical ideas for improving our system. If not, I hoped people would at least begin to appreciate the connections we have in this company and gain a better, deeper understanding of the model. I wanted them to realize that they really are the owners and that, as owners, they have all kinds of choices to make—choices that have been engineered into the system, choices that are available now because of the way we've been setting things up since the day our journey began.

Not that I'm looking for credit or gratitude. I just want people to know what they have. Most people don't realize what they have until they lose it. Sometimes they get it back, and sometimes they don't. I didn't want to take the chance that our people would squander a great opportunity because they didn't understand it, because they didn't appreciate the mechanisms we've put in place to help them succeed.

That's one of the strange things about this journey: You build a system, and your own people don't always see it. They use it. They benefit from it. But they don't get all the nuances, and they don't realize what a difference it makes. So when the time comes to make a decision, they may not make the right one. They may let an opportunity slip away because they don't know what they have.

I can't say for sure how much the leadership groups increased the participants' knowledge of our system, but it was obvious that they didn't see any need to change it. Instead of radical improvements, we got suggestions for doing the same things better—optimizing rather than innovating. Missing was the sense of urgency that I was feeling more and more strongly as time went by.

The Ultimate Challenge of Ownership

While the future leaders were exploring the six long-term issues they'd selected, I and the other senior executives had our own little project. We'd hired an accounting firm to come in and help us develop three different financial scenarios for the next five years, based on whether the economic environment would be good, bad, or mediocre. In each instance, we projected the cash flow we could reasonably expect to generate per year, factoring in the needs of our current businesses, the probability of shareholders cashing out, the sale of assets, and so on. We also tried to estimate what might happen to the stock value.

The results were sobering. If we kept on our current growth curve, the company's value could double in five years, from about $30 million in 2000 to about $60 million in 2004. At that point, we'd have little choice but to bring in outside investors to buy the stock of departing shareholders—which would be a giant step. Having outside investors could change the whole thinking of the business. For one thing, the employees would not have a controlling interest in the company anymore. Under those circumstances, it might not be possible to preserve the community or the culture.

Throughout our journey, we'd been guided by our desire to make the benefits of ownership available to everyone in the company. I had never wanted my success to come at the expense of other people, including those who'd be taking over when I left. So I felt obligated to come up with a plan that would at least give them a choice about whether or not to keep the equity inside the company. Then they could decide for themselves what they wanted to do.

In the meantime, there were other ownership issues we were struggling with. One of them involved the wealth gap between the old-timers and the newer people. That gap is a natural consequence of the leverage effect I discussed in Chapter 11. People who came in at the company's beginning got the benefit of the tremendous rise in our stock value as we paid down our debt during the first few years. There was simply no way that anyone who joined later could catch up. The result was that we had some people working side by side, doing the same job, and one person might have an ESOP stake of $150,000 while the other's shares may be worth $2,000. If there was a 10 percent increase in the stock price, moreover, the first guy would see his ownership stake rise by $15,000, and the second guy's would go up just $200.

Not surprisingly, such discrepancies were causing morale problems. An employee may not understand all the subtleties of stock ownership, but people always know when somebody else has something they don't have. Then again, how could we solve the problem without being unfair to the old-timers? They'd worked hard over a long period of time to build up the value of their stock. If we reduced the gap, say, by giving more stock to the newcomers, we'd dilute the old-timers' shares—in effect, taking away from them the wealth they'd earned.

We tried to attack the problem in a variety of other ways. For example, we put together a stock offering, taking advantage of a program that allows employees to get a 15 percent discount on stock they buy in their company. We even announced the offering a year in advance, so that people would have time to save up the cash they'd need to buy in. Although there were strict limits on what we could say about the offering, we knew we were having a good year, and the stock price might be rising as much as 40 percent. Combine the likely stock price increase with the 15 percent discount on the current price, and the offering was about as close as you can get to a sure thing: Employees who bought in were bound to earn a hefty return almost at once. Unfortunately, most people declined to buy in. They said they couldn't afford to.

We'd also set up an internal stock market. Anyone interested in buying or selling shares could contact the corporate finance department, which would match buyers and sellers. Relatively few people took advantage of that opportunity, too.

Then there was the challenge of putting more ownership in the hands of the up-and-coming leaders. It was essential that they have a stake commensurate with the responsibility we were asking them to take on. We'd already set up a stock option program (see "How to Design a Stock Option Plan That Works," page 248), but we still needed to make the stock exciting for people. Of course, stock becomes most exciting when its value starts to rise rapidly, but there are a limited number of ways to make that happen.

So all of these issues were on our minds as we tried to figure out how to orchestrate the transfer of ownership that we knew would have to occur in the next few years.

Taking the Plunge

What drove our thinking were the numbers in the financial scenarios. It was obvious that we could keep ownership inside the company only by moving fast. If we waited five years, we'd have no choice but to sell the company or bring in outside investors. In order for the next generation to have a shot at owning the business, we'd have to start cashing out major shareholders almost immediately.

As it happened, we had two large shareholders from the original buyout group who'd expressed interest in retiring. Together they owned 15 percent of the outstanding stock. Maybe, I thought, we could persuade them to cash out right away. If I and some of the other original shareholders agreed to sell a portion of our holdings as well, we could conceivably buy back 30 percent of the company's stock at a price we could still afford.

And then what? Suppose we retired the stock. We'd see an automatic increase in the value of every outstanding share. Even if our earnings were to remain flat in the coming year, we could pretty much count on our stock price rising at least 30 percent at the next valuation, from

$9.20 to almost $12. If profits rose as much as we expected, we could have a stock price increase of 50 percent or more. (In fact, it rose 48 percent, to $13.60 per share.*)

That kind of increase would have major ramifications. To begin with, it was bound to have an impact on morale. The guy with a $150,000 ESOP stake would see it rise $75,000 to $225,000, which would have to get him pretty excited. Even the guy with a $2,000 ESOP stake would realize a gain of $1,000—enough to get his attention and drive home the benefits of owning stock. As for the option holders, they stood to gain most of all. A key manager with 10,000 options issued at, say, $5 a share would be looking at a total increase in excess of $80,000 immediately, setting up a potential gain in the hundreds of thousands of dollars by the time the options had to be exercised in years eight through ten.

That's one of the tricks you learn in this journey. Sooner or later, you figure out there's another way to put more equity in the hands of employees that doesn't involve making a contribution to an ESOP or handing out more stock options. You can also do it by repurchasing stock from shareholders and retiring it. Since there are fewer shares outstanding, each remaining share automatically grows in value. The people who are still around—including members of the ESOP and stock option holders—wind up with bigger pieces of the pie.

So a plan began to take shape, but there was a catch, or actually two catches. For openers, the big shareholders might be reluctant to sell their stock now, figuring it would be worth substantially more at a later date. Then again, we could probably induce them to sell by agreeing to pay a substantial amount up front and the rest over five years instead of ten. We could also offer them a competitive interest rate on the unpaid balance.

If the shareholders accepted our proposal, however, we'd run into the second catch. We could get the big increases in stock value only by financing the buyout ourselves. To do that, we'd have to add an unsecured debt of $12 million to our balance sheet. Our debt-to-equity ratio

---

* By the way, I'm referring here to stock prices after six splits. To calculate the increase since 1983, you have to multiply the latest price by six. So a share bought for 10 cents in 1983 is now worth $81.60 (six times $13.60).

HOW TO DESIGN A STOCK OPTION PLAN THAT WORKS

There's a widespread myth that a company has to be public, or "prepublic" (that is, preparing to go public), for stock options to be effective. Unless you can offer the prospect of a public market for the stock, we're told, the options won't attract the kind of employees you're looking for or provide the ones you have with an incentive to go the extra mile. The rewards are just not big enough—or so it's said.

Don't believe it. Stock options can work just as well in a private company as in a public or prepublic company, provided you have a program that encourages the right kind of behavior. That means designing the program so that it rewards people for working hard to build the long-term equity value of the business. In fact, many start-ups have such poorly designed programs that they encourage exactly the opposite type of behavior and wind up damaging the company in the process.

It helps if you don't have to rely on stock options as your sole means of sharing ownership. Unlike most prepublic start-ups, we have an ESOP, and so we can reserve the options for the people we've identified as our future leaders. By giving them something extra, we send them an important message. We let them know that they're special, they're different from other employees, and they'll be called on to do different things.

I also want our future leaders to know we're looking for a long-term commitment. Under our options program, they earn their stock over seven years. The options don't even begin to vest until the thirty-seventh month—that is, the beginning of the fourth year. If people leave the company before then, their options are worth nothing. Thereafter, they become 10 percent vested in year four, 20 percent more in year five, 30 percent more in year six, and the final 40 percent in year seven.

So people get all of their stock options only if they stick around for the entire time. Then they have three years to convert their options to stock by purchasing shares at whatever the agreed-on price of the stock was when the options were issued. The options must be exercised before the end of the tenth year, but that still gives people plenty of time to work on increasing the stock price. Some of our current option holders, for example, will wind up paying less than $5 per share for stock that could be worth $40 per share ten years after the issuance of the options, assuming we hit our targets.

What's more, people don't necessarily have to come up with cash to buy the stock. We can decide to let them cover the cost, as well as whatever taxes are due, by selling some of the shares back to the company at the current, higher price. So the option holders wind up with real equity, and in all likelihood they won't have to spend any money out of their own pockets to pay for it. They just have to work as hard as they can to get the stock price up. The increase in the stock price from the time they receive the options will ultimately determine how well they do.

Now, I know some readers, especially those in Silicon Valley, will shake their heads at the idea of a seven-year vesting period. They think they have no choice but to offer a faster payout. Employees demand it. How can you compete for talent if you're asking people to wait two or three times longer to get their money than they'd have to wait if they worked for another company?

My response is that you get the behavior you design into the program. When you make it too easy for people to cash out, they don't take ownership seriously. Equity becomes just another perk of the job. People think they can make a quick score and leave. That's one reason we see so much turnover in Silicon Valley companies.

My goal is to reduce turnover, not promote it. I want to make sure people have to pay their dues before cashing out. I also want them to understand what it really takes to build equity value. To me, the first three years of our program are skin in the game. You need that much time just to appreciate what you've got. Once you realize how much your options could be worth someday and what you have to do to get the full payoff, something clicks. Your dream suddenly comes into focus. The psychic ownership kicks in, and you start getting the rewards that come from working together to make a bigger pie and from watching your piece of it grow.

I want our future leaders to have those dreams, and I want them to see that we're going to stand behind our words. We really are going to transfer the equity. The next generation of leaders will have a chance to acquire ownership in the company from my generation, and they won't have to come up with millions of dollars to do it. They can pay for the stock with the sweat of their brow.

would balloon from 0.8-to-1, which is very low, to about 3.5-to-1, which most lenders consider dangerously high. Every year, we'd need $2.5 million in cash flow to pay down the debt, in addition to the $2.5 million we needed for growing the company. In short, we'd have to generate $25 million over five years, which we'd never done before. The most cash flow we'd ever had in a five-year period was $15 million—and that was during one of the strongest economic periods in history. What if the economy went bad?

As it turned out, the shareholders did agree to our proposal, so we had an important decision to make. There was still a possibility of selling the stock to an outside investor. We certainly wouldn't want to bring in a venture capitalist who'd be looking to cash out in five years, thereby moving us straight from the frying pan into the fire, but we might be able to find a patient investor to buy the stock—an insurance company, for example. Was that the best route?

Or did we want to assume the debt and the risk that went along with it? We'd be making a commitment to generate $5 million a year for five straight years. If we couldn't do it, we'd have no choice but to go looking for outside capital, and at that point we might have trouble finding the kind of investor we wanted. We might also be in a much weaker position. The economy could be bad. The cost of capital could be high. A dozen things could go wrong.

Granted, we had some contingencies in place. We could sell the investment we had in a local bank we'd helped start. We also owned several million dollars' worth of property that we could unload in a pinch. For that matter, we could probably find buyers for several of our subsidiaries if necessary. You create those trapdoors without knowing how you're going to use them, or even *if* you're going to use them. The truth is, you'd prefer not to use them, but at least they're available.

They aren't fail-safe, however. We could still wind up with our backs to the wall. It was not the sort of risk that I and the other senior executives could take on our own. I talked it over with the leadership group on future capital needs, which began setting up focus groups throughout the company. There we laid out the choice as clearly as possible: sell 30 percent of the company to an outside investor, or take on the debt and pay it off by generating $25 million over five years.

People had a lot of questions and a lot of fears. "What if we can't do it?" they asked. "How would we pay off the debt?" We ran through the contingency plans, as well as the risk that more drastic measures might be required. We also explained the potential rewards.

Eventually, a consensus emerged: We should go ahead and take the plunge. People felt they at least had to try to keep the company for themselves.

The End of SRC

I had my own fears about the decision. In particular, I worried that people didn't really understand the magnitude of the challenge they faced. Here we were with a perfect balance sheet. At a debt-to-equity ratio of 0.8-to-1, we could handle any adversity. We could weather any economic downturn. If we needed cash, we could get it easily and fast. Frankly, we couldn't have been in better shape going into the recession that we all believed was coming.

Yet we were throwing away the safety net. We were taking on a huge amount of debt at precisely the wrong moment. Why? To give the next generation a shot at owning the business. It was a great opportunity, but it presented an enormous challenge. What's more, the challenge wouldn't end anytime soon. Cashing out shareholders would be an ongoing necessity as long as people wanted to keep ownership inside the business. There were still five members of the original thirteen waiting to be cashed out, after all, not to mention the people who would be exercising their stock options in the next five or six years and all the members of the ESOP. So we'd have the next round of buyouts to deal with when the first one was finished, and then many other rounds after that.

In thinking about our future financial needs, I'd come to the conclusion that we'd taken the company about as far as it could go without making major changes. We'd been very good at optimizing, but except in one or two of our businesses, optimization wasn't capable of producing the additional earnings, and therefore the additional wealth, we would need to take care of all the people in the game. There simply weren't enough untapped earnings left in most of our products and services.

We were also approaching the limits of financial engineering. You can boost a share price only so much by repurchasing stock and retiring it. Recall that we'd started with 1 million shares outstanding in 1983, and we'd had six stock splits since then, so you might expect that we'd have 6 million shares outstanding. We were actually down to about 2.4 million shares. When you factored in the more than $20 million we'd paid departing shareholders in principal and interest, it turned out that almost 40 percent of the increase in our stock value had come from retiring shares we'd bought back. Those big gains wouldn't be available in the future. As a practical matter, there wasn't enough stock that could be retired. Instead the big gains would have to come from big increases in earnings and from the sale of businesses with high price-earnings multiples.

So where would we get those earnings increases, and how would we create those high-multiple businesses? Clearly, we were going to have to innovate like crazy. We'd have to do over and over again what we'd done with Encore, and we'd have to do a lot of other things as well. We'd have to get into hot industries. We'd have to be attuned to market trends. We'd have to develop the kinds of stories investors were looking for. We'd have to use everything we'd learned about creating value if we were going to generate the wealth we'd need down the road.

What's more, we couldn't continue to be dependent on the same small group of people to come up with the new ideas—particularly since most of those people would be retiring in a few years. Their successors would have to step up to the plate.

But would they? Did they have any notion of what was required? After our experience with the leadership groups, I had my doubts. It looked to me as though the successors were stuck in the old SRC, the company that was so great at optimization. That company had had a fine run for eighteen years, but it wasn't going to cut the mustard in the future.

In a sense, the old SRC was already becoming a thing of the past. Step by step, the company was being transferred from one group of owners to another, and the new owners had no choice but to run it differently. Why? Because they faced an entirely new set of challenges, unlike any the previous owners had ever encountered. If the new owners didn't change the business, they'd eventually reach a point at which they'd be forced to sell it. Then change would definitely come, and it might not be to their liking.

The more I thought about it, the more convinced I became that we should formally declare the end of one company and the beginning of another. We should take credit for all the great things we'd accomplished over the previous eighteen years, and then we should let go of them. We should say, "Those things were part of the company we used to work for, and we're really proud of them, but now we're working for a company that has to take an entirely different approach. Let's figure out how we can make this new company even better than the old one."

Part of my motive, I admit, was personal. For years, I'd lived in fear of making a mistake that would be used to discredit the Great Game of Business. In our efforts to do right by our employees, I worried we'd inadvertently do something that damaged the company, and the cynics would pounce all over us, saying, "See, it doesn't work to run a business that way after all." The criticism would be unfair and untrue, in my opinion. SRC and hundreds of other companies have already proven that the system works. Nevertheless, I would sometimes wake up with night sweats over the possibility that a decision we'd made might come back to haunt us and undermine what we'd accomplished.

The decision to releverage the company definitely had that potential. Granted, a debt-to-equity ratio of 3.5-to-1 may not sound so bad for a company that was once at 89-to-1, but back in 1983 I hadn't known enough to be terrified. Now I did. In addition, I had more to lose.

On the other hand, I firmly believed that taking on the debt was the right decision for the employees, and so somehow I had to overcome my fears. That required a mental trick. By declaring the end of SRC, I realized I could get myself to accept that we'd completed our mission and proven what we had to, and now we could get on with the next challenge: creating a new company to compete in the new world of business. There would be no more night sweats. The old SRC had been a great success, but it was over and done with. I would acknowledge it and celebrate it and then leave it behind.

It's always hard to accept the necessity of changing something that has been successful over a long period of time—even if you recognize intellectually that change is essential. One way or another, you have to make the break in your own mind before you can let go and move on.

To be sure, I wasn't the only person who had to break with the past. It wouldn't do much good for me to move on if no one else came along. Then again, people weren't likely to come along unless they shared my sense of urgency. I decided we had to do something visible and dramatic to make them realize just how risky our situation was about to become.

At the same time, I wanted to make a strong statement about the future. I was absolutely determined to change our mind-set with regard to innovation. By hook or by crook, we had to make the move from short-term thinking to long-term thinking. Not that we'd abandon all the mechanisms and practices we had, but they weren't enough to carry us anymore. We needed a new company now that had the values of the old SRC, in addition to a great management system and ownership culture, but that could innovate as well as it optimized.

So on November 1, 2000, we bought back the stock, assumed the debt, and announced that the old SRC had officially ended—and that a new SRC had just been born.

Reinventing the Business

I'm sure a lot of people had no idea what we were talking about, but they quickly began to find out, as we launched a series of initiatives designed to demonstrate our new priorities as a business and to show everybody how we needed to operate from then on.

To begin with, we changed the huddle process. Previously we'd had weekly huddles in the subsidiaries and biweekly huddles for the company as a whole. In the companywide meetings, we would have each subsidiary forecast its numbers for the month, more or less as we'd been doing it from the start. I began to think, however, that the practice might be promoting short-term thinking by focusing so much attention on monthly performance. That was appropriate for the subsidiaries, but I wanted people to be thinking long-term on the corporate level. So we stopped doing the monthly numbers in the companywide huddles. Instead we focused on developing and implementing plans for the next three to five years.

We also revamped the leadership groups, establishing three training tracks—for entry-level leaders, middle managers, and senior managers of the subsidiaries. The first group learned basic management skills. The second followed a program similar to the one we'd had for the leadership groups in the first year. For the senior managers, we brought in a corporate entrepreneurship program developed at the University of Southern California, which took people through the entire process of starting up a new internal venture from scratch.

In addition, we made some management changes aimed at ensuring we'd get the $5 million in cash flow we needed each year. General managers had to be able to deliver what they'd promised, and everybody had to understand that missed forecasts were a luxury we could no longer afford. So we moved some key managers around—and let a couple of people go.

Mainly, though, I focused on initiatives that had the potential to provide huge payoffs while serving as informal learning tools for teaching people a different way of thinking about the business.

Engines Plus was a case in point. It had evolved considerably since the early days of oil coolers and power units. We'd put in a bright young general manager, Rich Armstrong, who had turned out to be an extraordinary innovator. The company continued to make power units, but

Armstrong had greatly expanded the number of applications and product lines, in the process driving the sales of Engines Plus from $9 million to $15 million.

The real opportunity lay in the future, however, because those power units could be used both for irrigation and for extracting natural gas. As a result, Engines Plus had the potential to become a player in two of the hottest markets around: energy and water resource management. With droughts and rolling blackouts in the headlines, investors were lusting after any technology that could address the energy shortage or help farmers manage their scarce supplies of water. Shares of public companies comparable to Engines Plus were trading at price-earnings multiples of 30 to 80.

I realized Engines Plus could have that kind of a multiple as well, provided we could build it into a stand-alone business with a good story to tell investors about the future. As part of SRC, its multiple would remain stuck at around 10. Before we could spin it off, however, we had to make some major changes. The company needed deeper and more experienced management. It needed engineers who were capable of developing hot products. It needed a strong, independent board of directors. In short, Engines Plus had to start operating like any other fast-growing company on a prepublic track.

So we began putting the pieces in place. Armstrong, who had always been a better innovator than optimizer, moved into a business development role, and we brought in a new general manager with the experience required to take the company to the next level. His mission was to get there in no more than three years, at which point we'd spin Engines Plus off, raising a substantial portion of the $25 million we needed over the next five years.

Hoping to find other such opportunities, we also launched Springfield's first venture capital fund, Quest Capital Alliance, with $6 million we'd raised in the community. The fund manager set up shop in our corporate headquarters. Before long we were looking at twenty-five to thirty deals a month, knowing that just one success could carry us a long way toward our goal.

Meanwhile, we kept looking for opportunities inside SRC. One of them we found in the lessons of the dot-com bubble. Like most other people, I'd been awed by the staggering valuations that companies with no profits had been able to achieve, if only for a couple of years. The phenomenon demonstrated, if nothing else, the power of an attractive business model to capture the imaginations of investors.

If we were going to create businesses with high multiples, I decided, we needed to be looking for new business models that were as attractive as the dot-com models had been, yet sustainable. That meant demonstrating not only tremendous potential for future growth but real, ongoing profitability.

It occurred to me that, just as the dot-com craze had passed, so eventually would the Internet funk. Sooner or later investors would realize that some types of e-commerce businesses had an extraordinarily bright future after all—notably the ones with a history of sales growth and profits.

What if we could put together such a business? We could set up a subsidiary to sell engine parts over the Internet. We could call it Plenty-Of-Parts.com, or POP Inc. Eventually we could merge POP Inc. with Encore, creating a dot-com with a five-year history of outstanding sales and profits. That could turn out to be an extremely marketable asset. Another dot-com might decide to buy it just for its earnings.

In fact, we did set up POP Inc., and we probably will merge it with Encore eventually. The two companies belong together. The point, however, is not just to provide us with another strategic option like the one we have with Engines Plus. I'm also trying to show people the kind of thinking we must do if we're going to build this new company.

Those lessons are very tough to learn. For one thing, they have a tendency to make people nervous. Consider the two top managers of Encore, Denise Bredfeldt and Rick Brandell, who have both grown up in SRC. They cut and bleed the Great Game of Business. They also run a wildly profitable company by the seat of their pants, and they're horrified at the suggestion that Encore might be sold—because they love what they're doing. Their first thought is "This is awful. We're going to be kicked out of the family."

I understand their reaction. Nobody likes to leave a comfort zone. Most of us think, "Why mess with success?" We've been trained to believe that, if you work hard, everything will come to you. It's one of the biggest fallacies our parents teach us: "Just keep your nose to the grindstone." Then we're caught completely unawares when the grindstone is replaced by something better and we suddenly can't pay the bills anymore.

That's why we need a long-term strategy. We may never sell Encore, but we have to be ready in case we can't meet our obligations at some point and we're forced to sell something. If we did sell it, moreover, we wouldn't necessarily have to include the people in the deal. That would be their choice.

As for the people, they need to make the mental break with the past. They need to take credit for the old world they've enjoyed for so long and get on with making the new world better—because the day will come when the baton has to be passed.

The End of the Rainbow

There's one other initiative I've taken. I informed our board of directors that I would remain as CEO for the next five years, but then I planned to step down.

I'll probably be the last of the original thirteen shareholders to cash out and move on. So my departure will officially mark the end of that chapter in SRC's history. The content of the next chapter depends a lot on what happens between now and the time I leave.

As challenging as it will be to pay off the debt we've assumed, there's a great opportunity for everybody if we can pull it off. It's an opportunity not only to increase our stock value, but to take our company, our management system, and our people to the next level. My hope is that, through the buyback, they'll finally grasp the full meaning of ownership. They'll see its potential to transform the lives of people throughout a company—provided enough of them understand the risks an owner has to take and accept the responsibility an owner has to shoulder.

It won't be easy. Some people won't get it. They'll complain about the money being taken out of the company by the guys who are leaving and bellyache about paying down the debt. We'll hear grumbling because bonuses won't be as large as they might have been if we'd brought in an outside investor instead of giving our people a chance to acquire the stock.

In the worst case, the markets could go to hell, and we might have to do what we've tried so hard to avoid doing all these years: lay people off. Whoever gets laid off will sit there saying, "Those greedy sons of bitches, they did this to me." Morale could plummet. We could find ourselves right back where we were in 1983, struggling not to destroy ourselves from within.

All that could come to pass—if people let it happen. But it doesn't have to happen. We have the tools we need to complete this transfer of ownership, and the benefits will be huge, absolutely huge, if people want to do it.

That's the key.

OWNERSHIP RULE #14

You gotta wanna.

It's one of the higher laws of business I wrote about in the last book, and it's a fundamental rule of ownership as well. If I've learned anything in this journey, it's that you make your own destiny in this world. You determine your own outcomes. If you have the will, there's almost always a way. It may not be the most direct route. You'll have to overcome a lot of obstacles. But you'll get there eventually.

Now our people have to decide if they want to take advantage of this opportunity we've created together. Do they think they're good enough to pull it off? Are they ready to test their mettle? It has to be their mission, their charge of the Light Brigade, and the future leaders have to show everyone else the way. They're the champions. I'm expecting them to carry the lessons they're learning back to the rest of the organization, so that people can make up their minds with full knowledge of the stakes and the choices.

As for me, I'm working on my own exit strategy these days. Assuming we hit our goal of $25 million, people will once again be able to decide in five years whether or not to keep the company for themselves. The debt will be available if they want to use it, and they should have higher earnings as well, provided they've done a good enough job of innovating and optimizing. In that case, they'll have more options than ever.

One option might be to eliminate the corporate offices altogether. We've built such a decentralized organization that I'm not sure corporate will be needed in a few years. Instead, each subsidiary could have a governing board of directors. Of course, if you eliminate corporate, you also eliminate a tremendous amount of overhead—and thereby increase earnings even more. So the value of SRC could actually increase as a result of the departure of me and my corporate colleagues.

Then the village could continue without us, stronger than ever. If you were standing on the hill overlooking the valley with the little huts, you'd see the lights in one of them go out, but the rest would keep right on blazing away.

And all the inhabitants would have the satisfaction of knowing that they've really achieved something. If nothing else, they've shown that it is, in fact, possible to build a company of owners. You can create wealth and make sure everybody gets part of it, and then you can take your share and leave guilt-free, leave without remorse or regrets, knowing that you haven't taken advantage of other people to get it but rather have given them the same opportunity you've had. You are turning over to them a system they can carry forward, repeating the process, fulfilling their own dreams, creating their own wealth, and eventually passing the torch to the next generation to do the same.

Of all the rewards business has to offer, that surely has to be one of the greatest.

Epilogue
The Long Road

On September 25, 2001—exactly two weeks after the horrific airplane hijackings of September 11—*The New York Times* ran an article about the one U.S. airline that had a chance of maintaining profitability in the wake of the terrorist attacks. Southwest Airlines, the article noted, had faced a similar situation during the Persian Gulf war and managed to earn a profit while the rest of the industry lost more than $6 billion over two years. Now investors were betting that Southwest could pull off a similar feat. Its share prices had fallen far less that those of other carriers following the attacks. And although it was only the seventh-largest airline in terms of passenger miles and revenue, its market value of $10.5 billion was about the same as the market value of all the other major airlines *combined.*

The *Times* article went on to note various factors that supposedly accounted for Southwest's success, such as its quick "turn times"—getting planes back into the air after just twenty minutes, compared with forty-five minutes for most other airlines. Also cited was its use of smaller, less-congested airports, thereby avoiding costly delays. Then there was its ample reserve of cash and readily available credit—not to mention its ability to operate so efficiently that, even in bad times, it burned cash at a fraction of the rate of other carriers.

What the *Times* article didn't mention, or even allude to, was the single factor that made all of Southwest's other competitive advantages possible—namely, its culture of ownership.

It's a common oversight, but I found it amazing nonetheless, particularly given the timing. Never has the strength of Southwest's culture been more apparent than it was in the weeks after the terrorist attacks. At other airlines, there was outrage as companies laid off thousands of people, said they couldn't afford severance pay, and then asked the government for billions of dollars in emergency aid, none of it destined for laid-off employees. At Southwest, employees came up with cost-saving ideas, donated profit-sharing money, and signed over federal tax refund checks to the airline. Some people even offered to work without compensation if it was necessary to keep the planes flying.

Of course, it wasn't necessary. Southwest's chief financial officer told the *Times* that the company had no plans for layoffs and didn't need them anyway. It had been operating shorthanded before the attacks. A reduced schedule would simply mean spending less on overtime—not that the airline was planning to cut back its schedule. "We don't want to do things in the short term that hurt in the long term," he said.

For some reason, a lot of people find all of this hard to grasp—including many otherwise intelligent and sophisticated observers of business. They think you have to explain Southwest's success in terms of its marketing strategy, or its financial management, or its operating efficiencies, or what have you. Those things are certainly important, but Southwest's strength comes first and foremost from its people and its culture, as cofounder and former CEO Herb Kelleher and his colleagues never tire of telling anyone who asks.

I remember reading an interview with Kelleher in *The Wall Street Journal* a few years back. The interviewer asked him what he meant when he said that Southwest's culture was its biggest competitive advantage. "The intangibles are more important than the tangibles," Kelleher replied. "Someone can go out and buy airplanes from Boeing and ticket counters, but they can't buy our culture, our esprit de corps."

So how, as a manager, did he build and sustain the culture? "I've tried to create a culture of caring for people in the totality of their lives, not just at work," Kelleher replied. "There's no magic formula. It's like building a giant mosaic—it takes thousands of little pieces. . . . You have to recognize that people are still most important. How you treat them determines how they treat people on the outside."

And, on one level, it really is just as simple as that. There are no gimmicks, techniques, or mechanisms that can produce an ownership culture if you don't have a real commitment to "caring for people in the totality of their lives."

That's where so many companies go astray. United Airlines is a good example. Back in 1994, magazines and newspapers were heralding United as a new model of employee ownership. With great fanfare, the airline had cut a deal with some of its unions to set up an ESOP that gave employees a 55 percent equity stake in the carrier's parent, UAL Corp., in exchange for steep wage concessions, seats on the board, and a role in corporate governance.

The deal did, in fact, help United gain a temporary competitive edge over its non-employee-owned rivals such as American, Delta, and Northwest, but the old divisions and conflicts remained. There were no fundamental changes in philosophy, limited attempts at business education, and no commitments to "caring for people in the totality of their lives." Instead of rebuilding the culture, both management and labor focused on the governance issues, making sure that each side lived up to its end of the bargain. And while people were called owners, they weren't asked—or shown how—to think like owners, and so most of them continued to think like employees. It's small wonder that they were bitterly divided on extending the ESOP when the issue arose in 2000. Even before the terrorist attacks, which led to massive layoffs at United, morale was extremely low.

Contrast United's experience with that of Southwest, which began giving employees stock ownership in the 1970s—and didn't ask for wage concessions in return. Over time, Southwest employees clearly came to understand the benefits of what they were getting, as was evident in January 1995, when the company and its pilots association signed an historic ten-year contract.

It was historic, in the first place, because the union agreed to a term of ten years, which is an eternity in collective bargaining. Even more unusual was the pilots' decision to freeze wages for the first five years in return for stock options. On top of that, the pilots agreed to freeze work rules for the entire length of the contract, apparently believing that the company would be willing to revise the rules if circumstances changed.

The contract showed an extraordinary degree of trust between the pilots and the company. As Kevin and Jackie Freiberg note in *Nuts!*, their fine book on Southwest Airlines, "Trust is a prerequisite to ownership because it strengthens self-confidence. . . . One of the reasons pilots are willing to assume ownership for Southwest's success is that they are confident they will have a crucial role in shaping the company's future."

But what I found even more striking was the business intelligence behind the contract.

That's a subject Herb Kelleher and I had discussed a couple of years before the contract was signed. Southwest had invited me to come speak about the Great Game of Business. After my talk, Kelleher had told me that he absolutely agreed about the importance of training people in business. The greatest dangers to Southwest, he said, were five contracts that had to be negotiated in the next couple of years. The employees' decisions in the contract negotiations would make or break the company. "We have to teach them to be good businesspeople," he said.

I didn't hear anything more about it until I read an article in *The Wall Street Journal* announcing the new contract between Southwest and its pilots. I immediately called up Southwest's director of human resources, who had been one of my hosts. "What happened?" I asked.

"Herb just sat down with the pilots and said, 'Let's do the math,'" he replied. Kelleher had shown them what would happen if, say, United was forced to increase its wages by x amount—how much it would have to increase ticket prices. So what if Southwest also increased ticket prices but didn't increase wages? Its profitability would obviously rise. And who would benefit most? The shareholders. Kelleher took the pilots through the numbers and showed them how much better they could do with stock options than with wage increases. Besides, they'd be investing in themselves, which was the best investment they could make. The result, after all, would be largely in their hands.

The pilots got the message, and the company was able to keep its costs low and its balance sheet strong during a period when it was competing head-to-head with United, Delta, US Airways, and other carriers trying to duplicate Southwest's success in serving smaller markets. The big payoff came following the terrorist attacks. The other airlines were so financially strapped that they had to eliminate their least profitable routes, including many of those on which they had been competing with Southwest. As a result, Southwest immediately began picking up market share and emerged from the crisis stronger than ever.

The pilots, for their part, got the full benefit of the deal they'd made in 1995. The long-term increase in the value of their stock options dwarfed any salary increase they might have received in the first five years.

What Trust and Business Education Can Do

That combination of trust and business intelligence is the hallmark of an ownership culture as well as an extraordinarily powerful competitive advantage. Over the past ten years, I've personally seen hundreds of companies use open-book management to build trust and spread business knowledge throughout their workforce, thereby developing the kind of culture that has allowed them not only to prosper in good times, but to respond quickly to adversity and take advantage of the opportunities that are available only when times are tough. In the process, those companies are helping to define the new management paradigm that will become the standard against which all others are measured in the twenty-first century.

That said, I have to add that this journey is not for the fainthearted. Ownership is a long, hard, lonely road. There is nothing more powerful in business than a culture that people are willing to fight for, but it takes years to build one, and there are no shortcuts. Every company with an ownership culture has put in its time and paid its dues. People have done the education, set up the systems, developed the disciplines, made the mistakes, worked through the problems, dealt with the doubters, overcome the obstacles, and kept on going—even when it must have seemed as though there had to be an easier way. Why? Because it was the right thing to do. Because it made sense. Because it was what they believed in.

That's what it takes to build and, most important, to sustain a culture of ownership. The payoff is a workforce full of people who care, who take responsibility for themselves and for one another, who will do whatever is necessary to protect their community and the business behind it.

There are lessons here that go beyond business, however, because ownership is a state of mind. Ownership is hope. It's curiosity, openness, an eagerness to learn and grow. It's caring about yourself and the people around you. It's wanting to contribute, to make a difference. It's the courage and conviction to face the future. It's confidence, self-esteem, and pride. It's the ability to handle diversity. It's giving back to your community and appreciating the gifts you've received.

Those are great qualities to have in a business, but they're also great qualities in a school, or a church, or a social service organization, or a nation. And they're the qualities we need now more than ever.

Index

For Further Information

The SRC Holdings Corporation and The Great Game of Business® are interested in helping you and your company build a profitable ownership culture through open-book management. We offer a variety of products, seminars and workshops, business coaching, and a professional speakers' bureau. To receive more information on these services, please contact us at 1-800-386-2752 or www.greatgame.com.

About the Authors

Jack Stack is president and CEO of the Springfield ReManufacturing Corporation (SRC), an employee-owned company that supplies remanufactured engines to major automotive companies. He lives in Springfield, Missouri. **Bo Burlingham** is the editor-at-large of *Inc.* magazine and lives in Cambridge, Massachusetts. They are co-authors of the best-seller *The Great Game of Business.*